Parent-Child Interaction and Parent-Child Relations in Child Development

The Minnesota Symposia on Child Psychology

Volume 17

Parent-Child Interaction and Parent-Child Relations in Child Development

The Minnesota Symposia on Child Psychology

Volume 17

edited by
MARION PERLMUTTER
University of Minnesota

Minnesota Symposium on Child Psychology
= (17th : 1982 : University of Minnesota,
Minneapolis)

LEA LAWRENCE ERLBAUM ASSOCIATES, PUBLISHERS
1984   Hillsdale, New Jersey   London

10230865
DLC

6-18-84 JH

Lawrence Erlbaum Associates, Inc., Publishers
365 Broadway
Hillsdale, New Jersey 07642

Library of Congress Cataloging in Publication Data
Main entry under title:

Parent-child interaction and parent-child relations in child
   development.

   "The Minnesota Symposia on Child Psychology, volume
17."
   Papers presented at the 17th Minnesota Symposia on
Child Psychology, Oct. 28–30, 1982, University of Minne-
sota, Minneapolis, sponsored by the Institute of Child
Development.

   Bibliography: p.
   Includes indexes.
   1. Developmental psychology—Congresses. 2. Parent
and child—Congresses. I. Perlmutter, Marion.
II. Minnesota Symposia on Child Psychology (17th :
1982 : University of Minnesota, Minneapolis) III. University of Minnesota. Institute of Child Development.
BF712.5.P37   1984   306.8'74   83-25347
ISBN 0-89859-380-8

Printed in the United States of America
10 9 8 7 6 5 4 3 2 1

Contents

Preface

This volume contains the papers presented at the seventeenth Minnesota Symposia on Child Psychology, held October 28–30, 1982, at the University of Minnesota, Minneapolis. As has been the tradition for this annual series, the faculty of the Institute of Child Development invited internationally eminent researchers to present their research and to consider problems of mutual concern to scientists studying development. For this symposium, there also were commentary papers prepared by members of the University of Minnesota community.

The theme of the seventeenth symposium, and the present volume, was parent-child interaction and parent-child relations. The choice of this topic reflects a long history of concern about parental influence on development, as well as a number of new issues and methods for addressing them. Some of the investigations that were discussed focused on determinants of parent-child interaction, whereas others focused on its consequences. The volume thus includes work involving fairly micro analyses of the very nature of interaction and the development of relationships, as well as more molar examinations of the impact of interaction or lack of it. In addition, the volume truly represents a life-span compendium. One chapter presents research on parent-child interactions with infants, while another presents work on parent-child interactions between adults. Finally, the breadth of perspectives that were brought to bear here are reflected in the commentaries, in which psychological, sociological, and family systems perspectives were considered.

The main presenters were Dr. Ina Užgiris of Clark University, Dr. Marilyn Shatz of the University of Michigan, Dr. Alison Clarke-Stewart of the University of Chicago, Dr. Lois Hoffman of the University of Michigan, and Dr. Gunhild

Hagestad of the Pennsylvania State University. The commentators were Dr. Jeylan Mortimer, Dr. W. Andrew Collins, and Dr. Willard Hartup.

Financial support for the seventeenth Minnesota Symposia on Child Psychology came from the Graduate School of the University of Minnesota as well as from the University's College of Education. Many individuals at the Institute of Child Development provided much help in carrying out the symposium, and their aid was deeply appreciated. They include Margarita Azmitia, Andy Collins, Ganie DeHart, Helen Dickison, Sue Fust, Marci Glicksman, Jan Goodsitt, Lu-Jean Huffman, Debby Jacobvitz, Kathy Kolb, Judy List, Bill Merriman, Margaret Miller, José Nañez, Caroline Palmer, Anne Pick, Herb Pick, Martha Robb, David Schmit, June Tapp, and Chris Todd. Finally, the contributors who presented their research, and the commentators who discussed it, are gratefully recognized. Their dedication and insights are of greatest import.

Marion Perlmutter
University of Minnesota

Parent-Child Interaction and Parent-Child Relations in Child Development

The Minnesota Symposia on Child Psychology

Volume 17

1 Imitation in Infancy: Its Interpersonal Aspects

Ina Č. Užgiris
Clark University

Throughout the history of psychology, the topic of imitation has attracted the interest of both theorists and investigators. Imitation has come to be recognized as a distinctive type of human activity. However, beyond the similarity of operational criteria used to identify instances of imitation in empirical studies, there has been little agreement about the range of phenomena to be defined as imitation, about the psychological processes that may be involved in acts of imitation, or about the significance of imitation for human development. Attempts to bring order to this topic by proposing different terms for distinguishable types of imitation (e.g., Aronfreed, 1969; Gilmore, 1968; Miller & Dollard, 1941) have met with little success. It may be necessary to acknowledge that imitation is not a theory-free concept; it takes on meaning within specific theoretical frameworks. Different theoretical frameworks highlight the various facets of imitation in distinct ways.

In general, imitation involves similarity, a temporal sequence, and dependence upon observation. An act is considered an instance of imitation if it resembles a previously observed act and if observation of the model act is a determinant for its occurrence. A distinction drawn by most theorists in one form or another separates those instances in which the observation of the model changes the likelihood of an act from those in which observation leads to the addition of a novel act to the observer's repertoire. For instances of the first type, an increase in the occurrence of the target act following observation of a model is sufficient to establish observation as a determinant for the act; for instances of the second type, it is necessary to ascertain that the target act was not in the observer's repertoire prior to observation. Practical difficulties notwithstanding, it

1

is instances of the second type that typically have been considered fundamental to imitation. They have been studied within the framework of social learning theory as examples of observational learning (Bandura, 1977). They also have been studied by researchers interested in cognitive development as a way to assess the child's understanding of actions differing in complexity and to evaluate the role of imitation in cognitive progress. In fact, similarity between imitative actions and spontaneous actions when dealing with specific tasks has been used to support the assertion that imitation depends on cognitive understanding of the model (Kuhn, 1973). In both cases, however, the focus has been individualistic; an individual's ability to understand, to represent, or to learn from the model has been emphasized.

When imitative activity is viewed as a means for one individual to profit from the knowledge, skills, or social wisdom of others, the emphasis on imitation of novel acts is understandable. But if imitative activity is viewed as an aspect of social interchange, the distinction between the two types of imitative acts mentioned previously becomes much less important. A joint focus on the model and the observer as participants in interaction makes the recognition of resemblance between their acts central (Užgiris, 1981b).

My goal in this chapter is to discuss imitation during infancy as interpersonal activity. A brief account of the emphases resulting from viewing imitation in its interpersonal context is followed by a discussion of imitation in the first 2 years of life. An overview of thinking about the origins of imitation is presented as background to the description of some empirical studies of imitation that we have conducted. The chapter concludes with a consideration of imitation during infancy as a form of communication.

In the last decade, there has been an upswing of interest in the study of infant imitation. Most of these studies have been directed at establishing (1) how early imitation can be observed in human infants; and (2) what kinds of acts infants are able to imitate at different ages or levels of development. These kinds of studies basically use the imitative act as a vehicle to reveal the infant's perceptual, cognitive, and integrative abilities (e.g., Maratos, 1982; McCall, Parke, & Kavanaugh, 1977; Meltzoff, 1982). Selective imitation of models varying along a dimension such as complexity is taken as a measure of the infant's competence in regard to that dimension. In only a few studies has there been consideration of the process of imitating a model and the possibility of changes in this process with development (e.g., Kaye & Marcus, 1978). Furthermore, there is relatively little information about the overall prevalence of imitation during infancy or the preferential imitation of different types of acts in different contexts. The emphasis on imitation as a mirror of the infant's abilities has deterred the study of imitation as an activity that is a part of the infant's interactions with the world.

An interpersonal framework suggests a different emphasis in regard to at least three facets of imitation. First, it highlights the dyadic nature of imitation.

Another person is most often the model whose act is imitated. Although there are scattered observations of infants imitating the sounds or movements of inanimate objects, it is the actions of other persons that normally serve as models for imitation. The person whose actions an infant imitates is likely to be engaged with the infant; the imitation by the infant will be observed and can influence the subsequent activity of the model. The effect of imitation on the person being imitated has been recognized in research with children (e.g., Fouts, Waldner, & Watson, 1976; Kauffman, Gordon, & Baker, 1978; Thelen, Dollinger, & Roberts, 1975; Thelen, Frautschi, Roberts, Kirkland, & Dollinger, 1981), but has not been studied with infants. Furthermore, when imitation is considered as a dyadic activity, it becomes clear that the roles can shift and the model can in turn imitate the observer. The sequence can extend through a number of turns for each participant. In informal reports, the occurrence of mutual imitation in the interactions of infants with adults has been noted, but imitation as a bi-directional activity has not been investigated systematically, except in one study by Pawlby (1977).

Second, an interpersonal framework suggests that in addition to the cognitive aspect, imitation has an interpersonal aspect. Piaget's (1945/1962) emphasis on the close tie between imitation and cognitive functioning was influential in focusing research on the relation between the observer's cognitive level and imitation of particular models (e.g., Harnick, 1978; Sibulkin & Užgiris, 1978). Typically, in the context of problem solving, the model was considered to be a circumscribed act rather than a person engaged in a specific activity with the child. However, with changing cognitive abilities, an infant's understanding of the interpersonal situation is likely to change as much as his or her understanding of a specific modeled act. The infant's interpretation of the interpersonal situation deserves consideration in relation to progressive changes in imitation.

Third, an interpersonal framework suggests the desirability of studying imitation during ongoing interactions. Most studies of imitation by infants have used highly controlled procedures. Typically, a person models a set of strictly defined acts in a prescribed manner and the infant is expected to respond to each during a short time interval. The infant is given little opportunity to influence the course of the interaction by his or her behavior. The choice of this procedure has been prompted by concern to demonstrate that observation of the model is in fact a determinant of the infant's behavior. These studies have shown that infants are capable of imitation. But in order to learn about the form, frequency, and function of imitation during interaction with others, it is necessary to study imitation in less artificial situations.

When imitation is located within ongoing interpersonal activity, it can be seen as a means of exchange, a way of conveying likeness with the partner. A brief review of some theoretical ideas concerning the origins of imitation in infancy is presented next as background for a discussion of the communicative function of imitation.

THE ORIGINS OF IMITATION

Historically, imitation has been considered an innate tendency (e.g., McDougall, 1914) as well as a capacity learned through standard learning mechanisms (e.g., Gewirtz, 1969; Miller & Dollard, 1941). Current demonstrations of imitation by neonates are again raising the issue of the biological roots of imitative ability. These positions have paid little attention to changes in imitation with development.

In contrast to such views stand conceptions of imitation as a process that itself undergoes development. Baldwin (1895) presented a view of this kind and it was taken up with modifications by Guillaume (1926/1971) and Piaget (1945/1962). The tendency for self-sustaining or repeating activity common to many organisms, called circular activity by Baldwin, was posited as the origin for imitation. Both Baldwin and Guillaume related development in imitation to changes in the child's understanding of the self as agent and of others as individuals like the self. Piaget built on their ideas and related development in imitation to the general course of development in sensorimotor intelligence.

Baldwin suggested that a motor act that results in a complex of sensory impressions similar to the one that instigated it tends to be repeated as an instance of circular activity. In the process, the complex of sensory impressions leading to the motor act becomes better delineated. Imitation appears when the complex of sensory impressions produced by the act of another person is assimilated to one already familiar to the infant through his or her own prior activity. The perceived complex of sensory impressions need not be identical to the one experienced by the infant as a result of his or her own activity, but must be assimilated to it, in order to ensue in the motor act. According to Baldwin (1895):

> The essential thing, then, in imitation over and above simple ideo-motor suggestion is that *the stimulus starts a motor process which tends to reproduce the stimulus and, through it, the motor process again.* From the physiological side we have a *circular activity*—sensor, motor; sensor, motor; and from the psychological side we have a similar circle,—reality, image, movement; reality, image, movement, etc. (p. 133, italics in original)

Two phases in the development of imitation were recognized by Baldwin: simple imitation and persistent imitation. Simple imitation was characterized as the production of the same motor act on each repetition irrespective of its degree of match to the model's act. Persistent imitation led to an improvement in the degree of match to the model with repeated attempts. Baldwin posited that this was due to an active comparison of the memory of the impressions of the instigating act with impressions resulting from the infant's own performance. Such active comparison made it possible to accommodate to new models and was thought by Baldwin to be important for learning in general. Baldwin did not address directly the question of what led to the active comparison process employed in persistent imitation, but he seems to have tied it to growth in attention and memory capacities and to cerebral maturation.

Baldwin's ideas were criticized by Guillaume (1926/1971), particularly for the handling of the transition from circular activity to imitation. Guillaume (1926/1971) did not accept the notion that the image of the act of another could substitute for a self-produced image in the instigation of a motor act:

> If the mental image of my own acts is not a primitive and adequate condition for their reproduction, there is additional reason to deny this role to the perception of other people's acts. Imitation therefore cannot be, even in the simplest cases, the immediate and spontaneous phenomenon that so many psychologists have described. We can no longer be content to say—at least as regards the young child— that example operates by virtue of its similarity with the image of one's own act, which would be the act itself recommencing. (p. 25)

Guillaume posited a discontinuity between the early ''self-imitations'' comprising circular activity and imitations of others, particularly in the case of imitation of movements. Many have found it easier to build the link between repetitive self-activity and imitation for vocalizations. Mead (1934/1962) put great stress on the fact that vocalizations and eventually language have a similar effect on the speaker and the hearer in his conception of the attainment of intersubjectivity, although otherwise he gave little importance to imitation in his theory of social development. Guillaume thought that early repetitive activities contributed to the acquisition of differentiated perceptions which were prerequisite for imitation, but he opted for trial-and-error learning as the main process leading to imitation of both movements and vocal sounds.

In keeping with the opinion of the times and in spite of some of his own observations, Guillaume assumed that imitation could not be shown by infants prior to the middle of the first year of life. He considered the motive for imitation to be the desire to achieve an interesting event suggested by the act of the model. Once perception was sufficiently differentiated, the totality of the model's act could become a goal, leading the infant to try out various acts to achieve it. Guillaume attributed considerable importance to the bodily similarity between adult and child so that, for example, the action of swinging a toy was likely to result in a similar arm movement by the child in order to get the toy swinging again, without any attempt on the part of the child to reproduce the model's action. Such instances may look like imitation, but they lack the specific intent to match the model's act.

Consequently, Guillaume used the term ''true imitation'' to refer to acts having the specific aim of matching the act of the model. He argued that immediate imitation of meaningless gestures (actions the child would not do for another purpose) offers the best evidence for true imitation. It was thought to appear rather late, at the end of the second year or into the third year of life, because it requires considerable cognitive capacity. That it may require a different view of the interaction with the model was not considered.

Although deemphasizing the role of circular activity, Guillaume saw a definite evolution in the process of imitation, which was related to the emancipation of imitation from control by extrinsic goals, habitual cues provided by the model or the self, and subordination to affective attitudes. "Naturally, even after the child reaches a higher level, the beginning and intermediate stages remain . . . In cases of pure imitation, the infant's state of mind is not the same as it is for an interested pseudo-imitative reaction; but the one has become possible only because of the other" (Guillaume, 1971, p. 122).

Piaget (1945/1962) built on both Baldwin's and Guillaume's ideas concerning development in imitation. He accepted Baldwin's notion that imitation originates in circular activity. To overcome the objection to Baldwin's view that it assumed an automatic triggering of the motor act by a percept of the prior acts of either the self or others, he elaborated the concept of "scheme." Piaget defined schemes as repeatable features of wholes that are both motoric and perceptive. In addition, he placed stronger emphasis on the functions of assimilation and accommodation than had been done by Baldwin, stating explicitly that "no new external element ever gives rise to perceptive, motor, or intelligent adaptation without being related to earlier activities" (Piaget, 1962, p. 80). As the assimilatory schemes integrate a greater variety of external elements, they become capable of greater generalization. When an observed act by another can be assimilated to a sensorimotor scheme, but the scheme has to be accommodated in the process, imitation takes place. Piaget objected to the role ascribed to trial-and-error learning and generalization by Guillaume, claiming that such processes were too limited to account for imitation. But he agreed to the close connection between development in imitation and in intelligence suggested by Guillaume and adopted some of the transitions in the development of imitation delineated by him.

The description of development in imitation given by Piaget still constitutes the main reference point for most of the recent research on infant imitation. By deriving imitation from accommodation of the assimilatory schemes, Piaget found a way to claim a continuity between the enhancement of circular activities in the earliest months due to the intervention of a model who repeats the infant's activity and the systematic imitation of new models by the infant that is observed much later. The system of six stages described by Piaget involves two main dimensions: the familiarity of the modeled act to the infant and the ease with which accommodation can take place. Initially, the activity of a scheme may be prolonged by a model's act that can be assimilated to it, but because of minimal accommodation, this kind of enhancement is only a precursor to even pseudo-imitation. At the second stage, matching of a familiar model may occur, but accommodation is very limited, so that similarity to the model depends mostly on the degree to which the infant's activity can be duplicated by the model. At the third stage, there is greater accommodation to the model, in that the infant can systematically match the familiar act selected by the model, but there is no imitation of novel acts. The matching achieved in these three stages was considered preparatory to true imitation by Piaget and would have been considered simple imitation by Baldwin.

At the fourth stage, imitation of novel acts may be observed, constituting a major transition in the development of imitation. The process of accommodation is vividly manifest in the gradual approximations to the novel model and fits the description of persistent imitation given by Baldwin. The fifth stage is marked by greater ease of accommodation, evident in the systematic imitation of new models. The occurrence of deferred imitation at the sixth stage may be taken as further progress in that the schemes accommodate to the model without overt activity. Thus, for Piaget, development in imitation is linked to cognitive understanding (or availability of schemes to assimilate the model) and capacity to accommodate (related to increasing differentiation of assimilation and accommodation). The kind of "imitation for the sake of imitation" discussed by Guillaume is not included in Piaget's system of stages.

This sequence for development in imitation is supported by research evidence only in very general terms. Most studies that have included several age groups of infants have found that older infants imitate a greater variety of models, more complex models, and do this more readily (for a review, see Parton, 1976; Užgiris, 1979a; Yando, Seitz, & Zigler, 1978). In general, however, studies have not addressed critical assumptions concerning either sequence or characterization of stages in this progression.

Most controversy has been generated by reports of neonatal imitation. The acts most frequently reported to be imitated are facial movements such as mouth opening or tongue protrusion (e.g., Burd & Milewski, 1981; Maratos, 1973; Meltzoff & Moore, 1977). In fact, reports of such imitations exist in the earlier literature (e.g., Valentine, 1930; Zazzo, 1957), but they had been discounted for one reason or another. The current reports have also been debated (e.g., Anisfeld, 1979; Hayes & Watson, 1981; Jacobson, 1979; Jacobson & Kagan, 1979; Masters, 1979; Meltzoff & Moore, 1979; Waite & Lewis, 1979). Critics suggest that the obtained matches may be due to general arousal, be nonspecific to the models used, or be part of a group of reflexive responses that decline with age.

The controversy makes it clear that the definition of imitation is also in question. If true imitation is tied to accommodation to novel models, these matching activities by infants may not qualify. No one has argued that the actions imitated by neonates are novel in the sense that they are not frequently performed by infants of this age. The facial gestures could be considered novel in the sense that neonates are not likely to have seen themselves performing them; in which case the judgment rests on assumptions about sensory integration, which is the point stressed by Meltzoff (1982). However, if it can be accepted that neonates match such gestures selectively (even if the gestures are considered familiar), these observations imply greater capacity to accommodate than was assumed by Piaget. Reports of matching of vocalized pitch (Kessen, Levine, & Wendrich, 1979; Papoušek & Papoušek, 1982) and of facial expressions of emotion (Field, Woodson, Greenberg, & Cohen, 1982) by young infants suggest that infants can contribute to establishing a similarity with another person. Whether such matching is to be considered part of imitative development is a conceptual issue.

It is striking that although most of the observations of infant imitation involve persons modeling human expressions or activities, they have been treated almost exclusively in relation to the infant's cognitive capacities: ability to integrate sensory information, understand relations between objects, coordinate actions sequentially, or remember activities for a period of time. Baldwin (1895) stressed that persons have the kinds of characteristics that make them especially likely to be imitated. In instances of persistent imitation, he saw the origin of volition and of selfhood. Imitation was implicated both in the genesis of subjectivity and of intersubjectivity. "My sense of myself grows by imitation of you, and my sense of yourself grows in terms of my sense of myself. Both *ego* and *alter* are thus essentially social; each is a *socius* and each is an imitative creation" (p. 338). However, Baldwin's statements regarding the role of imitation in this process were fairly general and they have not been elaborated on in subsequent research.

Piaget linked imitation with symbolization, but stressed imitation as a precursor to all representation. Because human communication is largely symbolic, a tie between imitation and communication might have been worked out within the framework of Piaget's theory, but the role of imitation in gaining cognitive understanding has been emphasized instead. The function that imitation may have in interpersonal interaction is just beginning to be discussed. In this context, Mead's comment that the importance of imitation lies in the fact that it helps pick out what is common in the behavior of the two interactants may deserve further consideration.

A number of investigators studying mother-infant interaction mention that imitation occurs during such interactions, but little quantitative data specific to imitation has been reported. In the earliest months it is typically the mother who matches the expressions or vocalizations of the infant (Papoušek & Papoušek, 1977; Trevarthen, 1977). From an interpersonal view, however, it is the congruence achieved through matching that is most important, and the identity of the partner whose action produces the match is secondary. The achievement of congruence seems to be significant for both partners. Papoušek and Papoušek (1979) have pointed out that imitation by the mother creates a situation through which an infant can perceive that his or her behavior regularly produces a response from the mother, and in view of the relatively small number of infant acts that can be reciprocated, the infant can soon recognize the mother's response. These maternal imitations often call forth smiles or joyful vocalizations. On the other hand, a matching response from her infant appears to be highly salient to the mother as well. Lewis (1979) reported that the majority of mothers of infants under 6 months of age have the impression that their infants engage in imitative games with them, even though in an experimental setting their infants were shown to match the mothers' behaviors no more often than might be expected from the general probability of those behaviors. The impression that the mothers have may be nonetheless important for sustaining interactions during which matching of responses actually does occur. An instance of matching can be a realization of mutuality for both the infant and the mother; it can confirm similarity of feeling, interest, or goal.

The communicative aspects of imitation became apparent to me while working with several students on imitation by infants in a laboratory setting. Our interest was mainly in the influence of cognitive development on imitative performance. However, repeated viewings of the videorecords of the infants' behaviors suggested that the kinds of dimensions we used to grade the acts that we modeled to the infants were not the only ones that seemed to matter to them. Although we started with a highly controlled situation, our observations suggested that data on imitation in the course of ongoing interactions was also needed. Some of these studies are described next.

IMITATION OF DELIBERATELY MODELED ACTIONS

In these studies, we were interested in the relation between different characteristics of modeled actions and imitation. Only manual acts were employed. The studies were carried out in a child study laboratory appropriately furnished for infants and young children and equipped with cameras for videorecording of sessions on decks located in an adjacent control room. The infants came from families who agreed to participate in our studies upon being contacted through a letter and a follow-up telephone call. Infants with a normal birth and health history according to parental report were accepted for study. The socioeconomic standing of these families ranged from lower-middle to upper-middle class. The infants were brought to the laboratory by a parent who remained with the infant throughout the session.

Specificity in Infant Imitation. Descriptions of development in imitation have been based on the assumption that there is an overriding commonality among the acts imitated at each developmental level. In terms of Piaget's scheme, the acts imitated at the third stage must be familiar to the infant and visible while being performed; at the fourth stage, the acts need not be visible; at the fifth stage, novel acts may be imitated. However, empirical studies have found that other characteristics of acts are also important. Abravanel, Levan-Goldschmidt, & Stevenson (1976) considered the possibility that actions which are accompanied by sound might be imitated more often than silent ones. Their data substantiated this expectation in some instances, but not in others. Subsequently, McCall et al. (1977) found no support for the importance of this variable. On a post hoc basis, Abravanel et al. concluded that acts in which objects are used are imitated more frequently than acts without objects. They even suggested that nonvisible acts may be difficult for infants because they typically do not involve objects.

We conducted a study to compare the imitation of manual acts performed using toys and the same acts performed without toys (Užgiris & Silber, 1976). A total of 24 infants were tested, divided equally into three age groups: 11 months, 14 months, and 18 months of age. Each age group contained an equal number of boys and girls. Four infants did not complete the session and others were recruited to replace them.

Four different acts were modeled by a female experimenter. When performed using toys, they consisted of striking a medium-sized bell with the palm of the hand, squeezing a soft toy between thumb and forefinger, pushing along a toy car with fingers placed on its roof, and making a pinwheel move in a circle with a forefinger. The same acts performed without the toys constituted the empty movements. All four acts were presented first as empty movements, then with the toys, and then again as empty movements. The order of the individual acts was counterbalanced across infants, but the same order was maintained across conditions for any one infant. Each of the four acts was modeled three times in each condition; there was a pause for the infant to imitate after each modeling.

The infants' behavior was scored from videotapes. Instances of full imitation, partial imitation, or irrelevant behavior were coded. The infant's highest performance in the three presentations of each act was taken as the infant's score in order to have the score reflect the infant's ability to imitate a particular act rather than his or her willingness to repeat this imitation across trials. From an interactive orientation, an argument could be made for taking the frequency of imitation across trials into account. In this study, however, the results remain essentially unchanged regardless of the type of scoring. The videorecords of three infants in each age group were evaluated by two independent scorers. They agreed on 85.8% of the 324 trials scored.

We expected the younger infants to imitate more readily when the acts were performed with toys, since they would resemble more the total unanalyzed acts familiar to the infants. Because older infants can imitate novel acts, we thought they might imitate the empty movements as well. Furthermore, we expected that the empty movements might be imitated more on the second presentation, because Guillaume had argued that actual matching helps the child to see the possibility of imitating an act.

In analyzing the data, we found no age differences and a strong condition effect. The mean imitation scores are given in Table 1.1. Although the means fit the expected trends, the individual variability was so large that only the condition

TABLE 1.1
Mean Imitation Scores (Summed for
Four Acts)

	Conditions		
Age Group	Empty Movement 1	Toy	Empty Movement 2
11 mo.	6.0	8.5	5.9
14 mo.	6.2	8.9	6.0
18 mo.	6.4	9.4	7.0

Maximum Score = 12.

effect was significant. The finding that infants imitate actions involving objects more readily has been obtained in several other studies as well (McCall et al., 1977; Rodgon & Kurdek, 1977). The data on the frequency of full and partial imitations are given in Table 1.2. The parallel trend in full and partial imitations across conditions and ages suggests that both imitation categories index the infant's engagement with the model.

In looking at the infants' performance, it was clear that there were large differences in the imitation of individual acts common to all age groups studied. The pushing of the toy car was imitated most often; it was also the act most often imitated without the toy, significantly more than any other act. An explanation in terms of the familiarity of the act did not seem adequate. The striking action was

TABLE 1.2
Mean Frequency of Full and Partial
Imitations (Summed for Four Acts)

Condition	11 mo.	14 mo.	18 mo.
Empty Movement 1			
Full	.78	.87	.75
Partial	.22	.50	.87
Total	1.00	1.37	1.62
Toy			
Full	1.33	1.87	2.00
Partial	1.44	1.13	1.37
Total	2.77	3.00	3.37
Empty Movement 2			
Full	.67	.75	1.12
Partial	.44	.50	.75
Total	1.11	1.25	1.87

Maximum Possible = 4.

certainly very familiar to the infants; the striking of the bell produced a clear result that could serve as goal; yet the striking act was the least often imitated of the four used. The second most frequently imitated act was squeezing, particularly in the presence of the toy. We began to consider that the infants imitated those acts that they saw as meaningful, in the sense that they recognized them as suggesting a play activity that they had previously shared with others. The added elaborations and vocalizations of the oldest group implied that they were viewing the actions of the experimenter as referring to a play activity even when no toys were being used.

Meaningfulness in Infant Imitation.   In a study with Melanie Killen (Killen & Užgiris, 1981), we attempted to demonstrate more directly the relevance of the dimension of meaningfulness to imitation. We assumed that among the variety of acts that are familiar to young infants, some will become socially meaningful through their use in interactions with adults. Among these meaningful acts some may be unique to individual families, but others are likely to be conventional gestures or acts toward toy objects common within a cultural group. We selected to study several play acts that we thought would be meaningful when carried out with conventionally appropriate objects and nonmeaningful when carried out with inappropriate objects. We also studied imitation of simple familiar acts conventionally less linked to specific objects. Four groups of 10 infants were tested: 7½ months, 10 months, 16 months, and 22 months of age.

Six different acts using toys were modeled. Two of these were simple manual acts frequently carried out by infants: shaking and banging. We thought these acts did not change in meaningfulness when performed either with a block or a doll, although for purposes of some analyses we designated banging the block and shaking the doll as the conventional actions. The other four acts consisted of taking to the mouth, sliding on a surface, sweeping down on the side of the head, and hopping along a surface. When these acts were paired with conventionally appropriate objects, they became drinking from a cup, driving a toy car, brushing the hair, and making a dog walk. When paired with conventionally inappropriate objects (e.g., taking the toy car to the mouth), we considered them less meaningful to young infants. Since exactly the same arm-hand movements are performed in each case, the familiarity of the acts themselves does not vary with the change of object.

A female experimenter modeled actions employing each of the six acts twice for all the infants, once with an appropriate and once with an inappropriate object. The order of the presentations was varied across infants. Before the modeling, the infants were given 2 minutes to play with each object. Then, either the conventionally meaningful or the counterconventional act was modeled three times with that object, and the infant had an opportunity to imitate the action after each modeling. Subsequently, three presentations of the same act with a different object were made. This procedure was continued for all objects. The infants' behavior was scored from videotapes as full imitation, partial imitation, or irrelevant behavior. Two scorers achieved 89% agreement in scoring a sub-sample of the videotapes.

We expected differential imitation of the three types of actions with age. The simple acts were familiar to even the youngest infants, so we expected them to imitate those acts. If the meaningfulness of the act is relevant for imitation, we expected infants to begin to imitate acts with conventional objects earlier than the same acts with counterconventional objects. The oldest group was considered likely to understand the action even with an inadequate substitute object and to imitate the counterconventional actions as well. Moreover, if imitation is a reflection of an active accommodation to an incompletely known event, we expected imitation of each type of action to peak and then to decline across the age groups.

Our expectations were mostly supported by the data which are shown in Table 1.3. The youngest group imitated the simple actions of shaking and banging the most and the counterconventional actions the least. The two oldest groups imitated the conventional actions the most, which produced a significant interaction effect between age and type of action. The counterconventional actions were imitated most often by the oldest group of infants, but not significantly differently from the conventional actions. The two middle age-groups imitated the conventional actions significantly more than the counterconventional ones, substantiating our hypothesis that meaningfulness of the action as a totality rather than familiarity of the acts themselves was related to imitation.

Since the simple and the conventional actions were ones the infants might have shown spontaneously in play with objects, we compared the frequency of these actions during the period of play with each object prior to modeling and their frequency following modeling. These results are shown in Table 1.4. Only full imitations were considered in this comparison. The modeling effect was found to be significant as well as the age effect; there was also a significant

TABLE 1.3
Mean Imitation Scores
(Summed for Four Acts)

Age Group	Simple Acts	Conventional Acts	Counterconventional Acts
7½ mo.	2.8	1.4	0.6
10 mo.	1.8	4.4	1.3
16 mo.	3.8	6.2	3.6
22 mo.	4.4	6.2	5.2

Maximum Score = 8.
(From Killen & Užgiris, 1981).

TABLE 1.4
Mean Number of Simple Acts and
Conventional Acts Observed in Play and
Imitation

	Simple Acts		Conventional Acts	
Age Group	Play	Imitation	Play	Imitation
7½ mo.	0.6	1.2	0.7	0.6
10 mo.	0.9	0.9	0.8	1.8
16 mo.	0.3	1.9	2.3	3.3
22 mo.	0.1	2.2	1.4	3.0

Maximum Possible = 4.
(From Killen & Užgiris, 1981).

interaction. With age, the trend for the frequency of these acts differed during spontaneous play and following modeling. The frequency of conventional actions increased in play and in imitation, while the frequency of simple actions decreased in play, but increased in imitation. For the two oldest groups of infants, the simple actions can hardly be considered a challenge to their cognitive understanding; nevertheless, they were imitated quite often. The behavior of the infants seemed to suggest that imitation for them was a format for interacting with the experimenter. It was a way of sharing an activity concerning objects with her.

The behavior of the infants following modeling of the counterconventional actions was also revealing. The youngest group was not very interested, as might be expected. The 10-month-olds watched attentively, but often performed a conventionally appropriate action, as if instructing the experimenter about the nature of the object. The 16-month-olds seemed to recognize the incongruity; some giggled and others gave the toy back to the experimenter rather than attempt the counterconventional action. The oldest group was most likely to follow the experimenter in the counterconventional activity. Some of them seemed to have reached the level of imitating for the sake of imitation described by Guillaume, although we would argue that the counterconventional actions are not meaningless acts for these infants.

These findings have been replicated and extended in another study (McCabe & Užgiris, 1983). Imitation of counterconventional actions was found to occur at roughly the age when infants begin to engage in pretend play. If the ability to substitute a different object for the appropriate one is involved in grasping the meaning of counterconventional actions, then modeling of those same acts with objects that are inappropriate to the act, but have no typical act associated with them, should produce a similar trend in imitation. We wanted to show that the difficulty in imitating acts paired with conventionally inappropriate objects was not due to interference from the tendency to perform instead the familiar, socially appropriate actions with them. Therefore, in this study, the same acts were modeled with conventionally appropriate, neutral, and conventionally inappropriate objects. In addition, several more complex actions (requiring joint use of two objects) were modeled in order to observe imitation of actions likely to be of interest to the older infants irrespective of the outcome of the meaningfulness manipulation.

Three groups of 12 infants in the second year of life were tested: 12 months, 17 months, and 22 months of age. The acts of hugging, drinking, sliding, and putting to the ear were modeled using three sets of objects. A doll, cup, car, and telephone receiver were used to produce the conventional and the counterconventional actions. Abstract-shaped pieces of wood and styrofoam were considered neutral objects and were paired with the same acts to produce the neutral actions. Complex actions involved putting together a two-piece puzzle, stirring in a cup with a dowel, putting clothespins through a slit into a can, and clapping together two styrofoam half-circles. The infants were given up to 2 minutes to play with each object prior to an action being modeled with that object. If a target action was performed spontaneously, it was not modeled and an alternate action was used. The fourth action in each category was employed as the alternate. The testing procedure was the same as in the Killen and Užgiris study, except that both the experimenter and the infant's mother modeled all the actions. However, there was little difference in imitation for the two models and data are presented averaged across the two.

Imitation was scored from videotapes. A third of the tapes was scored by a second scorer, with 83% agreement in scores assigned for each imitation trial. The highest score achieved on any of the three trials given for each action was used in data analysis.

Because the youngest infants in this study were a year old, there was no change in imitation of conventional actions with age, as would be expected on the basis of the Killen and Užgiris study. The 12-month-olds imitated the conventional actions significantly more than any of the other types. The 17-month-olds imitated conventional actions significantly more than counterconventional actions. The 22-month-olds imitated all three types of actions equally. In general, imitation of the neutral actions was more similar to imitation of counterconventional actions than of conventional actions. The mean imitation scores for the different types of actions are given in Table 1.5. We interpreted the results as indicating that both neutral and counterconventional actions come to be imitated when an atypical object can be integrated into a familiar action structure in a meaningful way. Both imitation and pretend play may be reflecting the child's ability to symbolize in action (Užgiris, 1981a). In the context of imitation, ability to symbolize extends the range of actions that can be meaningfully exchanged, since imitation of conventional actions is not given up, but retained, as it is also in play.

TABLE 1.5
Mean Imitation Scores
(Summed for Three Acts)

Age Group	Conventional Acts	Neutral Acts	Counterconventional Acts
12 mo.	6.5	5.1	5.2
17 mo.	6.4	6.0	4.9
22 mo.	6.2	6.8	6.1

Maximum Score = 9.
(From McCabe & Užgiris, 1983).

However, this is not to deny that cognitively challenging acts are also imitated. We found more imitation of the complex actions in each older age group of infants. Yet these were also actions that are suitable in the interpersonal context of play and were treated as such, particularly by the older infants. The repetitive pattern of demonstrations by the model and imitation by the infant fit the characteristic play format familiar to these infants. The imitative acts had a quality of exchanging statements in relation to the objects that were shared by the infant and model. In examining the records of these infants, we noticed that they engaged in relatively few approximate imitations; as shown in Table 1.6, they either imitated the act or engaged in a different activity. Only for the complex actions were there a number of approximate imitations. Being more difficult, these actions may have engaged the infant to cognitively understand them in addition to continuing the play activity.

The conclusion to be stressed from these studies is that infants imitate many acts that do not present a cognitive challenge to them. They may imitate simple acts that they no longer use when playing spontaneously with objects or new acts

TABLE 1.6
Mean Frequency of Full and Partial Imitations
(Partial Imitations in Parentheses)

Tasks	Age Group		
	12 mo.	17 mo.	22 mo.
Conventional	1.62 (.29)	1.79 (0)	2.00 (.14)
Neutral	1.04 (.21)	1.37 (.21)	1.95 (.14)
Counterconventional	1.00 (.29)	0.96 (.21)	1.64 (.09)
Complex	0.62 (.54)	1.58 (.79)	2.27 (.45)

Maximum Possible = 3.
(From McCabe & Užgiris, 1983).

that even seem incongruous as long as those acts are meaningful in the context of the interaction. Thus, imitation can be communicative and serves this function in interchanges between infants and adults. Thinking of imitation in this fashion, it seemed important to obtain data on the occurrence of imitation during ongoing interactions in which no deliberate attempts to obtain imitation would be made.

IMITATION DURING MOTHER-INFANT INTERACTION

Investigators with many different interests have been conducting studies of mother-infant interaction in the last decade. The measures taken and the level of analysis have varied widely, but the general consensus is that infants actively participate in the initiation and regulation of interaction (e.g., Tronick, 1982; Užgiris, 1979b). Many of these investigators mention that imitation takes place during dyadic interaction (e.g., Kaye, 1979; Papoušek & Papoušek, 1977; Trevarthen, 1977, 1979), but little data directly relevant to imitation has been presented.

Typically it is stated that in interchanges with young infants (2 or 3 months of age), the mother is the one who usually matches the acts of the infant. Experimental studies indicate that infants may also be able to match some modeled acts (Maratos, 1973; Meltzoff & Moore, 1977), facial expressions (Field et al., 1982), and vocal characteristics (Kessen et al., 1979) of adults, but the occurrence of such matching by infants during ongoing interactions has hardly been studied.

In a recent paper, Papoušek and Papoušek (1982) have presented some preliminary data on vocal matching during the first half year of life. They report close to five episodes of vocal matching per minute, on the average, for 2-month-old infants. These episodes are almost equally split between the infant matching the mother and the mother matching the infant. The great majority of these episodes involve matching of pitch. At older ages, other aspects of vocalization begin to be matched, with some differences emerging between the sequences in which the infant matches the mother and those in which the mother matches the infant. In a study concerned with display of facial expressions, Malatesta and Haviland (1982) found that mothers of both 3- and 6-month-old infants match about a third of the changes in facial expression shown by their infants, especially expressions of interest, surprise, and joy. Whether infants also match changes in their mothers' expressions was not determined. In addition, Field (1977) has reported that instructing mothers to imitate the actions of their 3½-month-old infants increases the attentiveness of the infants and frequently results in gleeful, gamelike exchanges. Such remarks suggest that the infant matches the mother's behavior in turn, but no data on the length of matching sequences were reported by Field.

The most extensive study of imitation in the context of relatively uncon-strained interaction has been performed by Pawlby (1977) in Britain. She studied eight mother-infant pairs at weekly intervals starting when the infants were 4 months old and continuing for about 6 months. She looked at matching episodes produced by the action of both participants. Overall, there were more sequences of mother matching the infant than of infant matching the mother during this period. Matching by the infants increased with age, but maternal matching did not decline, particularly for acts of object manipulation. Although about half of the episodes involved only one exchange, all pairs also engaged in longer match-ing sequences. The content of the matching episodes varied with the age of the infants. Pawlby's study indicates that matching by both partners does take place during ongoing interactions well into the first year of life and raises the issue of the role of such matching in development. Her view that imitation may function to establish a nonverbal communication code is in keeping with data from a few additional studies.

In describing their observations of mother-infant play, Hubley and Trevarthen have commented that when infants and mothers begin to coordinate their inten-tions and to engage in cooperative play, infants also begin to accept the mother as a teacher and to learn from her demonstrations (Trevarthen, 1980). In studies of mother-infant games (e.g., Gustafson, Green, & West, 1979; Ratner & Bruner, 1978) matching as part of the game structure also has been observed. In addition, Dunn and Kendrick (1979) have described considerable imitative play between infants and their older siblings. Imitative play has been found to be an important category of peer play among infants and toddlers as well (Goldman & Ross, 1978; Hvastja-Stefani & Camaioni, 1983). Taken together, these studies show that imitative acts have a place in the social interactions of infants where coordi-nation of goals and actions is required. It may be that reciprocal imitation has an important regulating role in the social interactions of even preschool children (Lubin & Field, 1981; Nadel-Brulfert & Baudonniere, 1982), but the data are meager for this age group.

At present, we are conducting a study to obtain more detailed data on the occurrence of matching behavior during ongoing interaction in a larger sample of mother-infant pairs (Užgiris, Benson, & Vasek, in progress). We are using the term matching behavior in order to emphasize the reciprocal nature of the activity in which we are interested. The matching of the infant by the mother as well as of the mother by the infant are viewed as aspects of imitative activity. There is evidence that behavioral matching does take place in such interactions, but it is uncertain whether it fits the definition of imitation. The infant acts that are matched by the mother are not novel for the mother, but observation of the infant performing them is most likely a determinant for their occurrence. On the other hand, acts that are matched by the young infant may not even involve a direct attempt on the infant's part to match the mother. Nevertheless, once the behav-ioral match is achieved, it is available to be experienced by both partners. We are suggesting that the opportunity to experience similarity may be an important beginning for communicative development.

Our underlying assumption in this research is that mothers and young infants interact as persons, mutually regulating their activities and sharing some of their interests and feelings. Matching is a behavioral means for sharing understanding with another and may be particularly important when other means of communication are not available. When variations are introduced into matching sequences, they can serve to expand the field of mutual understanding, while selectivity in matching the partner may serve to give particular direction to the interaction.

We have videorecorded 80 mother-infant pairs while engaged in face-to-face interaction in a laboratory. The infants fall into four equal groups with mean ages of 2½, 5½, 8½, and 11½ months, evenly divided by sex. About half of the infants are firstborn, another quarter have one older sibling, and the others have between two and five older siblings. The mean age of the mothers is 28.4 years and the mean age of the fathers is 31.1 years. With only four exceptions, both parents have at least a high school education; the great majority have had some education beyond high school. Data on 40 mother-infant pairs, sampled equally from all age groups have been analyzed and the results reported here are derived from this subsample.

All pairs came to the laboratory twice. During the first session, a period of face-to-face interaction was videotaped, followed by a period of interaction with toys. During the second session, mothers were interviewed about interaction with their infants while being shown portions of the videotape from the first session and the infants were tested for imitation of an experimenter modeling a standard series of imitation items. The topic of imitation was not mentioned in the letter inviting parents to participate in the study nor in any of the instructions during the first session, but was brought up in interviewing the mothers during the second session.

The face-to-face interaction was scheduled for 12 minutes, but pairs who completed at least 9 minutes of interaction were retained in the study. In the total sample of 80 pairs, 14 infants became fussy and had to be replaced and 3 additional pairs had to be replaced because of equipment failure. For the face-to-face interaction, infants were placed either in an infant seat on a low table, in a walker chair fastened to a small platform, or in a high chair; the mothers were seated on a low chair facing the infant. In all cases we attempted to have the eyes of the infant and the mother at about the same level. The mothers were asked to play with their infants the way they usually do, but to remain in the seats provided for them. The experimenter followed the interaction on a monitor in an adjacent room and the mother knew that she could signal the experimenter through the video system. Most mother-infant pairs had no problem with this procedure, although some sessions had to be interrupted to calm a fussy infant or to caution the mother not to move out of camera range.

The face-to-face interaction was followed by a period of play with toys. The mothers were given three toys (a wooden dog on wheels, a squeeze toy shaped like a clothespin with a painted-on face, and a string puppet representing a doll; alternates were used if the infant had any of these toys at home). Mothers were also asked to bring a small toy that the infant liked to play with from home. The mother was instructed to interest her baby in playing with each of the four toys in succession. Two minutes were allowed for play with each toy and the time to change toys was signaled by a knock from the experimenter. The order of the toys was varied across infants, but the interaction with toys always followed the face-to-face interaction.

The interactions were videorecorded by means of two cameras, one focused on the face and upper body of the mother, the other on the face and most of the body of the infant. The cameras were openly visible inside the room, but the rest of the equipment was located in an adjacent control room. A small microphone was hung from the ceiling between the infant's and mother's seats to pick up vocalizations. Output from the two cameras were combined by a special effects generator and recorded as a split-screen image on a single tape. A time generator was used to obtain a continuous time record on the tape.

The videotapes were scored second by second. First, periods of interpersonal involvement were isolated. Interpersonal involvement episodes were defined as periods during which the pair established eye-contact and had at least one member attempting to engage the other or periods during which the pair became mutually involved through the tactual or auditory modalities without prior eye-contact. Three types of interpersonal involvement were scored: Face-to-Face, characterized by initial eye-contact, continuing visual monitoring of the partner, and activity with the partner in a turn-taking or simultaneous format; Mutual Gaze, characterized by initial eye-contact and subsequent focus of gaze either in the same direction or on the same object while at least one partner engaged in other relevant activity; Mutual Involvement, characterized by periods of activity with the partner in a turn-taking or simultaneous format, without initial eye-contact and intermittent eye-contact, although one of the partners may visually monitor the other. The occurrence, duration, and type of interpersonal involvement were noted.

Within periods of involvement, all matching episodes were identified. A matching episode was said to extend from the beginning of the act which was subsequently reproduced to the last production of the act by one of the partners. An act was considered to be matched when it was exactly or approximately reproduced by the partner within a few seconds and without other intervening activity. The partner whose act was matched by the other was labeled the initiator of the episode. The performance of an act once by each partner defined one round and was the minimum unit for a matching episode. Episodes containing more than one round were considered a matching sequence. For each matching episode, the duration of the episode, the initiator, the sequence of turns, the number of rounds, the degree of matching (full or partial), and the act being matched were recorded.

Independent scoring of samples from the tapes of all four age groups by two judges yielded mean percentages of agreement of 83% averaged across categories of interpersonal involvement (range = 79% to 89%), and 86% averaged across aspects of matching episodes (range = 70% to 95%).

There were no significant differences across age in the proportion of the interaction time without toys spent in interpersonal involvement. On the average, interpersonal involvement accounted for 65% of interaction time. However, the interpersonal involvement time was accumulated slightly differently with age: the frequency of episodes increased and their duration decreased with age, as is shown in Table 1.7. The most marked change took place in the period between 3 and 5 months of age.

Proportion of time spent in different types of interpersonal involvement also varied with age, as shown in Table 1.8. The youngest infants engaged almost exclusively in Face-to-Face involvement: with age, a greater proportion of time was spent in Mutual Involvement, but Mutual Gaze involvement was low for all age groups. A significant age by type of involvement interaction resulted from the decrease in Face-to-Face and increase in Mutual Involvement interaction with age. There was considerable between-pair variability in the distribution of time across the three types of involvement. These characteristics of interaction give the frame for the occurrence of matching episodes.

The overall frequency of matching episodes increased with age from a median frequency of 3.5 in the youngest age group to a median of 13.5 in the 11½-month group, although there was considerable individual variation at all ages. This may appear to be a low overall frequency of matching. We probably missed many episodes of matching that lasted a fraction of a second; these would have become apparent had the tapes been analyzed microanalytically. In addition, we specifically excluded smiles from the category of acts that might be matched, because smiling generally tends to be reciprocated and might, therefore, overshadow matching of all other acts. Similarly, only facial expressions involving a change

TABLE 1.7
Changes in Interpersonal Involvement with Infant's Age

	Age Group			
Interpersonal Involvement	2½ mo. N = 10	5½ mo. N = 10	8½ mo. N = 10	11½ mo. N = 10
X̄ Proportion of Interaction Time	.71	.63	.61	.66
X̄ Number of Episodes	13.9	21.8	22.1	24.6
X̄ Duration of Episodes (in secs.)	38.8	21.6	18.5	20.3

TABLE 1.8
Mean Proportion of Time Spent in the Three Types of Interpersonal
Involvement

Interpersonal Involvement	Age Group			
	2½ mo. N = 10	5½ mo. N = 10	8½ mo. N = 10	11½ mo. N = 10
Type:				
Face-to-Face	.96	.56	.54	.65
Mutual Gaze	.01	.07	.18	.12
Mutual Involvement	.03	.37	.28	.23

in the whole countenance and held for a clearly noticeable moment were count-ed. The judgment of vocal matching was made intuitively on the basis of a combination of parameters and should not be compared with the frequencies derived by Papoušek and Papoušek (1982) through sophisticated spectral analy-sis. Our frequency of a mean of 9.5 matching episodes in 12 minutes of interac-tion is actually very close to the mean of 8.6 matching episodes in 10 minutes of interaction obtained by Pawlby (1977), who used a similar level of analysis. These results indicate that matching episodes are fairly frequent, but they do not make up a substantial portion of mother-infant involvement.

In all age groups, mothers matched the behavior of their infants, and the absolute frequency of episodes in which the mother matched the infant increased with age, most markedly between 6 and 8 months. However, as shown in Table 1.9, the proportion of such episodes declined, because infants themselves in-creasingly matched behaviors shown by their mothers. For the youngest group, episodes in which the infant matched the mother constituted 16% of all matching episodes, but for the oldest, such episodes increased to 31% of the total. This difference was equally characteristic of individual dyads, even though there was considerable variation in the overall frequency of matching episodes.

TABLE 1.9
Changes in Matching Episodes with Infant's Age

	Age Group			
	2½ mo.	5½ mo.	8½ mo.	11½ mo.
Median Frequency	3.5	5.0	8.0	13.5
Range	1–33	1–14	3–19	5–33
X̄ Proportion of Mother Matching Infant Episodes	.84	.86	.77	.69

The more active participation of the older infants in matching episodes is also demonstrated by the increase in the mean number of rounds per episode in the two oldest groups studied. As shown in Table 1.10, matching episodes in the two youngest groups generally extended only for one round. In the two oldest groups, one-round episodes were still the most frequent, but the number of longer matching sequences increased. The sequences extending beyond two or three rounds either took on a game quality or extended to include variations on the original act.

Over half of the matching episodes involved motoric acts. Vocal matching accounted for another third of these episodes, and the remainder were combinations of both vocal and facial or vocal and manual behaviors. These combined acts were more frequent in the older groups of infants.

Analysis of the interactions involving toys also showed a greater frequency of matching episodes in the dyads with older infants. Most mothers accepted the instruction to interest their infants in the toys by demonstrating several actions with each of the toys. The type of actions demonstrated varied with the age and capabilities of the infants. Nevertheless, there was at least one action with each toy that was demonstrated by almost every mother: squeezing the clothespin, rolling the dog, and pulling the string to move the puppet. However, the quality of the demonstrations varied considerably with the age of the infant. The demonstrations were essentially designed to create an interesting sight for the youngest infants, were much shorter and not very persistent for the two middle groups, and became significantly more frequent, directed, and having the tone of instruction for the 11½-month-olds. Only the oldest group of infants matched the acts demonstrated by the mothers regularly, while matching by the 5½-month- and 8½-month-old infants was quite infrequent. This trend paralleled the increase with age in episodes in which the infant matches the mother obtained in interaction without toys. Instances of episodes in which the mother matches the action of the infant were missing or very rare in interactions with toys. The instruction to interest their infants in the toys might have given the mothers a task which

TABLE 1.10
Changes in the Number of Rounds for Matching Episodes with
Infant's Age

Age Group	Mother Matching Infant Episodes $\bar{X}$ Number Continuing through			Infant Matching Mother Episodes $\bar{X}$ Number Continuing through		
	1 Round	2 Rounds	3 or More	1 Round	2 Rounds	3 or More
2½ mo.	5.0	0.1	0	0.7	0.4	0
5½ mo.	4.4	0.2	0.4	0.3	0.3	0.1
8½ mo.	5.6	1.4	0.6	1.6	0.4	0.2
11½ mo.	7.1	1.9	1.1	2.8	1.1	0.6

changed the mutuality of the interaction. Alternatively, such mutual interaction involving toys may be a later achievement.

During the second visit, each mother was shown up to five segments from the tape of her interaction with her infant, selected to consist of two segments of matching behavior, two segments of mother's verbal interpretation of the feeling state, desire, or behavioral intention of her infant, and a segment of a game sequence. The mothers were asked to describe what was happening on the tape and were questioned about the basis for any inferential statements. In addition, they were asked about the prior occurrence of such behaviors or interactions and the persons with whom this typically occurred. If the mother did not mention imitation spontaneously, she was asked at the end whether she thought imitative interactions had any importance in infant development.

A little over a third of the mothers mentioned the importance of imitation spontaneously and all of them agreed that imitation played some role in development. Most related imitation both to learning ("It's the mother's way to show the baby what he can do") and to social interaction ("to keep the baby entertained"; "it's a kind of game"). About two-thirds of the mothers said they made a conscious effort to elicit imitation from their infants. As might be expected, mothers of older infants reported more imitation on the part of their infants. Most of them were also aware that they were matching the behavior of their infants. The interview statements showed consistency with the interaction record. Mothers from those pairs who engaged in many matching episodes were the ones who mentioned the importance of imitation spontaneously: those who engaged in few matching episodes did not do so and, when probed, tended to characterize imitation as an "automatic response" that "just happens." These relationships between interactive behavior and views on imitation suggest that reliance on matching may be a style of interaction between mother and infant with roots in early infancy.

Results show that although there is wide individual variation, matching of behaviors between mother and infant is a regular and increasing part of mother-infant interaction during the first year of life. Most of the behaviors matched are not novel for either partner; modeling of what the infant's actions might be and what the infant should strive for accounts for a very small portion of the matching episodes and occurs most often in interaction with toys. These data support the hypothesis that behavioral matching has a communicative function. As one of our mothers put it: "It's the mother's and baby's way of talking to each other."

IMITATION AS A FORM OF COMMUNICATION

It has been argued that research on imitation during infancy has slighted the interpersonal context in which imitation usually takes place. Because of the nature of the imitative event, two distinct views are possible, one emphasizing the cognitive task of understanding the observed act, and the other emphasizing the aspect of interpersonal interaction in the imitative exchange (Užgiris, 1981b). Although the views are distinct, they are not contradictory.

The cognitive aspect of imitation is supported by evidence of a relation between the cognitive level of the observer and the complexity of acts that are attempted or imitated. It appears that optimal interest is aroused by models that are within the observer's range of understanding, but cannot be grasped fully, and the imitation of the model helps to extend the observer's understanding. Piaget (1962) has explicitly expressed this idea in relation to imitation of novel models. "The interest thus appears to come from a kind of conflict between the partial resemblance which makes the child want to assimilate, and the partial difference which attracts his attention the more because it is an obstacle to immediate reproduction. It is therefore this two-fold character of resemblance and opposition which seems to be the incentive for imitation" (p. 51). The age-related trends for imitation of conventional, counterconventional, and complex acts observed in our research support the view that some understanding of the modeled act is a requirement for its imitation.

However, as other results from our studies indicate, a great deal of imitation does not involve incompletely understood acts but, on the contrary, well-practiced acts that seem to be meaningful to the individual who does the imitating. The frequent imitation of simple and conventional acts by older infants as well as the matching of highly familiar acts during interactions with the mother imply that there are other incentives for imitation besides partial understanding. It is suggested that imitation or matching during interpersonal interaction serves a social function that is distinct from the individualistic function of attaining better understanding of the observed act. It is being claimed that in the context of interpersonal interaction, imitation is a means of communication with the partner. The basic message that imitation conveys is mutuality or sharing of a feeling, understanding, or goal. It serves to affirm the act of the initiator in the context of the ongoing interpersonal engagement and thereby promotes continuation of the interaction.

This function of imitation may be most evident when other means of communication are unavailable. In interaction with infants, where one of the partners lacks the ability to communicate through language, matching serves to affirm a shared state. Once communication by means of language becomes possible, such affirmation can be accomplished through linguistic means. However, in situations where there is a barrier to linguistic communication (e.g., in a foreign country when two individuals lack a common language), gestural and vocal imitation may be used to affirm that something is shared or mutually understood. It is possible to speculate that communication through matching is a basic human capacity that becomes manifest whenever communication is confined to a fairly primitive level. Moreover, in the context of infant-adult interaction, imitation may serve as a stepping-stone in the child's achievement of more conventional means of communication by helping to establish first, that some states and interests can be shared by others and, second, that specific acts can be mutually understood to express those shared states or interests. Thus, although the communication of mutuality may initially depend on matching of facial or vocal characteristics that have universal significance, it may be expected to gradually begin to rely on acts that derive meaning from the history of previous interactions with a constant partner. If the partner is an adult member of a cultural group, the interactions in which the infant is engaged would be expected to follow cultural patterns.

In addition to affirming mutuality, imitation may provide direction to the exchanges that follow. Matching of the act of the partner is selective in that only some actions that could be matched are in fact matched. As the response to a statement in a conversation gives direction to the conversation by focusing on a particular part of a previous statement, so, analogously, the matching of a particular act of the partner highlights that act and suggests a direction for the interaction. We know little about the factors that influence partners to select particular acts for matching during an ongoing interaction. However, it is suggested that in the long run, selective matching by the adult partner may help the infant to adopt more conventionalized acts for sharing meaning with others.

Four related characteristics of imitation can be used to describe more fully its role in communication: imitation is interpersonally meaningful, it is reciprocal, it is selective, and it is progressive during development.

Imitation or matching that occurs in interpersonal interactions with young infants involves acts that pertain to the expression of feeling, intent, or engagement with the other. That most such matching episodes result from the mother matching the infant has been commented on by other investigators of mother-infant interaction and is shown by our data as well. The most frequently matched acts are vocalizations, facial movements, and head orientations. The infants are reported to respond with joy to such maternal matching (Field, 1977; Papoušek & Papoušek, 1977). It may be that the contingency of the mother's act on the infant's behavior and the control perceived by the infant is the initial source of the joy (cf. Watson, 1972). But the similarity itself may be significant also. Kaye (1979) has mentioned that mothers use both a maximizing and a minimizing matching strategy depending on their desire to encourage or to discourage a particular state in the infant; since the strategy works at least some of the time, the infants must actively adjust to the maternal model. Studies needed to disentangle the effects of contingency from similarity for highlighting matching episodes have not been conducted.

Even if instances of similarity are initially highlighted as a result of the predictability inherent in the adult's matching of the infant, the acts that come to be mutually matched gain meaning for both partners participating in such interactions. The argument for the meaningfulness of acts that are imitated in the context of interpersonal interaction is two-pronged. First, it rests on the nature of acts comprising such imitative exchanges. At each age level, they seem to be primarily acts that are recognized by both partners, ranging from facial and vocal play during the first 6 months of life to a variety of game routines in subsequent months (e.g., Gustafson et al., 1979; Malatesta & Haviland, 1982; Ratner & Bruner, 1978; Ross & Kay, 1980). For example, in our studies of deliberately modeled actions, the types of acts that were imitated by the youngest infants continued to be imitated by the oldest ones even though they also imitated more complex acts. Similarly, in our observations of mother-infant interaction, the majority of matching episodes consisted of hand games or vocal routines that were well known to both partners. Such highly practiced acts would seem to offer few difficulties for their reproduction, so that the source of their attractiveness must be elsewhere. It is suggested that it lies in their interpersonal meaning. Such acts may be considered not only familiar, but meaningful, because they are linked in specific ways to either objects or other acts within an action totality and mark that totality. Second, the argument for the importance of meaningfulness rests on the function of imitation in interpersonal exchanges. If, as has already been suggested, imitation is a way to indicate sharing of something with another, then there should be qualitative aspects of imitative exchanges correlated with changes in the infant's understanding of interpersonal interaction. There are no relevant data for infants. Even the effects of the infant's relation to the model on imitation have hardly been studied. We have made informal observations suggesting that during the second year, infants begin to understand imitative interactions as a form of interpersonal exchange in which one can make an indication and have it affirmed by the other through action. In our studies of deliberately modeled actions, the oldest infants seemed to have the clearest grasp that the situation was one of imitative exchange: They were most ready to imitate even the simplest acts, to wait for their turn, to shift from one act to another, as well as to reverse roles and to introduce some action for the experimenter to imitate. To use Guillaume's phrase, they seemed to be imitating for the sake of imitation. An understanding of imitation as a type of interpersonal exchange may facilitate the kinds of processes that Baldwin implicated in the development of one's sense of self and of others as persons. Furthermore, a basic understanding that imitative interactions are a format for exchanging meanings may be required for using imitation in linguistic interactions. Recent studies of children learning language have noted that imitation occurs fairly frequently in verbal dialogues and may contribute to linguistic progress (cf. Kuczaj II, 1982). It is also interesting that facility in matching counterconventional actions has been found to be predictive of verbal production at least in the early phases of language development (Bates, Bretherton, Snyder, Shore, & Volterra, 1980).

Imitation is also reciprocal and tends to become more reciprocal with the infant's development. Inherently, it is a format within which the roles of model and imitator tend to be reversed, either successively or over time. The increasing reciprocity during imitative activity is demonstrated by the increasingly even distribution of mother-initiated and infant-initiated matching sequences during interpersonal interaction obtained in our sample and by Pawlby (1977). The increasing number of matching sequences that extend through several rounds may be taken as another expression of increasing reciprocity. However, it may be noteworthy that most matching episodes remain one round in length; when they become fairly long sequences, they begin to include variations introduced by one or both partners. To the extent that imitations are communicative, it makes sense that they would not be repeated many times. Turn-taking sequences in games often involve complementary turns; in such games, the understanding is conveyed not directly through the action, but indirectly, through proper adherence to the script of the game. In imitation, the match achieved through the successive turns conveys understanding between the partners concerning the action being imitated. Thus, imitative sequences provide the format for checking on subjective accord within the larger framework of interaction. Moreover, the role reversals between the model and imitator that take place over time may also be important in helping the child gain understanding of the reciprocity essential to all modes of communication.

If matching on the part of the child can be considered selective as a result of what the child finds meaningful, maternal matching is selective in the direction of more conventional and arbitrary means of sharing understanding. Papoušek and Papoušek (1982) have pointed out that in vocal matching, mothers begin to focus selectively on speech-related characteristics in contrast to singing-related characteristics even before the infant begins to practice syllabic vocalizations. Out of the infant's realm of activities that potentially could be matched by the mother, only some are picked out, reproduced, and made meaningful; they are highlighted by the mother, practiced by the infant, and come to constitute a token in their interpersonal exchange. In our observations of mother-infant interactions using toys, we found that mothers matched relatively few infant actions. Also, they demonstrated relatively few actions, but for older infants these demonstrations converged on conventionally meaningful ways of treating the objects. With the younger infants (particularly the 5- to 6-month-olds) mothers tended to incorporate the toys into games that seemed to be well known and understood by the pair, but for which the nature of the toy was really irrelevant (e.g., flying a toy through the air in a pattern of a well-practiced buzzing routine even though the toy in hand was a wooden dog on wheels). With the older infants, the toy dog was much more likely to be used in a back-and-forth rolling routine, making use of the wheels on the toy. The process of selective matching of infant actions and of selective modeling of actions when it is the adult's turn to initiate an imitative exchange may play a role in the conventionalization of gestural communication.

The sharing of understanding through matching is progressive in the sense that it approaches more advanced forms of communication. Symbolic forms of communication permit reference not only to the here and now, but also to the past, to the distant, and to the imaginative. To the extent that matching moves from the replication of fleeting expressions, orientations toward objects of interest, and explorations of available toys to games of distinct roles and pretend actions, it can be said to approach more advanced modes of communication. Moreover, to the extent that the actions that are matched become mutually shared, conventionalized, and differentiated from the ongoing situation, they can also be said to share aspects of more advanced forms of communication. Symbol construction is evident in imitation as well as in other forms of activity and may be the link between imitation and other forms of communication.

The role of mutual imitation or matching in the process of verbal language development is also beginning to be explored much more directly. As the link between gestural communication and verbal language is coming to be appreciated (Lock, 1980; McShane, 1980; Volterra, 1981), the relation between the whole structure of interpersonal understanding in infancy and language development is beginning to be looked at in a new light. Even at the level of verbal language development, conversational exchanges that include repetition, reproduction, and sequences of mutual matchings are beginning to be studied as constructive for language development (e.g., Moerk, 1977; Ramer, 1976; Ryan, 1973). The role of matching or "specularity" (Camaioni, in press) is coming to be discussed regarding language viewed in the communicative context. Although now concerned with verbal routines and speech repetitions, the role of imitation may again be to communicate and to check understanding between the two participants in the dialogue.

Taken within an interpersonal framework, imitation or matching may be seen as a means for communicating shared experience or understanding. In earliest infancy, matching of vocalizations and affective expressions establishes the sharing of the current state by the two participants. Later in infancy, matching of play activities affirms the shared understanding of the direction or structure of the play interaction. In early verbal dialogues, matching indicates the realm of shared focus. Even in adulthood, imitation can serve to communicate understanding or sharing of experience in contexts where more advanced means for communication are unavailable (e.g., in a foreign country) or are set aside (e.g., in intimate relationships). The actual behavioral matching affirms mutual comprehension. With development, however, imitative interactions make use of a much greater variety of acts. Due to selectivity and reciprocity in imitative interactions, acts that are linked to specific experiences only by virtue of prior individual history or acts that have conventional meaning may come to express mutual understanding. The relation between participation in imitative exchanges and the development of symbolization is a topic awaiting to be fully explored.

ACKNOWLEDGMENTS

The writing of this paper and the research on imitation during mother-infant interaction has been supported by a grant from the Spencer Foundation. Thanks are extended to Melanie Killen, MaryAnn McCabe, Maria Fafouti-Milenković and Marie Vasek for their comments on an earlier draft of this paper. Appreciation is also expressed to the students and collaborators in research who shared their ideas on imitation with me and to the numerous parents and infants whose willingness to cooperate made the investigation of those ideas possible.

REFERENCES

Abravanel, E., Levan-Goldschmidt, E., & Stevenson, M. B. Action imitation: the early phase of infancy. *Child Development*, 1976, *47*, 1032–1044.

Anisfeld, M. Interpreting imitative responses in early infancy. *Science*, 1979, *205*, 214–215.

Aronfreed, J. The problem of imitation. In L. P. Lipsitt and H. W. Reese (Eds.), *Advances in child development and behavior*, (Vol. 4). New York: Academic Press, 1969.

Baldwin, J. M. *Mental development in the child and the race*. New York: Macmillan, 1895.

Bandura, A. *Social learning theory*. Englewood Cliffs, N.J.: Prentice-Hall, 1977.

Bates, E., Bretherton, I., Snyder, L., Shore, C., & Volterra, V. Vocal and gestural symbols at 13 months. *Merrill-Palmer Quarterly*, 1980, *26*, 407–423.

Burd, A., & Milewski, A. E. *Matching of facial gestures by young infants*. Paper presented at the meetings of the Society for Research in Child Development, Boston, Mass., 1981.

Camaioni, L. Piaget's theory of child language research. In L. Camaioni & C. de Lemos (Eds.), *Questions on social explanation—Piagetian themes reconsidered*. Amsterdam: John Benjamin, in press.

Dunn, J., & Kendrick, C. Interaction between young siblings in the context of family relationships. In M. Lewis & L. A. Rosenblum (Eds.), *The child and its family*. New York: Plenum, 1979.

Field, T. Effects of early separation, interactive deficits, and experimental manipulations on infant-mother face-to-face interaction. *Child Development*, 1977, *48*, 763–771.

Field, T. M., Woodson, R., Greenberg, R., & Cohen, D. Discrimination and imitation of facial expressions by neonates. *Science*, 1982, *218*, 179–181.

Fouts, G. T., Waldner, D. N., & Watson, M. W. Effects of being imitated and counterimitated on the behavior of preschool children. *Child Development*, 1976, *47*, 172–177.

Gewirtz, J. L. Mechanisms of social learning: some roles of stimulation and behavior in early human development. In D. A. Goslin (Ed)., *Handbook of socialization theory and research*. Chicago, Ill.: Rand McNally, 1969.

Gilmore, J. B. Toward an understanding of imitation. In E. C. Simmel (Ed.), *Social facilitation and imitative behavior*. Boston: Allyn & Bacon, 1968.

Goldman, B. D., & Ross, H. S. Social skills in action. In J. Glick & K. A. Clarke-Stewart (Eds.), *The development of social understanding*. New York: Gardner, 1978.

Guillaume, P. *Imitation in children*. Chicago: University of Chicago Press, 1926/1971.

Gustafson, G. E., Green, J. A., & West, M. J. The infant's changing role in mother-infant games. *Infant Behavior and Development*, 1979, *2*, 301–308.

Harnick, F. S. The relationship between ability level and task difficulty in producing imitation in infants. *Child Development*, 1978, *49*, 209–214.

Hayes, L. A., & Watson, J. S. Neonatal imitation: fact or artifact? *Developmental Psychology*, 1981, *17*, 655–660.

Hvastja-Stefani, L., & Camaioni, L. Effects of familiarity on peer interaction in the first year of life. *Early Child Development and Care*, 1983, *11*, 45–54.

Jacobson, S. W. Matching behavior in the young infant. *Child Development*, 1979, *50*, 425–430.

Jacobson, S. W., & Kagan, J. Interpreting imitative responses in early infancy. *Science*, 1979, *205*, 215–217.

Kauffman, J. M., Gordon, M. E., & Baker, A. Being imitated: Persistence of an effect. *Journal of Genetic Psychology*, 1978, *132*, 319–320.

Kaye, K. Thickening thin data: the maternal role in developing communication and language. In M. Bullowa (Ed.), *Before speech*. Cambridge: Cambridge University Press, 1979.

Kaye, K., & Marcus, J. Imitation over a series of trials without feedback: age six months. *Infant Behavior and Development*, 1978, *1*, 141–155.

Kessen, W., Levine, J., & Wendrich, K. A. The imitation of pitch in infants. *Infant Behavior and Development*, 1979, *2*, 93–99.

Killen, M., & Užgiris, I. C. Imitation of actions with objects: the role of social meaning. *Journal of Genetic Psychology*, 1981, *138*, 219–229.

Kuczaj, S. A., II. Language play and language acquisition. In H. W. Reese (Ed.), *Advances in child development and behavior*, (Vol. 17). New York: Academic Press, 1982.

Kuhn, D. Imitation theory and research from a cognitive perspective. *Human Development*, 1973, *16*, 157–180.

Lewis, M. *Issues in the study of imitation*. Paper presented at the meetings of the Society for Research in Child Development, San Francisco, Calif., March, 1979.

Lock, A. *The guided reinvention of language*. New York: Academic Press, 1980.

Lubin, L., & Field, T. Imitation during preschool peer interaction. *International Journal of Behavioral Development*, 1981, *4*, 443–453.

Malatesta, C. Z., & Haviland, J. M. Learning display rules: the socialization of emotion expression in infancy. *Child Development*, 1982, *53*, 991–1003.

Maratos, O. *The origin and development of imitation in the first six months of life*. Paper presented at the British Psychological Association annual meeting, Liverpool, 1973.

Maratos, O. Trends in the development of imitation in early infancy. In T. G. Bever (Ed.), *Regressions in mental development*. Hillsdale, N.J.: Lawrence Erlbaum Associates, 1982.

Masters, J. C. Interpreting imitative responses in early infancy. *Science*, 1979, *205*, 215.

McCabe, M., & Užgiris, I. C. Effects of model and action on imitation in infancy. *Merrill-Palmer Quarterly*, 1983, *29*, 69–82.

McCall, R. B., Parke, R. D., & Kavanaugh, R. D. Imitation of live and televised models by children 1–3 years of age. *Monographs of the Society for Research in Child Development*, 1977, *42*, No. 5 (Serial No. 173).

McDougall, W. *An introduction to social psychology*. Boston, Mass.: Luce, 1914.

McShane, J. *Learning to talk*. Cambridge: Cambridge University Press, 1980.

Mead, G. H. *Mind, self and society*. Chicago: University of Chicago Press, 1934/1962.

Meltzoff, A. Imitation, intermodal coordination, and representation in early infancy. In G. Butterworth (Ed.), *Infancy and epistemology*. New York: St. Martin's Press, 1982.

Meltzoff, A., & Moore, M. K. Imitation of facial and manual gestures by human neonates. *Science*, 1977, *198*, 75–78.

Meltzoff, A., & Moore, M. K. Interpreting imitative responses in early infancy. *Science*, 1979, *205*, 217–219.

Miller, N. E., & Dollard, J. *Social learning and imitation*. New Haven: Yale University Press, 1941.

Moerk, E. L. Processes and products of imitation: evidence that imitation is progressive. *Journal of Psycholinguistic Research*, 1977, *6*, 187–202.

Nadel-Brulfert, J., & Baudonniere, P. M. The social function of reciprocal imitation in 2-year-old peers. *International Journal of Behavioral Development*, 1982, *5*, 95–109.

Papoušek, H., & Papoušek, M. Mothering and the cognitive head-start; psychobiological considerations. In H. R. Schaffer (Ed.), *Studies in mother-infant interaction*. New York: Academic Press, 1977.

Papoušek, H., & Papoušek, M. The infant's fundamental adaptive response system in social interaction. In E. B. Thoman (Ed.), *Origins of the infant's social responsiveness*. Hillsdale, N.J.: Lawrence Erlbaum Associates, 1979.

Papoušek, H., & Papoušek, M. *Vocal imitation in mother-infant dialogues*. Paper presented at the International Conference of Infant Studies, Austin, Tex., 1982.

Parton, D. A. Learning to imitate in infancy. *Child Development,* 1976, *47,* 14–31.
Pawlby, S. J. Imitative interaction. In H. R. Schaffer (Ed.), *Studies in mother-infant interaction.* New York: Academic Press, 1977.
Piaget, J. *Play, dreams and imitation in childhood.* New York: Norton, 1945/1962.
Ramer, A. L. H. The function of imitation in child language. *Journal of Speech and Hearing Research,* 1976, *19,* 700–717.
Ratner, N., & Bruner, J. Games, social exchange, and the acquisition of language. *Journal of Child Language.* 1978, *5,* 390–401.
Rodgon, M. M., & Kurdek, L. A. Vocal and gestural imitation in 8-, 14-, and 20 month old children. *Journal of Genetic Psychology,* 1977, *131,* 115–123.
Ross, H. S., & Kay, D. A. The origins of social games. *New Directions in Child Development,* 1980, *9,* 17–31.
Ryan, J. Interpretation and imitation in early language development. In R. Hinde & J. Stevenson-Hinde (Eds.), *Constraints on learning.* New York: Academic Press, 1973.
Sibulkin, A. E., & Užgiris, I. C. Imitation by pre-schoolers in a problem-solving situation. *Journal of Genetic Psychology,* 1978, *132,* 267–275.
Thelen, M. H., Dollinger, S. J., & Roberts, M. C. On being imitated: Its effect on attraction and reciprocal imitation. *Journal of Personality and Social Psychology,* 1975, *31,* 467–472.
Thelen, M. H., Frautschi, N. J., Roberts, M. C., Kirkland, K. D., & Dollinger, S. J. Being imitated, conformity, and social influence: An integrative review. *Journal of Research in Personality,* 1981, *15,* 403–426.
Trevarthen, C. Descriptive analyses of infant communicative behaviour. In H. R. Schaffer (Ed.). *Studies in mother-infant interaction.* New York: Academic Press, 1977.
Trevarthen, C. Communication and cooperation in early infancy. In M. Bullowa (Ed.), *Before speech.* New York: Cambridge University Press, 1979.
Trevarthen, C. The foundations of intersubjectivity: Development of interpersonal and cooperative understanding in infants. In D. R. Olson (Ed.), *The social foundations of language and thought.* New York: Norton, 1980.
Tronick, E. Z. (Ed.). *Social interchange in infancy.* Baltimore: University Park Press, 1982.
Užgiris, I. C. Die Mannigfaltigkeit der Imitation in der Frühen Kindheit. In L. Montada (Ed.), *Brennpunkte der Entwicklungspsychologie.* Stuttgart: Verlag W. Kohlhammer, 1979. (a)
Užgiris, I. C. (Ed.). *New directions in child development* 4: *Social interaction and communication during infancy.* San Francisco: Jossey-Bass, 1979. (b)
Užgiris, I. C. Experience in the social context: Imitation and play. In R. L. Schiefelbusch & D. D. Bricker (Eds.), *Early language.* Baltimore: University Park Press, 1981. (a)
Užgiris, I. C. Two functions of imitation during infancy. *International Journal of Behavioral Development,* 1981, *4,* 1–12. (b)
Užgiris, I. C., & Silber, S. *Imitation with and without objects in infancy.* Unpublished manuscript, Clark University, 1976.
Valentine, C. W. The psychology of imitation with special reference to early childhood. *British Journal of Psychology,* 1930, *21,* 105–132.
Volterra, V. Gestures, signs, and words at two years: When does communication become language? *Sign Language Studies,* 1981, *33,* 351–362.
Waite, L. H. & Lewis, M. *Early imitation with several models: an example of socio-affective development.* Paper presented at the meetings of the Society for Research in Child Development, San Francisco, Calif., March 1979.
Watson, J. S. Smiling, cooing, and 'the game.' *Merrill-Palmer Quarterly,* 1972, *18,* 323–340.
Yando, R., Seitz, V., & Zigler, E. *Imitation: A developmental perspective.* Hillsdale, N.J.: Lawrence Erlbaum Associates, 1978.
Zazzo, R. Le probleme de l'imitation chez le nouveau-ne. *Enfance,* 1957, *10,* 135–142.

2 Contributions of Mother and Mind to the Development of Communicative Competence: A Status Report

Marilyn Shatz
University of Michigan

The normal child's acquisition of language is recognized as one of the most impressive feats of childhood. It is more remarkable still when we consider not only the complex grammar a typical child acquires in his first decade, but also the social rules for appropriate language use that require mastery. What factors allow the child to accomplish so much in such a short time is a question that has received much attention from both psychologists and linguists. More often than not, the context for investigating the question has been one of controversy, pitting environmentalists against nativists, or mother against mind, as it were. Now, after more than a decade of empirical research and theoretical discussion, it is clear that any adequate and specific answer to that question must be complex, involving descriptions of the information available in the environment. the nature of the child's processing procedures for accessing that information, and the nature of the cognitive and/or linguistic constraints that assure the efficient development of a functional human communication system.

We have yet to achieve full understanding of the process of communicative growth; but we know at least what sorts of answers will not suffice, and we have some excellent descriptions of environmental input and even some beginning understanding of intake and construction mechanisms in the child. In particular, it appears that for the acquisition of a variety of phenomena, nuances of environmental differences have little effect on rates of acquisition. Above some threshold of environmental support, differences in rate of growth often depend more on differences in children than on differences in environments. Moreover, some aspects of maternal behavior thought to be facilitative do not appear to serve that function.

The research program carried out by me and my students and colleagues has contributed to our burgeoning knowledge. What follows is an integration and summary of our various projects and a discussion of how our findings have influenced our current thinking about the development of communicative competence. In particular, I focus on: (1) the properties of parent-child discourse that may influence the child's behavior; and (2) the internal properties of the child which constrain the course of communicative development.

In the next section, the knowledge components involved in communicative skill are considered along with a discussion of the rationale and methods of our research. The next two sections present first our findings on the maternal behaviors that are potentially relevant to communicative development and then our findings on children's responses to those behaviors. The fourth section contains a discussion of the implications of our findings for a theory of the development of communicative competence, and takes up once again the issue of the roles of mother and mind in this process. Finally, the relevance of this sort of research for the general topic of parent-child interaction is addressed in the last section.

STUDYING THE DEVELOPMENT OF COMMUNICATIVE COMPETENCE

It is commonly recognized that communicative competence involves more than having a lexicon and a list of syntactic rules. As Hymes (1972) and others have pointed out, a competent speaker knows what to say to whom, when to take a conversational turn and when to give one, how to interpret paralinguistic information, and how to interpret nonliteral speech acts such as indirect directives, metaphors, and sarcasm. There is less agreement, however, on the question of how various aspects of communicative knowledge are related to one another. The classical transformational grammar position is that syntactic competence can be investigated apart from questions of knowledge of language use. Theorists taking a more functionalist position have argued that form and use are intimately tied and that separation of them, even for analytic or investigative purposes, is misleading. Analogous issues can be raised with regard to the course of acquisition. For example, how common are the factors that mediate the courses of the acquisition of syntax and communicative skill? Some researchers have postulated an intimate relation between communication and language development. In particular, communicative understandings have been presumed to precede linguistic accomplishments, somehow easing the path of linguistic development (see, e.g., Bruner, 1975).

The believers in this view have been the chief users of microanalysis to investigate environmental influences on acquisition. This method involves describing in detail the interactive patterns observed between mothers and children of different ages and then using these descriptions to make inferences about the role of parent-child interaction in communicative and linguistic growth (e.g., Ratner & Bruner, 1978; Zukow, Reilly, & Greenfield, 1980). The other method used to study environmental influences, correlational analysis, has been used by researchers from a variety of perspectives, primarily to investigate syntactic growth (e.g., Furrow, Nelson, & Benedict, 1979; Newport, Gleitman, & Gleitman, 1977). This sort of study involves correlating the frequencies of some variables occurring in maternal speech at one time of measurement with the frequencies of the same or hypothesized related variables in children's speech measured at a later time.

The studies using each of these methods have had some weaknesses. Correlational analyses do not permit determination of causation and are unreliable with small sample sizes; sample sizes are typically uncomfortably small in the language studies using correlation. Moreover, despite sophisticated attempts to overcome them (e.g., Newport et al., 1977), problems such as the difficulty of making comparable assessments of growth rates for children at different stages of development still remain (see Bates, Bretherton, Beeghly-Smith, & McNew, 1982; Gleitman, Newport, & Gleitman, in press; Hoff-Ginsberg, 1981; and Hoff-Ginsberg & Shatz, 1982; for discussions and reviews). Microanalytic techniques are extremely time consuming and costly, and studies relying on them generally have resulted in plausibility proofs, rather than clear evidence for parental effects (Shatz, 1982). That is, they usually indicate whether a particular account of facilitation is possible, without demonstrating just what information is necessary and sufficient for growth.

There are several things that distinguish the work done by me and my students from the work discussed above. First, we have used a variety of methods, including microanalysis and quasi-experimental and experimental techniques to overcome some of the difficulties associated with the use of only one method. Second, our use of microanalysis on data from naturalistic settings was not motivated by a belief in a necessarily close relation between communicative and syntactic development. Indeed, I have argued elsewhere that such a position is untenable (Shatz, 1981, 1982, 1983a, b). Briefly, I make two kinds of arguments to support this view. The first is that different knowledge bases underlie syntactic and communicative knowledge, and the mapping between those bases is nonobvious. For example, one can generate utterances that are grammatically acceptable but communicatively inappropriate because the listener's perspective has been ignored. Children are often reported to produce such utterances, as when they call out to a listener in an adjacent room, "What is this?" Conversely, they sometimes demonstrate conversational understandings in the absence of syntactic knowledge, as when 2-year-olds take their turns in dinner-table conversations but produce word salad. The second point is that the acquisition of communicative knowledge is itself a complicated process, requiring an explanatory developmental account as much as does the acquisition of syntax. Such an account is not now available. Thus, nothing of explanatory significance is immediately gained by yoking the acquisition of syntax to communicative progress.

Recognizing the separability of accounts of communicative development and syntactic development does not, however, preclude acknowledging that there are similar questions that can be asked about the acquisition of each. For each it is necessary to describe both the environmental input available to the child and the use the child makes of that information. We have studied the role of mother and mind in both the acquisition of syntax and communication, treating them as potentially separable but related systems. Our goal has been to identify processes used by the child to extract information from the environment and then to consider the implications of those processes for both the acquisition of syntax and the development of communicative skills. To achieve this goal we have established a multifaceted research program that draws on a variety of techniques.

At the outset, it is important to note that for much of our work the outcome measures of interest are not growth rates but types of responses to varying inputs. The rationale for this focus is that examining immediate responses to different inputs gives us a more precise characterization of the information in the communicative context which children take up. Especially when we manipulate input conditions experimentally, we can see the direct impact of those manipulations on child behavior. There is, of course, an obvious disadvantage to making inferences about the factors influencing development from knowledge of the factors influencing responses: The two sets of factors need not be the same. Yet, given the methodological problems associated with correlational work, it seems reasonable to try to get some direct, explicit evidence for the kinds of information that children actually do take in. The question of whether children use such information to expand their systems is a subsequent one to that of uptake.

Moreover, the inferences we can make about influences on development from an understanding of influences on responding are not without some foundation. First, we will see that what we discover about the child's intake processes bears on the plausibility or implausibility of particular accounts of developmental influences. That is, the more we know about the processes available for information extraction, the more we can constrain possible accounts of acquisition. Second, the nature of the child's responses to input gives us descriptions of the stages of development through which the child passes on the way to adult competence, thus providing another sort of constraint on viable accounts of acquisition. Finally, to the extent that a common account can be given of response data and growth data from sources such as correlational studies, a more reliable picture of the mechanisms of development can be obtained.

In sum, we use data on maternal behavior and children's responses to varying sorts of input to build a picture of potential influences on the development of communicative competence. The enterprise is much like puzzle solving: each piece of knowledge constrains the alternative solutions for the remaining puzzle pieces. This paper summarizes the current status of the enterprise, reporting our results to date and drawing the implications of our work for an understanding of the influences of mother and mind on the development of communicative competence.

THE NATURE OF THE INPUT

Our interest in describing the communicative environment to which children are exposed has focused on the kinds of speaker behaviors that might make the entrée into linguistic interactions easier for the child. Hence, we have concentrated the bulk of our efforts on examining how syntactic information in maternal speech is related to other aspects of their communicative behavior. It is practically impossible to investigate all other aspects of communication separately. Therefore, our strategy has been to select several of particular interest and to examine their relation to the formal properties of maternal speech.

In the process of our work, we have also made many informal observations about other factors in maternal speech that might influence child productions. These are discussed as well. Both our formal and informal observations have led to an account of the character of the maternal behavior found in child-directed conversations. This account is presented in the last part of this section. In a later section, we consider how these properties of maternal communicative behavior influence the behavior of the child.

Gesture-language Mappings

One of the nonlinguistic aspects of the communicative setting that has received considerable attention from researchers in the last half-dozen years is the gestural behavior of mothers. The reason for this attention is the commonly held belief, going back at least to St. Augustine, that gestures help the child understand what is being said. Thus, several researchers have described the characteristics of the hand gestures mothers produce during speech directed to their children (Garnica, 1978; Murphy, 1978; Schaffer, Hepburn, & Collis, 1983; Schnur & Shatz, 1984; Shatz, 1982; Zukow, Reilly, & Greenfield, 1980). There is considerable agreement about the basic features of maternal behavior under these circumstances. Gestures accompany roughly 30–50% of the utterances mothers address to their children. The gestures are typically discrete, and they are drawn from a fairly restricted set. That is, they are not the sort of fluid, flowing gestures more often observed accompanying speech to other adults, and their types are fairly limited in number. In particular, there are pointing and holding-out gestures as well as demonstrations of actions. There are, of course, flourishes on these basic types. For example, one can merely point at an object, or one can tap with an extended index finger on the object. Both are points of a sort. Similarly, one can actually spin a toy carousel, or one can produce the action iconically above the object under consideration. Both demonstrate actions on objects, one more concretely than the other.

Whereas the descriptive characteristics of the maternal gestural system are fairly well documented, the function of such gestures has been less thoroughly examined. Our work has focused on the question of whether and how such a system could facilitate the child's performance in communicative settings. To do this, we have gone beyond the description of maternal gestures to examine the relation of those behaviors to the form, meaning, and intentions of the accompanying maternal speech. We have also examined how maternal speech changes when mothers are asked to sit on their hands and kept from gesturing. Finally, as is discussed later, we have examined children's responses to gestured and ungestured speech.

Gesture, Form, and Meaning. One fairly obvious way that gestures might facilitate a child's understanding of the spoken language is through one-to-one mappings between some type of gesture and some characteristic, either syntactic or semantic, of the accompanying speech. For example, if points only occurred as the speaker uttered "cat" as in "That's a cat," "Here's a cat," and so on, then the child could take the point as a cue that the accompanying sound was to be associated with the object designated. Note that this mapping still does not account for the knowledge that associated strings of sounds are *names* of objects. As Dore (1978) has noted, the idea of reference has a linguistic component that is difficult to derive from nonlinguistic understandings alone. Yet, one can see how, if the child had the idea that names were possible, the regular relation between pointing and naming would at least cue the child into the status of the sound string he was hearing without his having to understand referential frames such as "That's a . . . ." In fact, the point could be an entrée into the understanding of such referential frames.

Such an account turns out to have no basis in fact. Points are not uniquely associated with named objects, nor are any other gestures uniquely associated with particular semantic roles. Moreover, particular gestures are not uniquely associated with particular syntactic forms (e.g., questions, imperatives, or declaratives). Instead, fairly complex patterns of gestures tend regularly to be associated with either referential or action activities that are expressed by a wide variety of forms (Shatz, 1982). For the youngest children we have studied so far (16-month-olds), the patterns are even more complex than they are for slightly older children (Schnur & Shatz, 1984). Thus, any simple or straight-forward account of how gesture might facilitate language comprehension or acquisition seems ill-founded.

Further findings from the Schnur and Shatz (1984) study on four mothers of 16-month-olds support the notion that gestures are not a particularly useful entrée into language, at least on any specific level. In that study, mothers were observed twice talking to and playing with their children. During the first observation, mothers were simply asked to behave as they normally would with their children. During the second session, mothers were asked to conduct similar interactions, but this time to sit on their hands while doing so. That is, they were told not to gesture. Thus, it is possible to compare the speech of the same mothers when they were able to gesture and when they were not.

In the no-gesture condition, mothers used explicit terms of reference 71% of the time, whereas they did so only 58% of the time when they were free to gesture. The use of pronominal reference and deictic terms such as *this* and *that* rose correspondingly in the free condition. It appears, then, that the use of a gesture and a deictic pronoun is often a substitute for more explicit linguistic reference. This way of expressing reference is a common one, even among adults (Pechmann & Deutsch, 1982). That parents use it to their young children is remarkable only if one holds that parents are continuously concerned with language tuition and should instead be pairing gestures and labels in order to facilitate their children's linguistic development. Parents and older children do indeed make adjustments in their speech for young children: that is a well-documented fact (Newport, 1976; Shatz & Gelman, 1973; Snow, 1972). Apparently, however, not all such adjustments are done with the teaching of the language in mind (see, e.g., Shatz & Gelman, 1977; Snow, 1977). Given the other concerns operating in a communicative situation, such as getting an appropriate response from one's listener, as well as producing an utterance with undue effort, parents' use of habitual ways of making reference, even when talking to their young children, is understandable.

Gesture and Expectations of Response.   If gestures are not serving to clarify accompanying language, then why do mothers produce so many of them? Several of our studies suggest that gestures have a tendency to capture the child's attention (Allen & Shatz, 1983; Schnur & Shatz, 1984); hence they are a good device for keeping the child focused on selected aspects of the interaction, in particular, those relating to maternal actions or specific objects. If parents intuitively know this, then perhaps they selectively gesture when they are interested in drawing their child's attention to something in particular, rather than in giving the child free rein to respond in any way the child chooses. Interestingly, in a recent study we found just this sort of selective gesturing among mothers of two groups of children, with mean ages of 19 months and 26 months (Shatz & Schnur, in preparation). We identified those places in maternal behavior (called openings) where the mother seemed to be eliciting some sort of response from her child. Then we coded the openings for the type of response the mother seemed to expect: observation only, general action, some explicit action, some general verbal response, an explicit verbal response, or a *yes* or *no*. Table 2.1 shows the preliminary maternal data grouped according to the ages of the chil-

TABLE 2.1
Mean Percent of Each Type of Maternal
Openings That Were Accompanied by Gesture

| | Directed to | |
Type of response expected	26-month-olds	19-month-olds
Observation only	78	77
General action	70	63
Explicit action	47	70
General verbal	21	36
Explicit verbal	36	22
Yes/No only	14	31

(From Shatz & Schnur, in preparation).

dren. Mothers gestured more when they attempted to elicit observation or action than when they tried to elicit verbal responses.[1] Apparently, mothers have some understanding, however tacit, that gestures capture the child's attention. (Their understanding stands them in good stead, as our later discussion of children's responding will suggest.)

Summary.   There appear to be two reasons for the sort of maternal gestural behavior we observed. One is that mothers employ a rather habitual way of making reference, combining gestures and deictic pronouns. The other is that mothers are intent on capturing their children's attention, especially insofar as they expect their children to respond by watching or by acting in turn. There is no support for the view that gestures create an easy mapping between nonlinguistic and linguistic phenomena and hence function importantly as an entrée into an understanding of language per se.

Form-Function Relations

Part of the motivation in examining gesture-language relations was to look for simple mappings between them that might facilitate the breaking of the linguistic

---

[1]The analysis described here is somewhat different from the one presented in one of our earlier gesture studies (Shatz, 1982). In that study conversational units called cycles were coded according to whether the mother's chief topic involved action or reference. In that analysis, the mother's making reference herself and her attempts to get her child to name would have both been coded as reference cycles. Later studies (Schnur & Shatz, 1984; Shatz & Schnur, in preparation) moved to a coding scheme centered more on the mother's expectation of a particular sort of response. In that case, a mother's object reference would (ceteris paribus) be coded as *observation expected* whereas her attempt to have her child name would be coded as *explicit verbal response expected*. This later way of coding data revealed the selective occurrence of gesture as a function of response expectation whereas the cycle-based analysis did not.

code. A similar goal motivated the investigation of form-function relations in maternal questions (Shatz, 1978a, 1979). Questions are a particularly interesting form to study for several reasons. Different forms of questions take different sorts of answers; for example, yes/no questions have different canonical answer-hood conditions from wh-questions. In addition, questions serve a variety of functions in conversation besides literally requesting information. Thus, questions can be requests for action ("Can you shut the door?") or cessation of action ("Why don't you stop that racket?"), where no verbal response is required or expected. As is obvious from our few examples, the function of a question is not in one-to-one relation to its form: directives can be expressed by a yes/no question or a wh-question. The relevant issue is whether mothers provide a simple system of form-function mappings that might ease the child into the linguistic system.

There are several ways that mothers could simplify the system. They could pair particular forms only with their literal functions, using questions, for example, only to express requests for information and imperatives whenever they wished to convey a request for action. Given the frequency in English with which forms other than the imperative are used for the directive function, such a strategy might be a real conversational burden to mothers, whose ordinary ways of expressing requests for action would then be considerably disrupted. It should come as no surprise, then, to find that mothers do not adopt the literal form-function mapping strategy. Instead, they produce a variety of forms to express requests for action (Shatz, 1978a, 1979). Whereas mothers of younger children tend to produce more imperative forms for their directives than mothers of older children, about half of their directives are still expressed with other forms (Schaffer et al., 1983; Schneiderman, 1980).

Another way mothers could simplify the system is by producing fewer kinds of form-function pairs, even though some of them would not be literal. To assess the variety of question forms and the functions they expressed, I examined the types of form-function pairs that 17 mothers of children aged 18–34 months produced in child-directed, naturalistic conversations (Shatz, 1979). Mothers of beginning language learners produced as many different kinds of form-function pairs as did mothers of more advanced children. Mothers of younger children did make one sort of adjustment more frequently than mothers of older children: They tended to use certain pairings more frequently, namely, those composed of forms that served a particular function more than any other and that were found in the speech of more than half of the mothers studied. An example of these characteristic pairs is a directive expressed by a *can-you* sentence, as in "Can you shut the window?" Most of these characteristic pairs are highly conventionalized ways of expressing particular functions in middle-class English, for example, calling the listener's attention to something by saying, "See (the) X?" It appears, then, that mothers of younger children tend to make adjustments not toward more literal messages but toward more conventional ones.

Forms, Functions, and Routines.   One possible reason for the increased frequency of characteristic pairs in the speech of mothers of younger children is that these pairs are good candidates for linguistic routines in which parents typically engage children at this age. For example, two of the typical frames for the testing function, where mothers elicited specific information they already had and expected the child to have as well, were ''What is this?'' and ''What does an X say?'' where X stands for the name of an animal. I do not know how commonly children are engaged in these kinds of standardized short sequences of dialogue, although several researchers have reported that they occur with some frequency (Grief & Gleason, 1980; Ratner & Bruner, 1978). When we interviewed parents about the linguistic games they played with their children, four of five parents of children 16–18 months of age reported that they had at least one sort of routine interactional game that they played frequently with their children (Allen & Shatz, 1983).

Such games seem to be designed more to elicit talk than to teach language, at least insofar as syntax is concerned. Hence, the adjustment of the form-function mapping system that results as a consequence of focusing on characteristic pairs seems to some extent to be a by-product of the attempts to elicit talk in linguistic games and not a direct grammar teaching or simplification strategy on the part of the mothers. Regardless of their motivations, mothers are fairly successful at getting their children to talk. As we will see later, these linguistic exercises may be an important part of the child's first conversational efforts.

Conversational Styles

Whereas most parents report the use of conversational games and make use of gestures in talking with their young children, the inter-dyad variety of patterns of interaction is large. For example, some parents choose to play the ''where's your body part?'' game, and others the animal sounds game (Allen & Shatz, 1983). Also, although it is possible to characterize individual mothers' patterns of gesturing, it complicates the descriptive system to try to find one description to characterize the gestural behaviors of a group of mothers (Shatz, 1982). This kind of intra-individual consistency but inter-individual variety is typical too of the maternal conversational styles I have noted on the basis of more informal observation. For example, some mothers make heavy use of tag questions or rising intonation on declaratives as a way of testing their interpretations of their children's utterances or actions and of maintaining the interaction. The following are examples of that sort of style.

1.   C: Doggie
     M: Doggie? Yeah.
2.   C: Can't. (trying to fit one object into another)
     M: You need some help, don't you?

Other mothers have different devices for keeping a conversation going. One mother I observed used *hmm* with falling intonation to acknowledge child utterances or with rising intonation to prompt a response (Shatz, 1981). Other researchers report that some parents imitate their children's utterances when they respond to them (Folger & Chapman, 1978; Seitz & Stewart, 1975). What is notable is that whatever device a mother uses to fulfill these interactive functions, she tends to use it with some regularity. For example, in a short transcript the mother who used *hmm* produced 23 of them.

I know of no studies directly comparing these aspects of conversational styles of mothers when they talk to their children with when they talk to adults. I suspect that if there were, they would demonstrate some differences in frequency rather than differences in kind. That is, I suspect that mothers who use a larger number of tag questions with their children, compared to other mothers, also use a larger number when talking to interlocutors other than children, although generally frequency of tag questions to children might be different from the frequency of those directed to other listeners. This conjecture awaits empirical support, but the notion that conversational style is not wholly dependent on the characteristics of the listener, but rather is fairly consistent in individual speakers regardless of listener seems like a reasonable hypothesis. Without it, it would be difficult to explain why mothers of the same-aged children display so many different devices for maintaining interaction with their children.

Summary: The Influences on Maternal Behavior

In the input literature, considerable attention has been paid to the characteristics of maternal speech as a special way of talking to young children (see, e.g., Snow & Ferguson, 1977). The focus on the differences in maternal speech addressed to children and to adults was entirely appropriate, given the interests of researchers in showing that the nature of the environment to which young language learners are exposed is not hopelessly degenerate (see Snow, 1972). However, when accounting for the nature of speech to children, one must not forget that speech production is a highly automatic process. Parents talking to their children do make adjustments, but they do so within the framework of their overall linguistic competence. It would be surprising to find that their patterns of child-directed speech were entirely different from those directed to other listeners.[2] There is, after all, effort involved in modifying one's customary way of talking. Witness how difficult it is to talk to foreigners for whom one consciously tries to avoid

---

[2]It is not even clear that a very different input would be the maximally useful one for acquisition. Too simple an input might lead children down a garden path of grammatical construction, from which it would be difficult to recover (see Wexler, 1978). Certainly, if children are to achieve mature status, they must ultimately be exposed to a reasonable sample of adult language. Whether this is best done sooner or later in development depends on one's theory of language acquisition.

idioms and rapid speech. Indeed, the increase in loudness often reported as a characteristic of speech to foreigners may be more a symptom of the stress induced by having to speak in unaccustomed ways than the result of a speaker belief that increased intensity will aid understanding.

My contention is that the maternal behaviors I have described are not a direct result of mothers trying to create an environment that controls their child's language growth. Their behaviors are the outcome of several other factors. As I and others have noted elsewhere, mothers are concerned primarily with maintaining an interaction with their children. As such, devices like questions, which are good facilitators of interaction with any listener, are likely to have a high rate of occurrence. Mothers, too, seem to know something about what their children can and cannot do, and they adjust the frequency of requests for action and test questions to accord with their expectations of the child's responses (Shatz, 1979). Mothers enjoy having their children respond linguistically, and their use of language games to teach even the youngest tot a few performance routines may be as much for their pleasure as to instruct the child in language. As for their gestural behavior, they seem to think that a gesture is a good device for capturing a child's attention, and they apparently make use of it for that purpose. Premack, (personal communication) reports that gesture has the same effect on chimpanzees.

However, within the framework of these constraints on talking to and with their children, mothers are also well-practiced speakers of a language, accustomed to using certain devices to refer, to make requests, and to acknowledge a prior remark. It is from this same repertoire of conversational devices that they draw when talking to their children. Thus, they refer with gesture and deictic pronouns, they use a variety of indirect directives, and they maintain somewhat idiosyncratic conversational styles. Mothers, then, do not necessarily precisely tailor their output to maximize either their children's complete understanding of everything they hear or their language growth. Instead, they draw selectively on their own communicative experience and expertise to initiate and maintain interaction with their children. The consequence of this for the children is that they are exposed to some communicative phenomena that they deal with only partially successfully, as we will see as we turn to the children's data.

CHILDREN'S USE OF INPUT

I argued in the prior section that maternal behavior was not the result of mothers force-feeding their children bits of simplified grammar in an orderly fashion, but instead was the result of their attempts to carry on successful interactions with them in fairly conventional ways. The child's task, then, is to deal with this fairly complex and varied array of information about language and language use. Our studies of children's responses in conversational settings lead to the conclusions that children have several strategies for easing their way into participatory roles in conversations, some of which involve fairly little knowledge of grammar and, on occasion, nonstandard uses of the input. Our studies have also suggested several characteristics of the information-processing system children bring to the language-learning task. In this section I report on both of these sorts of findings. The section begins with an examination of children's responses to the input characteristics considered in the prior section, starting with gesture and then going on to form-function relations and conversational style.

Responses to Gestured and Ungestured Language

To date, five different studies done in my laboratory have examined the influence of gesture on the children's responses to language. The findings are remarkably consistent across studies. The main points are that only for the youngest children studied so far (16–18 months) does gesture seem like a useful device for keeping the child focused on the interaction. Generally, the inclusion of gesture in a message somewhat lowers the probability that children will produce an appropriate verbal response and raises the probability that some nonverbal response (either observation or action) will be produced. Finally, only the older children we have studied (those over 24 months) seem to expect that gesture and language will function together in conventional ways. In sum, it appears that gesture does not lead the child to better linguistic responses initially; instead, the child must learn the conventional relations between gesture and language before gestures can be anything more than attentional devices.

More specifically, in our first study we examined children's responses to sequences of natural conversation in which mothers focused the conversation either on some action-related or reference-making activities (Shatz, 1982). Reference-making activities were segments of interaction involving one or more maternal utterances during which mothers talked about the names of objects or their attributes ("That's a duck," "That's a smiling face") or tried to elicit such talk from their children ("What is it?" "Is that yellow?"). Action-related activities were those segments of interaction during which mothers talked about actions on objects as they or their children performed them ("Can you put the blocks in there?"). The basis for isolating a segment of the interaction as an instance of an action-related or reference-making activity was that one object or activity was involved. Children's responses were coded as appropriate if they indicated that they knew what kind of response was required. For example, an answer of "basket" in response to a mother who asked "what is this?" while holding out a picture of a bag was coded as appropriate because it indicated that the child understood a verbal label was required. Eight children 19–34 months of age were as likely to give evidence of understanding what was expected of them when conversational segments were gestured as when they were not. They responded appropriately about 75% of the time on action sequences and about 65% of the time on reference sequences. Only for the three youngest children was there any hint of an effect of gesture, and then only for reference sequences. The three youngest children (mean age = 20 months) responded appropriately twice as often to gestured as to ungestured reference sequences.

To examine further this slight suggestion of a facilitating effect of gesture on very young children, we studied the responses of four 16-months-olds in two conditions of input. In the first, the mothers were simply told to act as they normally would with their children; in the second, they were asked to sit on their hands as they talked to and played with the children (Schnur & Shatz, 1984). Our analysis for this study (and a later one) differed from the first one in that here we examined the children's responses at times when the mother seemed to be leaving a place for the child to respond rather than at the ends of her sequences of action-related or reference-making discourse. The revised coding scheme gives, we believe, a more accurate account of the problem of response timing and appropriateness from the point of view of the participants (see footnote 1).

The children's responses were categorized as action, vocalization, observation only, or no attention. Responses were also coded as appropriate, inappropriate, or indeterminate, according to the degree to which they corresponded to the mother's expectations. (Maternal expectation was assessed by coders' evaluations of mothers' behaviors prior to and following children's responses.)

Our analysis of responses occurring in the natural condition showed that children were highly responsive even when response openings were not preceded by gesture. Generally the children were significantly more likely to respond than not, regardless of whether a gesture had occurred. Only one child gave some indication that gestures increased the rate of responding. We then went on to examine whether the presence of gesture affected the kinds of responses produced. There was some tendency for observing and action behaviors to occur after gestures more frequently than vocalizations, whereas vocalizations occurred more than observations in the absence of gestures. As for the appropriateness of the children's responses, action responses were very frequent and were appropriate roughly 80% of the time, whether preceded by gesture or not. Appropriate vocalizations also showed no effect of gesture presence, but it is important to note that vocal responses generally were low in frequency.

Another interesting finding in this study was that in the ungestured condition children tended to be somewhat less responsive than they had been in the natural condition, even when mothers occasionally forgot themselves and produced limb movements. It appears that the overall lack of movement on the part of the mothers had a deleterious effect on keeping the children engaged. Further evidence that gesture's main influence is on the engagement of the child's attention comes from the finding that observing responses dropped from 41% in the

2. THE DEVELOPMENT OF COMMUNICATIVE COMPETENCE   47

natural condition to 23% in the ungestured condition. Again, there was some tendency for the children to produce more vocalizations when gestures were absent than when gestures occurred.

The children examined in this study also participated (along with an 18-month-old) in an experiment in which the effect of gesture on nonverbal and vocal responses was investigated more closely (Allen & Shatz, 1983). In that study each child was asked a series of *what* questions of the sort that mothers typically produce as they play with their children at home, for example, "What does a dog say?" "What says moo?" and "What lives in a barn?" The same questions were asked under four different input conditions: (1) with a gesture directed at a relevant object (e.g., a dog for the first sample question); (2) with a gesture at an irrelevant object (e.g., a toy airplane for the first question); (3) no gestures but the relevant object present on the floor near the child; and (4) no gesture and no relevant object present. The questions were dispersed throughout non-test conversation. Moreover, neither the same question in different conditions nor two different questions in the same condition were allowed to occur in sequence.

Findings from this study confirmed the children's tendency to vocalize when no gestures were present in the input. Children were more nonverbally responsive when gestures were present; they produced a nonverbal response over 80% of the time when a gesture accompanied a question, regardless of whether the experimenter's gesture was consonant with the language or not. Interestingly, most of the nonverbal responses were not appropriate answers to the question. (An instance of an appropriate response would be holding out a cow (or even a horse) in answer to "What says moo?") Only 14% of the nonverbal responses were appropriate. Because two-thirds of the questions could have been answered appropriately nonverbally, one cannot argue that the children were merely using a nonverbal rather than a verbal mode to produce appropriate responses. Further evidence against this argument is the fact that the large number of nonverbal responses varied considerably in kind, from picking up a gestured-at object, to putting something on it, to tossing it away. Verbal accuracy too was low, and it was unaffected by condition of input. The lack of differences in action responding in the consonant and conflictful gesture conditions and the indifference of verbal accuracy to input conditions suggest that children of this age do not process the linguistic and gestural information together as a single message.

Results from a similar experiment with 14 children aged 18 to 26 months (Shatz, Allen, & Raizman, in preparation) lend support to our earlier findings. In this study, there were three conditions; consonant gesture, conflictful gesture, and no gesture. In addition, the kinds of questions that were asked could be divided into those for which a gesture at an object designated the object to be labeled (the appropriate response) and ones for which the gesture designated only the object that was the topic of the question. A sample sentence for which a gesture could designate a response is "What says woof-woof?" with a gesture at a dog; a sample topic-designated utterance is "What does a dog say?" again with a gesture at the dog.

Even the younger group of children (aged 18–20 months) generally were responsive, regardless of condition. However, the proportion of responses that included a correct verbal response was significantly higher for both groups in the ungestured condition than in either of the gestured conditions. Older children (24–26 months) produced a correct verbal response on 43% of the ungestured trials as compared to 33% on the consonant gesture ones and 25% on the conflict trials. Younger children produced fewer correct answers overall but similarly performed better in the ungestured condition. To some extent, the condition effect is due to the facts that the children produced better verbal responses when they did not also produce action, and they were significantly less likely to produce action responses when there was no gesture in the input. In addition, the responses of the younger children to both types of questions were largely unaffected by differences in the consonant and conflictful gesture conditions, whereas the responses of the older children revealed an interaction between gestural condition and sentence type. The older children were helped a bit by gesture on the answer-designating sentences when the gestures were consonant with the language, and they were hurt when the gestures were conflicting. On the topic-designating sentences, conflictful gestures had no detrimental effect at all. In other words, the older children expected the gestures and language to be consonant, but only for those sentences where the language suggested that an accompanying gesture would designate the object to be labeled.

Summary.   Our studies of children's responses to gestured and ungestured language suggest that children progress from an early period (before 18 months of age) during which their attention is captured by gestural movements to one where they tend to respond with action to gesture and with vocalization to language somewhat independently (18–24 months) and then to one where they recognize that gesture and language can be part of the same message and require an integrated response (more than 24 months). Interestingly, we found no evidence that attention to gestural input actually blocks intake of the linguistic input (Shatz, Allen, & Raizman, in preparation). Our data, then, cannot be taken as definitive proof that gestures accompanying language cannot possibly facilitate language acquisition. Instead, our data seem to reveal that the gestural system is not a completely transparent one that children naturally and easily use to help them understand the spoken messages they hear. Part of what they must learn are the conventional relations between the gestural and linguistic components of messages. Apparently, they must learn to integrate the components of their own modes of response to produce integrated answers as well. Until they do, it appears that gestured input can be as much a detractor as a facilitator, leading children to act rather than respond verbally and directly to the language they hear.

Responses to Form-Function Pairs

Action Responding. The propensity of young children to act in response to language stands them in good stead when they are presented with an array of directives of varying form. Because they are inclined to produce action, they are likely to respond in reasonably appropriate ways even when requests for action are not expressed directly by imperatives. Even children as young as 17 months are as likely to give action responses to their mothers' question directives as to imperatives (Shatz, 1978a). Young children are also as likely to respond with action to noncharacteristic directive form-function pairings as to characteristic ones (Shatz, 1979).

Moreover, questions that refer to actions also induce action responses, even when they are uttered with no definite directive intent. In a study examining the responses of 18 children aged 19–34 months to sentences like "Can the ball fit in the truck?" I found that, in the absence of any interpretive linguistic context, the children were very likely to produce action responses and not informational ones, regardless of the form of the sentence (Shatz, 1978b). To investigate further the limits of this propensity to act, I presented some of these same children with identical questions, but this time the questions were preceded on one occasion by a series of imperatives that were clearly requests to act ("Touch your nose"), and on another occasion they were clearly requests for information ("Is this apple red?"). The inclusion of a context in which to interpret the ambiguous function of sentences like "Can you put the ball in the truck?" had an effect on the children's behavior. In the sequences with imperatives preceding the test sentence, both the less linguistically advanced and the more advanced children produced action responses almost exclusively. On the informational sequences, both groups showed a decline in action responding, but more than half of the less sophisticated children's responses were still action, whereas only about one quarter of the responses of the more sophisticated children were action. Taken together, the studies suggest that young children have a fairly simple strategy for responding to interaction, which is to act unless some cue in the context, linguistic or nonlinguistic, leads them to do otherwise. Apparently, both the linguistic context and the presence or absence of gesture affects the tendency to act. Other findings of ours suggest additional factors that lead the child away from action and toward linguistic responding.

Routines as Stop-Action Cues. The one type of form-function pairing that seems to facilitate appropriate responding is the test question that is asked in a stereotypic style ("What is that?" "What does an X say?"). For the less advanced children I have studied, these characteristic test questions have some tendency to facilitate the production of appropriate verbal responses (Shatz, 1979). As noted earlier, such pairs are typical of the linguistic sequences found in the language routines in which mothers engage their children. As children become more linguistically sophisticated they answer test questions that are expressed noncharacteristically as well as the characteristically expressed ones, but for the younger children, the set form of the question may be an important factor in leading the child to discover that something other than action is required as a response. Further support for this view comes from the fact that when we examined 16–18-month-olds' responses to what-questions in an experimental setting, four of the five children exhibited response behavior that could be directly related to both observations and parental reports of mother-child language routines (Allen & Shatz, 1983). That is, the children were using their prior experience with language routines to help interpret (sometimes incorrectly) the what-questions in the new conversational setting.

The Influence of Conversation: Dialogic Form without Function

Children's attention to information in the conversational context on how to respond apparently goes beyond the learning of routines that parents intentionally teach. I have reported elsewhere that some children learn very early that questions take a yes/no response, and children often produce such a response even when it is not functionally or semantically appropriate. Children also pick up the speech patterns of their regular conversational partner; hence, one finds that children who imitate frequently have parents who do too, and the mother who used *hmmm* frequently had a child who did so (Shatz, 1983a, for a review). Often, however, these devices are adopted by the child without the attendant functional constraints governing parental use. For example, the child who picked up *hmmm* from her mother used it differently from the way she did. Older children also make use of frequently heard phrases before they fully realize the functional limits on their use. Thus, a 5-year-old said, "Nice of you to stop by" to his mother as she was leaving for work one morning. It took the mother several minutes to realize that the child was not sarcastically complaining about her being away from home. These sorts of unintentional violations of the functional relations in conversation suggest that the learning of the social relations governing language use are as extended a process as the learning of the grammatical relations governing the forms of language.

Processing Language in a Conversational Setting

There are several noteworthy implications to be drawn from our findings on children's responses with regard to the nature of the processing children do in the context of the conversational setting. That they have some representation of the forms of dialogue to use in selecting responses is suggested by the influence of routine interactions on experimental performance in the studies on what-questions. The informal observations of children's adoption, and sometimes inappropriate use, of conversational devices confirm this and suggest further that the acquisition of maternal forms is not tightly bound to the acquisition of maternal functions for those forms. In other words, children learn something about form in the absence of learning about function. They may even adapt forms to their own functions.

Moreover, children's functions may be quite limited in comparison to those of adults. Children's reliance on action responses may be an easy way to take a turn in an interaction despite very limited linguistic and interactive skills. The tendency to respond with action to a variety of forms suggests that children make little effort to try to map unique forms of initiation to unique kinds of responses (although the studies of gesture suggest that children tend to match mode of output to mode of input). Rather, they have the strategy of acting, other things being equal. The virtue in the linguistic routines or games that mothers play with their children seems to be that those instances provide information on some other ways to respond appropriately. The form-function units created in such games may be the first such instances that are narrowly enough defined and frequently enough used that they become mutually shared and commonly understood by both parent and child. It should be noted, however, that such language games give children information primarily about response appropriateness under certain conditions. It is not clear how much they might provide (or uniquely provide) information about linguistic structure.

The finding that the linguistic contexts in which identical test sentences are embedded influence the nature of the responses to those test questions indicates that children as young as 20 months do process linguistic information across sentences. A recent finding by a dissertation student in my laboratory shows that such processing is not limited to functional information. Hoff-Ginsberg (1981) reports that the rate of children's verb growth is positively related to the frequency with which mothers illustrate whole-constitute substitutions and deletions in adjacent sentence pairs in their speech to their children. Because these sorts of formal constituent changes do not occur all that frequently with function held constant over sentence pairs (Shatz, 1982), it appears that some syntactic advantage can be gained with such pairs even when function is not held constant. That finding is less surprising in light of the earlier discussion showing that form and function are not necessarily tightly bound up in the child's use of the input.

The results of the gesture studies make even more plausible the evolving picture of a child who does not process all the communicative information presented to him on one integrated level, but rather analyzes the data on several different levels or in several different ways. As I have already noted, gestural and linguistic information are not treated early on as elements of a single message, requiring a unified, consonant interpretation and an integrated response. It appears that one task of an adequate theory of communicative development will be to give an account of these several levels of processing as well as an account of how the child ultimately arrives at the mature procedures for speech comprehension and response behavior that are more integrative.

THE ROLES OF MOTHER AND MIND IN A DEVELOPMENTAL THEORY OF COMMUNICATIVE COMPETENCE

Constraints on a Theory of Communicative Development

A theory of the development of communicative competence will be adequate if it provides an account of how the child acquires and uses the knowledge necessary to be a competent member of a social group, and that account is consonant with what is known about the environment in which acquisition occurs and about the capacities of the child to make use of that environment. In other words, the characteristics of both the child and the environment constrain the sorts of theories that can plausibly account for development. In this section, I consider what it is that must be accounted for, what we know is available in the environment, and what characteristics the child brings to the task of acquiring communicative competence.

What Must Be Acquired. As noted earlier, to be adequate speakers of a language, children must learn not only the grammar of the language, but they must also gain knowledge of patterns of use. This knowledge includes information on when to speak, what to say to whom, and how to interpret utterances under different contextual circumstances. The blending of grammatical with social knowledge that results in the ability to produce appropriate speech acts is the crux of communicative competence. Some of this knowledge is culture-specific and some is more general. In many cultures, one might hear a request from a stranger like "Can you tell me the time?" and rightly infer it to be a request for the time and not for information about one's ability to read a clock. On the other hand, the Dutch habit of greeting other diners in the hotel dining room with a loud "goede morgen" when one enters for breakfast is an instance of more culture-specific knowledge of when to talk and what to say. In both cases, however, appropriate behavior depends on more than a knowledge of grammar. The questions for a theory of communicative development are what underlies such behavior and how is it acquired.

Clearly much of communicative development must wait on the development of cognitive abilities, as well as on the acquisition of a store of social experiences on which a conversational participant can draw. For example, much of successful conversation relies on the ability of the listener to draw inferences from what is said in combination with what is known about the speaker, the way people usually behave, the circumstances of the conversation, and so on. One would not expect very young children to have either the experiential store or the inferential ability to carry on conversation at that level.

Yet, there is much communicative information that a child conceivably could acquire with even limited abilities. Much of the way language is used in a society is very conventional and standardized, if not literal. For many kinds of speech acts, there are fairly standard ways to initiate and ways to respond, and these seem to be understood easily by adults whether or not they are literal expressions of those acts (see, e.g., Gibbs, 1979). What the child may need to learn early on is the range of speech acts that can be performed and the range of ways, as well as the most standard ways, of performing them. In other words, he may need exposure to the speech act lexicon.

The Communicative Environment.   In light of what needs to be acquired, the environment that is provided for the child would seem to be rich in the requisite information. Parents who talk fairly naturally and often to their children appear to use a wide variety of common forms and functions in their speech. Moreover, they do some explicit teaching of what to say when,[3] and they provide opportunities for their children to practice taking part in linguistic interactions, however stereotyped and formulaic. They do not, however, provide this information in a bit-by-bit fashion over time. Their speech act behavior does not change very greatly or frequently during the child's second or third years. Thus, it is unlikely that parents are governing in a very tightly paced fashion just what their children learn when. (For an extended argument in this vein, see Shatz, 1982.) Consideration of the characteristics of the child confirms this.

The Characteristics of the Child.   Children are quite naturally social creatures. They are attracted by action and sound, and normal children respond in kind spontaneously to both action and vocal stimuli. Their propensity for action responses has both positive and negative consequences. Their high rate of responding to parental overtures, even before they can say much, is undoubtedly positive reinforcement for parents who like to think they are communicating with their children. The same tendency, however, seems sometimes to suppress the children's verbally adequate responses. It is unclear at this time what causes the children's early tendency to match input mode and output mode, or how they

---

[3]The tendency to instruct the child in particular socially appropriate ways of responding is not limited to Western middle-class mothers. Although the specifics of both the messages and the communicative situations differ from Western settings, mothers in Papua New Guinea also instruct their children in the proprieties of conversational interaction (see Schieffelin, 1979).

learn to integrate better the linguistic and nonlinguistic aspects of their behavior and relate them to the intent of the message to which they are responding. What is clear is that the mature way of using gesture and language in an integrated fashion is not adopted straightaway by mimicking parental behavior. In other words, as in other aspects of language acquisition, the process of development includes some selective intake of the input provided and utilization of it in ways conforming to the child's abilities or purposes at the time. The child's use of forms found in maternal speech in ways functionally different from their parental roles is another instance of partial uptake sifted through the child's own devices.

Whereas the discussion of partial uptake suggests limitations on the amount and, possibly, the complexity of information the child can ultiize at once, the finding that children do process some information across sentences suggests that the amount of information on which the child operates is not necessarily small. A more plausible explanation for why the child seems to be able to process across sentences even though he cannot necessarily integrate all kinds of within-utterance information such as a gesture-utterance pair is that gesture-utterance pairs, and form-function pairs, mix two kinds of information. When children focus across utterances on either the functional or syntactic import of the sentence pairs, they may be staying within the same realm of analysis. It is possible that some degree of competence at within-level analysis is necessary before across-level analysis can proceed very far. The distinctions being made here are, of course, speculative and require further research. It is important to keep in mind too that levels of analysis would have to be defined from the perspective of the child. The point of importance for our current discussion is that the child brings some constraints to the communicative situation with regard to the kind of information in the environment he will take up and the way he will utilize it.

The Nature of Adequate Theories of Communicative Development

The kinds of theories that will be most consonant with the findings to date are ones that will focus heavily on the capacities of the child to extract, use, and integrate information to construct a communication system. The role of maternal behavior is perhaps more limited than some might have expected. The parent is more a data base for a self-directed learner than an active organizer and selector of the material to be learned at particular stages. Whereas it is important to remember that the research I have presented has dealt only with the early stages of verbal communication, it is unlikely that the maternal role grows at later stages of development, because it is at the point at which the child enters the verbal communication system that one might expect to see the greatest efforts made to assist that entrée. Moreover, some of what mothers do may be to provide preparatory or facilitative conditions for interaction more than to facilitate understanding or development. Gesturing, for example, serves the purpose of keeping the child engaged in interaction but does not appear to be necessary for the child's understanding of verbal messages.

The importance of considering a child's processing capacities and predispositions in any explanation of communicative development is reminiscent of arguments about the child's acquisition of syntax (Newport, Gleitman, & Gleitman, 1977). As with syntax, there may be some aspects of the communicative system that are more influenced by the fluctuations of the environment than others. For example, there may be certain types of speech acts (such as declaring and directing) that are universal and that the child need not learn. What he would have to learn is the range of forms acceptably expressing such acts in his language. Thus, the time at which a child gives indications of understanding or expressing such acts might be quite independent of the frequency to which he has been exposed to them. However, his way of expressing them might, to some extent, depend on the nature of his exposure to possible forms for doing so in the language.

Still another similarity between the communicative domain and other aspects of language learning concerns similarities to word acquisition. The children's production of conversational forms in contexts that are only partially appropriate seems much like the phenomena of over- and under-generalizations of words. Learning all the constraints on the conditions of use may be somewhat like learning all the constraints on a semantic system. Apparently, production of the forms does not wait on either.

In sum, the shape of a theory of communicative development may not be too different in general outline from that which seems most promising for other aspects of language acquisition. No theory that puts the burden of acquisition primarily on the environment can account for the selectivity and creativity of the child's performance. Nor can any theory that assumes ready understanding of communication on nonlinguistic gounds account for children's behavior. Nevertheless, just as children obviously learn the grammar of the language to which they are exposed, so they also learn their culture's rules for using that language. The data base for doing so must necessarily come from the speakers with whom the child regularly interacts, and one of these is most often the child's mother. The task of the mother, then, is to keep the child engaged while she provides a rich enough environment from which her child can extract the material needed to develop a communicative system consonant with the model provided. For the child's part, he uses the analytic and integrative techniques and capacities that may be similar, at least in part, to those he uses to develop a syntax. Yet, the two processes appear to go on separately (but possibly in parallel) rather than as one integrated operation. Only future work can tell us more specifically how similar the mechanisms of acquisition are across the various aspects of language learning and how separate are the courses of development over time.

PARENT-CHILD INTERACTION: LESSONS FROM
COMMUNICATIVE DEVELOPMENT RESEARCH

A child is the most sophisticated learning device yet created. Over time children manage to acquire with remarkably little direct tuition a variety of complex systems, for example, language, social rules, problem-solving strategies, and knowledge of the physical world. Unfortunately for the researcher interested in the mechanisms driving this remarkable device, its workings are not directly available for inspection. One way of gaining insight into the properties of the device is to manipulate the conditions in which it operates and to observe the consequences, in other words, to alter the environment. Parental behavior constitutes a large part of the young child's environment, and differences among parents in their styles of interaction with their children provide the opportunity for a natural laboratory. Examining the effects (and non-effects) of differences in parental behavior on child development is an appropriate way of gaining insight into the nature of the child's capacities, not only for the study of language or communicative development, but for a large array of other topics as well.

The misfortune of such research in the past has been that findings have often been interpreted too simplistically. Differences in development frequently have been interpreted as direct and simple functions of differences in parenting. More recently, researchers have recognized that the observed parental behaviors themselves may have been influenced by the children. Thus, replicating for other children the parental environments associated with high levels of development does not guarantee their appropriateness for those children and will not necessarily result in comparable development.

Researchers in language and communicative development are gradually coming to accept the possibility that optimal environments may vary depending on the children who utilize them. Katherine Nelson in 1973 suggested that children's early language development was best facilitated when parent and child matched on communicative styles, regardless of which style, referential or expressive, they preferred. Recently, researchers working with populations disadvantaged in one way or another have suggested that parental interaction styles having no particular effect on developmental patterns in normal children may nonetheless affect development in disadvantaged children (Nelson, Denninger, Bonvillian, Kaplan, & Bakes, 1983; Rocissano & Yatchmink, 1983). Similarly, providing a reasonably rich environment for the child and drawing his attention to it may not be sufficient to ensure language acquisition if the child is deficient in the analytic and integrative abilities apparent in normal children.

The point is not merely that individual differences among children need to be taken into account when determining the influences of parental behavior on development. If children generally did not actively participate in their own learning process, then the individual difference issue would not even arise. The point is that the child has to be a *serious* component in the study of parent-child interaction. The primary task of interaction researchers is not to uncover the parental environments of successful children so that similar ones can be provided for less successful children; rather it is to discover how children learn. Studying the parental environment and the child's uses of it are part of that endeavor. Once we understand the learning process, we presumably will be able to design not only facilitative environments, but efficient ones as well, for parents of even the most successful children may do things that are unnecessary to achieve the results we value.

The notion of efficiency introduces another moral to be derived from the communication research. In our work we found that some parental behaviors were more a consequence of habits of speaking than of teaching goals. It seems reasonable to assume that in other areas too, parental behavior is not completely governed by parents' perceptions of the needs of their developing children. In trying to understand why they behave the way they do, we should remember that parents are people too, subject to the constraints of habit and information-processing capacity.

In summary, much of what we have discovered about the communicative process is probably applicable to other areas of parent-child interaction. The need to go beyond feasibility arguments in determining the role of the parent in development, the importance of examining the capacity of the child to utilize the information provided by the adult, and the motivation behind the adult behavior are aspects of the study of parent-child interaction that should be addressed in attempting to understand the roles of mother and mind in development generally.

ACKNOWLEDGMENTS

Several students and assistants have made important contributions to the empirical studies described herein. Most are cited in the references, but I happily acknowledge again the efforts of Rhianon Allen, Zoe Graves, Erika Hoff-Ginsberg, Clare Raizman, and Elizabeth Schnur. Support for the research was provided by NIMH grants 28574 and 30996, a grant from the National Science Foundation, BNS-8020335, and a grant from Rackham Graduate School, University of Michigan.

The first version of this chapter was prepared while the author was a visiting scholar at the Max Planck Institute for Psycholinguistics, Nijmegen, The Netherlands. I thank Werner Deutsch of the Institute for his comments on that draft and the staff there for assistance in preparing the manuscript.

REFERENCES

Allen, R., & Shatz, M. "What says meow?": The role of context and linguistic experience in very young children's responses to what-questions. *Journal of Child Language*, 1983, *10*, 321–335.
Bates, E., Bretherton, S., Beeghly-Smith, M., & McNew, S. Social bases of language develop-

ment: A reassessment. In H. W. Reese & L. P. Lipsitt (Eds.), *Advances in child development and behavior* (Vol. 16). New York: Academic Press, 1982.

Bruner, J. S. The ontogenesis of speech acts. *Journal of Child Language*, 1975, 2, 1–20.

Dore, J. Conditions for the acquisition of speech acts.In I. Markova (Ed.), *The social context of language*. New York: Wiley, 1978.

Folger, J. P., & Chapman, R. S. A pragmatic analysis of spontaneous imitation. *Journal of Child Language*, 1978, 5. 25–38.

Furrow, D., Nelson, K. E., & Benedict, H. Mother's speech to children and syntactic development: some simple relationships. *Journal of Child Language*, 1979, 6, 423–442.

Garnica, O. Non-verbal concomitants of language input to children. In N. Waterson & C. Snow (Eds.), *The development of communication*. New York: Wiley, 1978.

Gibbs, R. W. Contextual effects in understanding indirect requests. *Discourse Processes*, 1979, 2, 1–10.

Gleitman, L. R., Newport, E. L., & Gleitman, H. The current status of the Motherese hypothesis. *Journal of Child Language*, in press.

Grief, E. B., & Gleason, J. B. Hi, thanks, and goodbye: More routine information. *Language in Society*, 1980, 9, 159–166.

Hoff-Ginsberg, E. *The role of linguistic experience in the child's acquisition of syntax*. Unpublished Ph.D. dissertation, The University of Michigan, Ann Arbor, 1981.

Hoff-Ginsberg, E., & Shatz, M. Linguistic input and the child's acquisition of language. *Psychological Bulletin*, 1982, 92, 3–26.

Hymes, D. Models of the interaction of language and social life. In J. J. Gumperz & D. Hymes (Eds.), Directions in sociolinguistics. New York: Holt, Rinehart & Winston, 1972.

Murphy, C. M. Pointing in the context of a shared activity. *Child Development*, 1978, 49, 371–380.

Nelson, K. E., Denninger, M. M., Bonvillian, J. D., Kaplan, B. J., & Bakes, N. Maternal input adjustments and non-adjustments as related to children's linguistic advances and to language acquisition theories. In A. D. Pellegrini & T. D. Yawkey (Eds.), *The development of oral and written languages: Readings in developmental and applied linguistics*. Norwood, NJ: Ablex, 1983.

Newport, E. L. Motherese: the speech of mothers to young children. In N. Castellan, D. Pisoni, & G. Potts (Eds.), *Cognitive theory* (Vol. 2). Hillsdale, N.J.: Lawrence Erlbaum Associates, 1976.

Newport, E. L., Gleitman, H., & Gleitman, L. R. Mother, I'd rather do it myself: Some effects and non-effects of maternal speech style. In C. Snow & C. A. Ferguson (Eds.), *Talking to children: Language input and acquisition;* Cambridge: Cambridge University Press, 1977.

Pechmann, T., & Deutsch, W. The development of verbal and nonverbal devices for reference. *Journal of Experimental Child Psychology*, 1982, 34, 330–341.

Ratner, N., & Bruner, J. S. Games, social exchange and the acquisition of language. *Journal of Child Language*, 1978, 5, 391–402.

Rocissano, L., & Yatchmink, Y. Language skill and interactive patterns in prematurely born toddlers. *Child Development*, 1983, 54, 1229–1241.

Schaffer, H. R., Hepburn, A., & Collis, G. M. Verbal and non-verbal aspects of mothers' directives. *Journal of Child Language*, 1983, 10, 337–355.

Schieffelin, B. Getting it together: An ethnographic approach to the study of the development of communicative competence. In E. Ochs & B. Schieffelin (Eds.), *Developmental pragmatics*. New York: Academic Press, 1979.

Schneiderman, M. H. *"Do what I mean, not what I say": Mothers' action-directives to their young children*. Unpublished Ph.D. dissertation, University of Pennsylvania, 1980.

Schnur, E., & Shatz, M. The role of maternal gesturing in conversations with one-year-olds. *Journal of Child Language*, 1984, 11.

Seitz, S., & Stewart, C. Expanding on expansion and related aspects of mother-child communication. *Developmental Psychology*, 1975, 11, 763–769.

Shatz, M. Children's comprehension of question-directives. *Journal of Child Language*, 1978, *5*, 39–46. (a)

Shatz, M. On the development of communicative understandings: An early strategy for interpreting and responding to messages. *Cognitive Psychology*, 1978, *10*, 271–301. (b)

Shatz, M. How to do things by asking: Form-function pairings in mothers' questions and their relation to children's responses. *Child Development*, 1979, *50*, 1093–1099.

Shatz, M. Learning the rules of the game: Four views of the relation between social interaction and syntax acquisition. In W. Deutsch (Ed.), *The child's construction of language*. London: Academic Press, 1981.

Shatz, M. On mechanisms of language acquisition: Can features of the communicative environment account for development? In E. Wanner & L. R. Gleitman (Eds.), *Language acquisition: The state of the art*. Cambridge: Cambridge University Press, 1982.

Shatz, M. Communication. In J. Flavell & E. Markman (Eds.), *Cognitive development*. P. Mussen (Gen. Ed.), *Handbook of child psychology*, 4th ed. New York: Wiley, 1983. (a)

Shatz, M. On transition, continuity, and coupling: An alternative approach to communicative development. In R. M. Golinkoff (Ed.), *The transition from prelinguistic to linguistic communication*. Hillsdale, N.J.: Lawrence Erlbaum Associates, 1983, (b)

Shatz, M., Allen, R., & Raizman, C. Show doesn't lead to tell: The effects of dual input on children's responses to test questions. Manuscript in preparation.

Shatz, M., & Gelman, R. The development of communication skills: Modifications in the speech of young children as a function of listener. *Monographs of the Society for Research in Child Development*, 1973, *38* (5, serial No. 152).

Shatz, M., & Gelman, R. Beyond syntax: The influence of conversational constraints on speech modifications. In C. E. Snow & C. A. Ferguson (Eds.), *Talking to children*. Cambridge: Cambridge University Press, 1977.

Shatz, M., & Schnur, E. Gesture, form, and expectation: A study of mother-child communication patterns. Manuscript in preparation.

Snow, C. E. Mothers' speech to children learning language. *Child Development*, 1972, *43*, 549–565.

Snow, C. E. The development of conversation between mothers and babies. *Journal of Child Language*, 1977, *4*, 1–22.

Snow, C. E., & Ferguson, C. A. (Eds.). *Talking to children*. Cambridge: Cambridge University Press, 1977.

Wexler, K. Empirical questions about developmental psycholinguistics raised by a theory of language acquisition. In R. Campbell & P. T. Smith (Eds.), *Recent advances in the psychology of language*. New York: Plenum, 1978.

Zukow, P., Reilly, M., & Greenfield, P. Making the absent present: Facilitating the transition from sensorimotor to linguistic communication. In K. E. Nelson (Ed.), *Children's language*, (Vol. 3). New York: Gardner Press, 1980.

3 Day Care: A New Context for Research and Development

Alison Clarke-Stewart
with the assistance of Christian Gruber
University of Chicago

According to projections given in the *Federal Register,* November 1981, nine out of ten households in the United States with children under 4 years of age will use some form of day care in the 1980s. This is mainly the result of the recent trend, unprecedented except in times of war, for women, including mothers of young children, to enter the work force. Currently, 48% of the preschool-aged children in the United States have mothers who are employed. This number has more than doubled in the past 15 years and it is expected to continue to rise throughout the decade. For the children of working mothers this social phenomenon presents a new context for development, a context that is, at least on the surface, distinctly different from the previous norm of exclusive or primary care by mother. For psychologists, who are being asked questions about just how this new context affects children's development, it presents a new challenge for research.

And challenge it is. For the question of day-care "effects" is one of the most complex environmental issues developmental psychologists have yet faced. It took many years to begin to be able to describe the complex and subtle connections between maternal behavior and children's development. It took even longer to recognize and examine systematically the contributions of fathers and siblings. Now, in order to understand children's development as it may be affected by day care, we must put together these family relations with a totally unknown—and unruly—set of extra-familial factors.

The problems this poses include, to begin with, *defining* "day care." "Day care" can refer to any kind of supplementary (i.e., non-parental) care, be it provided by Aunt Mary or Maria Montessori. It is often assumed to mean full-time attendance in a day-care center, but this is a serious misrepresentation of the real world of alternative care. Only about 15% of the children whose mothers are employed attend day-care centers, the rest are cared for in their own or someone else's home. If the reason to study day care is that it represents a major shift in the ecology of early childhood in this country, then limiting the definition of day care to one particular form of care seems unjustifiably shortsighted.

The problems facing the researcher of day care also include all those of any field study, in which it becomes necessary to give up a large degree of scientific elegance in the pursuit of social relevance and to sacrifice considerable simplicity and control in order to tap richness and reality. The laboratory approach to studying day care, in which one sets up a model day-care program, answers only questions about the effects of "what might be," not "what is." In the field, the day-care researcher must wrestle with problems of finding and keeping subjects and programs that are representative of "what is."

The possibility of applying a true experimental design and randomly assigning children to attend day-care programs or to stay home seems out of the question for other than atypical subject populations, such as poor, single mothers on welfare, for whom employment, the usual reason for day care, is not an option. As a result, the study of day-care "effects" involves not only the messiness of field research but the uninterpretability of correlational analyses, as self-selection puts inescapable restrictions on causal inference.

Longitudinal designs can go some way toward alleviating this problem by checking for pre–day-care differences between groups and then charting developmental changes over time. But when such designs are applied to this real world phenomenon there are problems in locating "pre–day-care" families and in tracking children's progress through what turns out to be a morass of unstable care arrangements. Add to these design problems those of the unreliability of observational methods, the lack of standardized instruments for assessing developmental outcomes, the difficulty of recruitment and the likelihood of attrition of subjects, and the plethora of problems grows.

Developmental researchers have not, however, shirked the challenge, and a number of innovative partial solutions to the research problems have been put forward in the last 10 years. A few researchers have gone the route of experimentation and set up exemplary day-care programs to which they randomly assigned subjects (e.g., the Abecedarian Project at the Frank Porter Graham Center, Ramey & Mills 1977, and the Milwaukee Project, Heber, 1978). Others have skirted the self-selection problem by studying only variations among day-care settings or programs, including experimentally induced ones (e.g., Ruopp, Travers, Glantz, & Coelen, 1979). Some researchers have observed children prior to day-care entry and then after (e.g., Roopnarine & Lamb, 1980). Yet others have looked at children in day care in countries where day care is more readily available and widely used (like Sweden, Cochran, 1977, or Bermuda, Scarr, 1981). None of these solutions is perfect, but progress is being made. It is no longer necessary to extrapolate from studies of animals, institutions, or Israelis (e.g., Fraiberg, 1977). We are beginning to collect some answers to urgent questions about day-care as it exists today.

In this chapter, I discuss one further effort to document and understand day-care effects, a study my students and I have been working on in Chicago for the past several years. It differs from these other studies of day care by including subjects from a wide range of existing day-care arrangements and programs in the United States, by assessing both the experiences and the abilities of these children, and by observing them at home as well as in day care.

THE STUDY

We started the study by conceptualizing a *continuum* of child-care arrangements varying in location and intensity, and running from full-time care at home alone with parents to full-time care in a day-care center. In between, we placed care at home with parents and siblings; care at home with a babysitter; care in a day-care home (in the babysitter's home, with at least one other child); and part-time care (10–25 hours/week) in a day-care center or nursery school. As soon as we started recruiting subjects, however, we found to our dismay that children were not fitting so neatly into our preconceived conditions—children were spending two mornings a week with grandma, three afternoons in a playgroup, going to a friend's on alternate Thursdays and six cousins were coming to spend the summer. Therefore, one very popular complex arrangement was added to the continuum: day care part-time in a center and part-time with a sitter. We ended up with a multidimensional continuum of "quantity of day care" that increases in the number of hours of nonmaternal care, the number and variety of children encountered, the number and variety of adults providing care, and institutionalization of the physical setting and activities (Table 3.1).

The sample located for the study consisted of 150 families with 2- to 4-year-old children distributed across these care arrangements. The families were selected to be intact, English-speaking and self-supporting. Beyond these criteria, they were not restricted except for the elimination of those living in certain areas of Chicago considered unsafe for nighttime travel by female graduate students. The names of potential subjects were found by a variety of methods, but the same

TABLE 3.1
Child-Care Arrangements

1	2	3	4	5	6	7
At Home With Parents	At Home With Parents And Siblings	At Home With Babysitter	Day-Care Home	Nursery School (Part-time)	Day-Care Center (Full-time)	Nursery School And Babysitter

methods were used to obtain subjects in all seven child-care groups, in order to rule out confounding effects of differential recruitment strategies. Doctors, churches, referral agencies, and supermarkets were used to get the names of parents with preschool children; the single source providing the largest number of names was a purchased mailing list for the Read-About-Me books. All subjects were approached first through a letter to the parents and then, for those children in day care, through telephone contact with the day-care director or provider. Only a small handful of the day caregivers contacted did not allow us to visit and observe children once the parents had agreed to participate in the study. To ensure a broad sampling of day-care settings, no more than four children from any one setting were recruited. The more than 80 different day-care settings represented in the study, therefore, seem likely to reflect the range of day-care facilities available to middle-class parents in Chicago in the late 1970s.

The general research plan was to find children who were in their first non-parental-care arrangement and had been there for 3 to 6 months (a period we thought would be long enough for the children to have adjusted to the new situation and brief enough not to have produced any permanent "effects" on development); to observe the children (at home, in their day-care settings, and in a standard laboratory playroom) at that time and then one year later; to document changes in their development over that year; and to relate those changes to observed variations in their home and day-care environments. Although this design is subject to the usual problems of self-selection into care arrangements, it was our hope that any differences found in children's development could be thought of not as pure "day-care effects" perhaps, but as "day-care effects-in-the-context-of-free-parental-choice."

Because of this plan to link children's development with environmental variation, we assessed both the abilities and the experiences of individual children. To assess children's experiences, an observer visited each child three times each year: morning, afternoon, and dinnertime, wherever the child was at the time. For a child in Group 7, for instance, the morning observation was likely to be in nursery school, the afternoon visit with a babysitter, and the dinnertime observation at home. The dinnertime visit was scheduled to be at a time when the whole family, including father, was together. Each observation lasted 2 hours. During that time the observer kept a running record of the child's activities, including all the social interactions he or she participated in, physical encounters with peers or adults, and play and learning activities. In addition, at 15-minute intervals the observer filled out a "snapshot" checklist of the people who were present and had interacted with the child during the preceding period. At the end of the observation she completed a checklist about aspects of the physical environment (its decor, equipment, messiness, dangerousness, etc.).

To find out more about the child's experiences beyond what could be observed in these relatively brief observations, a detailed interview was given each year to each child's mother, father, and caregiver(s). The interview included questions about the adults' backgrounds (occupation, education, religion, ethnicity, family income, work history, etc.); their attitudes (toward the child, day care, discipline, socialization, etc.); the child's social activities outside of day care (outings with family members, friends, etc.); and aspects of the day-care program not easily observed (including curriculum, adult-child ratio, and cost).

A clearer and more accurate picture of the sample was derived from these interviews (Table 3.2). The majority of families in the study were Anglo-Saxon, European, or "American" in ethnic orientation; only 12% were black, 2% Oriental, and 1% Hispanic. Over half the fathers were native Chicagoans; nearly two-thirds of them were college graduates. Most mothers (80%) were between 25- and 35-years-old; 60% were college graduates. Slightly over a third of them worked full-time, another third did not work, and the rest worked part-time. Most households consisted of mother and father and one or two children.

The fathers all claimed to spend some time in child care, actively involved with their children or responsible for them; half of them claimed this was at least 4 hours a day (taking the average of the previous weekday and weekend day). During the year-long investigation 30 families moved (half of them out of town) and 6 couples got divorced.

There were two "surprises" in the demographic data collected in these interviews. First, although we had not deliberately restricted subject recruitment according to social class, the families turned out to be disproportionately high in their socioeconomic status. Nearly half were of professional-class status, with professional or executive positions and graduate training. Only about a quarter of the sample was of lower than middle-class status. Also surprising was the large number of mothers who had worked or were working professionally with young children (one quarter of the sample). These "surprises" likely reflect both a limitation imposed by our sources of subjects' names and a differential willingness of parents to participate in a study of child care and development. Given this sample bias, we must be especially cautious in generalizing our results to the day-care population at large. The rationale for being interested in these results at all is that these are the kinds of parents who would be most likely to read and to "apply" the results of a study like this one.

To assess children's abilities, an elaborate battery of structured and semistructured tasks was designed and administered each year in a laboratory playroom, and, the first year, at home. The emphasis in these tasks was on children's social skills, since it was our expectation that if day care did have an effect on development, it most likely would be in the social domain. Children's social competence was assessed in staged encounters with unfamiliar adults (male and female), with an unfamiliar peer (of the same age, sex, and type of care arrangement), with a familiar playmate (selected by the child's mother), and with the mother. In addition, ratings of the child's social behavior during the dinnertime observation were made by the observer at the conclusion of those visits. Besides social skills two other domains of development were assessed: intellectual ability

TABLE 3.2
Sample Characteristics

Education	M	F
HS Graduate	15%	15%
Some College	27%	21%
College Graduate	26%	18%
MA +	34%	46%

Occupation (Father)	
Unskilled	5%
Skilled	11%
Blue Collar	8%
White Collar	11%
Middle Class	19%
Professional Class	47%

Family Income/Month	
$ 400–1,000	22%
1,000–1,400	29%
1,400–2,000	28%
2,000 +	21%

Ethnicity (Father)	
Anglo	21%
Afro	12%
Oriental	2%
Hispanic	1%
Western European	17%
Eastern European	14%
Southern European	3%
Northern European	5%
"American"	24%

Age of Mother	
21–25y	9%
26–30y	44%
31–35y	35%
42–52y	5%

Religion (Mother)	
Protestant	37%
Catholic	26%
Jewish	16%
Other/None	22%

Work Status (Mother)	
None	38%
Part-time	25%
Full-time	37%

Age of Child	
22–30m	31%
31–36m	23%
37–42m	21%

Experience with Children (Mother)

None	20%
Babysitting or Sibs	45%
Non-professional Child Care	11%
Professional	24%

Time in Child Care per Day (Father)

Less than 1 Hour	1%
1–2 Hours	6%
2–3 Hours	19%
3–4 Hours	23%
4–5 Hours	16%
5–6 Hours	19%
More than 6 Hours	15%

Length of Time in Chicago (Father)

Since Childhood	58%
More than 6 Years	22%
Less than 6 Years	20%

Sex of Child

Boys	56%
Girls	44%

Household Size

Number of Children

1	44%
2	44%
3	9%
4	3%

Number of Adults

Parents Only	78%
Parents + 1	15%
Parents + 2–5	6%

TABLE 3.3
Study Variables

Short Name	Full Name	Description
		OUTCOME VARIABLES
PROX M	Proximity to mother	Child-initiated physical contact and proximity to mother in lab session when stranger is present or after brief separation.
SOC M	Sociability to mother	In laboratory situations, positive, reciprocal, social interaction with mother during free play; cooperation with mother in joint tasks; positive interaction and greeting after separation; comforting of mother when "hurt."
SOC COG	Social cognition	Visual perspective taking; conceptual perspective taking; nonegocentric communication; emotional labeling and problem solving; knowledge of sex roles (tested).
SOC STR	Social competence with adult stranger	In laboratory situations, friendliness to unfamiliar adults; cooperation in joint tasks; comforting and helping; trust in "dangerous" situations; stranger's liking of child and rating of social competence.
SOC PEER	Social competence with peer stranger	In laboratory situations, positive interaction with peer (talk, play, affection); cooperation in joint tasks and in free play with toys.
NEG PEER	Negative to peer stranger	In laboratory situations, negative behavior to unfamiliar peer; taking away toy, controlling, insulting, refusing, withdrawing, avoiding.
SOC HOM	Social competence at home	At dinnertime observation at home, ratings of obedience, self-confidence, sociability, autonomy, assertiveness, playfulness, cheerfulness, and nonaggression.
COG	Cognition	Language comprehension; verbal fluency; object recognition; knowledge of concepts; digit span (tested).
SOC VIS	Social competence with visitor	At home session, comforting, helping, trusting unfamiliar adult; showing toys, following instructions (giving message, teaching game).
SOC FRIEND	Social competence with friend	At home session, positive social interaction with a familiar peer; cooperation in joint tasks and free play.
		FAMILY VARIABLES
SES	Socioeconomic status	Mother's occupation; father's occupation; mother's father's occupation; mother's education; father's education (2×); mother's highest wage, family income.

STABLE	Geographic stability	Length of time in Chicago, midwest, present house, neighborhood, marriage, for mother and father.
FAMILY	Extended family	Number of persons in household, in extended family; frequency of activities together and amount of participation in child care.
P TRAD	Traditional family values	Parents value as "ideal family": doing things together (eating, church, vacations, games), living in house in country, in same town as grandparents, father taking sons to football, making decisions, mother and daughters staying home, doing the cooking, having many children. Parents see day care as responsible for disintegration of families; think mother and father should and do have greatest influence on children (compared to other adults, sibs, friends, media); would ask friend or relative rather than doctor, professional, or book for advice about childrearing; believe home offers child better care. Mother's preferred activities involve family. Parents are opposed to women's lib and employment for women.
NIT PEOPLE	Number of people at home	Number of different people interacting with child during dinnertime observation.
HOM TOY	Number of toys at home	Number of types of toys and educational equipment in home or day-care setting (checklist), e.g., stuffed animals, trucks and other vehicles, story books, puzzles, instructive games.
HOM DANGER	Number of dangerous objects at home	Number of dangerous things observed (checklist), e.g., unprotected heights, sharp objects, cleaning supplies, medicines.
HOM STRUCTURE	Amount of structure in home	Clearly defined activity areas in the house, specific routines for each area, planned activities, by-the-clock schedule (checklist).
HOM DECO	Stimulating decor at home	Decorative elements in the house (checklist), e.g., rugs, ornaments, books, plants, pictures, lamps, piano, curtains, TV, fireplace.
HOM MESS	Messiness in home	Dirty and disorganized aspects of environment (checklist), e.g., toys, food, clothes out, dead plants, pet food, ashtrays, stained rug, dirty floor, peeling paint.
M.F in DC	Parents in day care	Time mother or father was in day care or nursery school as a child.
M ROL SAT	Mother's overall role satisfaction	Mother's satisfaction and enjoyment of overall role (including juggling job and motherhood. satisfaction with time for self, with accomplishments).
M M ROL SAT	Mother's satisfaction with maternal role	Mother's satisfaction with role as mother, including child care, teaching, playing with child, sharing child care with husband.
M ALIEN	Mother's feeling of alienation	Alienation questionnaire; e.g., "Most of my life is spent doing meaningless things;" "I feel no need to try my best for it makes no difference anyhow;" "Everyone is out to manipulate you

(*continued*)

TABLE 3.3 (*Continued*)

Short Name	Full Name	Description
		toward his own ends;'' prefers to spend time alone, in selfish pursuits rather than with family or on work.
M EXPER	Mother's professional experience with children	Mother's experience in child care from none to professional.
M, F GOOD CD	Parent's knowledge of child development and childrearing	Parent's education and training in child development; amount of reading about child care; value the child-care arrangement for child- and education-oriented reasons (staff, program, learning opportunities, play, educational toys, diversity); aware of individual differences among children; agree with experts' solutions to child-care problems concerning how and when to discipline.
M, F POS EXP	Parents' positive expectations	Parents have high expectations of child by time would start school (checklist); e.g., child should know own name, address, name of President and Attorney General, and what a pomegranate is; should be able to answer phone, decide what to wear, count to 20, read a few words, apologize when hurts someone, go downtown on bus alone. Parents rate child high on bright, loving, lively, fun.
C SOC ACT	Child's social activities	Frequency and variety of child's social activities outside of day care.
C SOC M	Child's social interaction with mother	Amount of time child spends with mother (dinner, outings, physical care, playing, learning, with mother responsible)
F INVOL C	Father's involvement in child care	Amount father is involved in child care: time spent responsible for child, in dressing, bedtime, outings, eating, playing for child, participation in and decisions about child's care arrangements.
M TIME	Mother spends time on:	Time mother spent per day, last week, on parents, work, child, etc.
M CAREER	Mother's career orientation	Mother wishes she were (still) working—or is glad she is working; liked working because of type of work, career, job; worked a long time; prefers work activities to family, friends; thinks work activities important, meaningful; chose child-care arrangement in order to work.
M WORK	Amount mother works	Amount of time mother has worked (year 1: since child born; year 2: in past year).
FAM TRAD	Traditional family and family values	FAMILY + TRAD.
M SAT ROL	Overall maternal role satisfaction	M ROL SAT + M M ROL SAT − M ALIEN.

NEG HOM	Negative physical environment at home	HOM DANGER + HOM MESS.
STIM HOM	Stimulating physical environment at home	HOM DECO + HOM TOY.

DAY CARE VARIABLES

MONEY DC	Cost of day care	Amount of money parents spent for day care per month.
CG TIME	Caregiver time in setting	Length of time caregiver has been in day care setting.
CG EVAL	Caregiver evaluation of child-care arrangement	Caregiver's evaluation of the child-care arrangement as high overall (on all of: opportunity for child to learn, to play with adults, with children, with educational materials, to be given discipline, socialization, love and affection, training in own culture, experience with people of other backgrounds; opportunity for parent involvement, opportunity for mother to pursue own interests).
HETERO	Heterogeneity of class	Heterogeneity within child-care arrangement in terms of children's ages, sexes, number, ethnicity, and SES.
MATCH ETH	Ethnic match	Proportion of people in child-care arrangement that are of child's own ethnic group.
CHILDREN	Children interacted with	Number of different children child interacted with during daytime observations.
CH-CCA	Children in child-care arrangement	Number of children in the child-care arrangement.
CH-CLASS	Children in class	Number of children in child's class.
CH/CG	Children per caregiver	Number of children per adult in child's class.
ADULTS	Adults interacted with	Number of different adults child interacted with during daytime observations.
AD-CCA	Adults in child-care arrangement	Number of different adults in the child-care arrangement.
AD-CLASS	Adults in class	Number of different adults in child's class (in regular contact with child).
YOUNG CH	Young children in class	Number of children in class more than one year younger than child.
OLD CH	Older children in class	Number of children in class more than one year older than child.
MESH	Home day-care mesh	Agreement or similarity between parents and caregiver on: SES, solutions to hypothetical child-care problems; discipline; teaching; affection; importance of opportunities for child in child-care arrangement; level of expectations for child; and involvement of parents in the child-care arrangement.

(continued)

71

TABLE 3.3 *(Continued)*

Short Name	Full Name	Description
DCC LENG	Length in day-care center	Amount and length of time child has spent in day-care center.
DCH LENG	Length in day-care home	Amount and length of time child has spent in day-care home.
BS LENG	Length with babysitter	Amount and length of time child has spent with babysitter.
MC PROP	Proportion of class middle class	Proportion of children in day-care class who are of middle or professional class SES.
CG TRAD	Caregiver's traditional family values	Same as P TRAD, for caregiver.
DC TOY	Number of toys in day-care	Same as HOM TOY, for day-care setting.
DC DANGER	Number of dangerous objects in day-care	Same as HOM DANGER, for day-care setting.
DC STRUCTURE	Amount of structure in day-care	Same as HOM STRUCTURE, for day-care setting.
DC DECO	Stimulating decor in day-care	Same as HOM DECO, for day-care setting.
DC MESS	Messiness in day-care	Same as HOM MESS, for day-care setting.
CG EXPER	Caregiver's professional experience with young children	Same as M EXPER, for caregiver.
CG GOOD CD	Caregiver's knowledge of child development and child rearing	Same as M, F GOOD CD, for caregiver.
VARIETY	Variety of people in day-care	HETERO − MATCH ETH.
PROGRAM	Educational program in day-care	CG EVAL + DC STRUCTURE + DC TOY.

and emotional behavior. Intellectual ability was assessed in tests of language comprehension and production, social cognition, knowledge of concepts, and memory. Emotional behavior was assessed in situations designed to elicit attachment, empathy, and aggression.

Data Reduction and Variables

Our first task was to reduce the abundance of information thus collected into a sensible set of variables that would reflect individual differences in abilities and experiences. In general this was done through a combination of conceptualization and correlation. Most variables were conceptualized as comprising various related components, and if the components were found to be empirically as well as conceptually related, they were combined into a single variable. This process was used to reduce the extremely large number of individual measures collected in the interviews (separate items), in the standard assessments (separate tasks), and in the observations (checklists and ratings) to a reasonable number of "family," "day-care," and "outcome" variables. The procedure is still being applied to the running records from the observations, so, unfortunately, this report lacks the results from that component of the study. The set of variables arrived at and analyzed so far is presented in Table 3.3.

RESULTS

Outcomes and Child-Care Arrangements

In the first major analyses of the study we attempted to find out how individual differences in "outcomes" were related to child-care arrangements. Table 3.4 presents the results of three multivariate analyses of variance (MANCOVAs) for the three standard assessments (Year 1 laboratory, Year 1 home, and Year 2 laboratory) and the two dinnertime observations, with the child's age and the family's socioeconomic status (SES) covaried out. These analyses and the specific contrasts between selected child-care groups show a high degree of consistency.

There were no significant differences in outcome variables for children cared for by their parents at home alone versus those at home with siblings (Group 1 vs. Group 2), suggesting that simply the presence of another child does not have a strong influence on the development of children's competence. There were no significant differences between children cared for by a babysitter in their own homes versus those in day-care homes (Group 3 vs. Group 4), suggesting that location of the care arrangement is not critical. There was only one significant difference between children in center care part-time versus those in center care full-time (Group 5 vs. Group 6 or Group 6 vs. Group 7), suggesting that there is

TABLE 3.4
Mancovas for Child-Care Arrangements

	MEANS							SIGNIFICANCE LEVELS	CONTRASTS			
	1 P	2 P + Sibs	3 BS	4 DCH	5 NS	6 DCC	7 NS + BS	Overall	1-2 / 3-4	1-2 / 3-7	3-4 / 5-7	1-4 / 5-7
TIME 1 n:	23	26	14	20	22	25	14	.000	.01	.01	.000	.000
LAB												
PROX M	0.34	0.98	0.08	0.80	-0.45	-1.01	-0.30					.002 >1
SOC M	-1.16	0.32	-0.12	-1.13	-0.22	0.83	1.22					
SOC COG	-0.38	-0.74	0.13	-0.08	0.62	0.15	0.43	.000	.000<	.01<	.03<	.003<
SOC STR	-1.33	-1.97	0.22	0.08	1.24	0.20	2.74	.03	.01<	.01<	.000<	.000<
SOC PEER	-1.01	-0.80	0.62	1.23	0.69	0.47	0.85	.000		.05<	.02<	.001<
NEG PEER	-0.08	-1.05	0.36	-0.31	0.01	0.41	0.91	.01		.04<	.01<	.001<
HOME												
SOC HOM	6.99	6.82	6.89	6.74	10.01	6.41	5.69					

TIME 2								.000		.000	.000
HOME											
COG	-0.36	0.16	0.05	-0.25	0.32	-0.04	0.24	.000		.000<	.000<
SOC VIS	-1.06	-0.54	0.10	-0.91	1.29	0.27	1.20	.000		.000<	.000<
SOC FRIEND	-0.30	-0.40	-0.10	-0.15	0.62	-0.04	0.52				
TIME 3 n:	5	18	6	7	39	31	22	.000	.02	.000	.000
LAB											
PROX M	0.25	1.12	-0.40	0.09	0.33	-0.71	-0.25	.001	.05>	.000>	.000>
SOC M	1.05	-0.11	-1.83	-0.21	0.68	-0.46	-0.32	.03			
SOC COG	-0.26	-0.46	-0.49	-0.26	0.35	-0.62	0.24	.000		.000<	.000<
SOC STR	-0.45	-1.10	-1.41	-1.99	1.31	-0.07	0.47	.004		.001<	.001<
SOC PEER	-3.34	-0.82	-0.34	-1.19	-0.23	0.29	0.59	.000		.000<	.000<
NEG PEER	0.32	0.00	1.77	-0.49	-0.40	0.29	-0.28				
HOME											
SOC HOM	5.44	6.47	6.71	6.88	6.82	6.92	6.82	.04		.000<	.000<

¹Direction of difference.

not a close link between children's development and the intensity of their day-care experience.

Numerous significant differences did appear in these analyses, however, when comparisons were made between children in parent care and those in day care (Groups 1–2 vs. Groups 3–7) in the first-year assessments, and between children in home care (with parent, babysitter or day-care home provider) and those in center care (part- or full-time) (Groups 1–4 vs. Groups 5–7) in all three assessments. Comparisons between intervening sets of child-care groups (Groups 1–2 vs. Groups 3–4 and Groups 3–4 vs. Groups 5–7) fill out the picture of a continuum of outcome differences paralleling our continuum of day-care arrangements. Linear trend analyses across child-care Groups 1–7 for the three MANCOVAs were also statistically significant. These consistent and highly significant differences favored children in day care and particularly children in center care on all measures of competence or maturity: Children in center care were higher on measures of competence expressed in interactions with parents, with strangers, and with unfamiliar peers, and in tests of intellectual abilities and social knowledge. The only variables that did not differentiate between center and home care were positive social interactions with a peer friend and negative interaction with a peer stranger.

Center children also sought less physical proximity and contact with their mothers than did home-care children. While some researchers (e.g., Blehar, 1974: Vaughn, Gove, & Egeland, 1980) have interpreted differences in maternal proximity seeking in their studies as indicating a pattern of avoidant attachment in day-care children, given the context of uniformly greater competence on other measures in the present study, a more reasonable interpretation of the proximity-seeking difference in this study would seem to be that it reflects greater maturity in day-care center children: That is, day-care children are displaying greater independence, not greater avoidance, of their mothers. This interpretation finds further support in Fig. 3.1, which plots, on the basis of cross-sectional age groupings, the course of development for this measure of proximity in home-care and center-care children. The developmental "paths" for the two groups were remarkably parallel, with the center group ahead by about 9 months until the highest age assessed, at which point the two paths coverged. This pattern suggests that the difference in proximity seeking between day-care and home-care children is one of timing rather than quality.

Similarly the graphs for cognitive development (Fig. 3.2) and social competence (Fig. 3.3) show parallel paths for center-care and home-care children, with center children ahead by an approximate average of 9 months until the age of 5 years. After 5, paths for cognitive development, like those for proximity to mother, converge, whereas those for social competence with strangers diverge. A plausible interpretation of all these results showing the greater competence of children in day care is that experience in a day-care center or nursery school

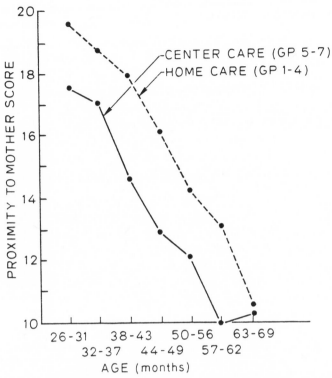

FIG. 3.1. Children's physical proximity to mother in two laboratory assessments, sample divided cross-sectionally into 6-month age periods.

encourages a more advanced level of functioning in the areas of social competence, intellectual knowledge, and emotional maturity over the age period 2 to 5.

However, in all these analyses the two assessment points year 1 and year 2 were treated as independent. What about changes over time? Contrary to our best-laid schemes, three quarters of the children in our sample changed care settings between our first- and second-year assessments; 61% changed not only particular setting but *type* of care arrangement (i.e., child-care group). This made it difficult to find a large enough sample that was stable in its care arrangements between the two assessment periods, so that changes in children's performance might be attributed to their care arrangement.

Although they were disconcerting to us, however, the changes in care arrangements were both systematic and practical for parents—the change almost invariably was from a home arrangement to a group or center one, as befitted the increasing age of the children. To examine the ''effect'' of changes over the year, another set of analysis of variance comparisons was performed to examine

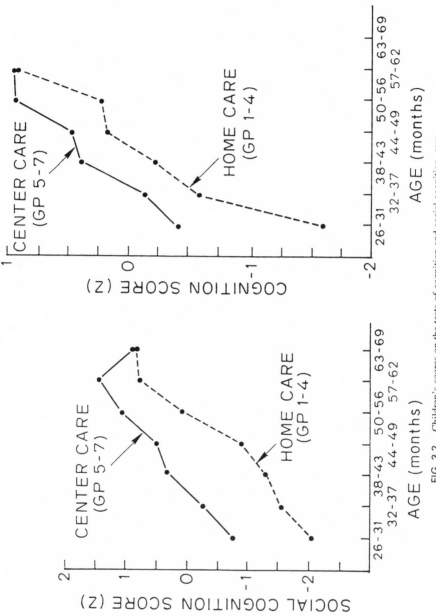

FIG. 3.2. Children's scores on the tests of cognition and social cognition, sample divided cross-sectionally into 6-month age periods.

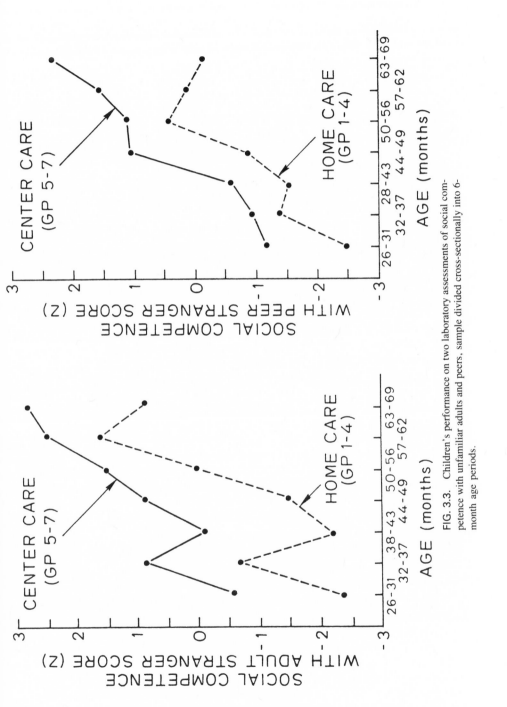

FIG. 3.3. Children's performance on two laboratory assessments of social competence with unfamiliar adults and peers, sample divided cross-sectionally into 6-month age periods.

differences among three groups of children: those who stayed in a home arrangement (Groups 1, 2. 3, or 4), those who stayed in a center arrangement (Groups 5, 6, or 7), and those who shifted from a home arrangement to a center arrangement. Three new outcome variables were also examined in these analyses: The *gains* between Year 1 and Year 2 in social competence with a peer stranger, social competence with an adult stranger, and social cognition. The results of these analyses are shown in Table 3.5.

Results comparing the stable subjects who stayed in either home or center arrangements reflect the results already discussed, albeit at lower levels of significance: The children in center care were higher on measures of independence (first year) and cognition and social competence (second year) than the children who stayed in home arrangements. There were no significant differences in their gain scores. More interesting is the second comparison, that between children who stayed in home care versus those who changed to centers. Differences on the first-year assessment speak to the issue of pre-day-care differences or self-selection. In this assessment the only significant difference was that children who were going to be switched to a center arrangement were less sociable toward their mothers than those who stayed in home arrangements. If there is any evidence of self-selection, then, it might be that the mothers of these less sociable and cooperative children decided to send them to day-care centers to increase their social skills. This seems unduly speculative, however, and we have no evidence to support it in the reasons given by parents for their selection of child-care arrangements. It is not the case that the mothers of more highly social and cooperative children kept them at home because they were nicer to be with, or that mothers of unsociable children sent them to day care to get rid of them; children in day-care homes and with babysitters were at the same low level of sociability toward mother as children in parent care. The weight of evidence from these analyses, then, is against systematic selection of center care on the basis of the child's level of development.

Analyses of differences in the second-year assessment for children who stayed in home arrangements versus those who shifted to centers speak to differences that may be due to day care. Here the only significant difference was in the gain in cognitive ability. Children who made the shift from a home to a center, as would be predicted if experience in a day-care center advances development, increased more in their cognitive scores than children who stayed at home. The results for gain scores in social competence, although not statistically significant, were in the same direction.

The third comparison was between children who had been in a center less than a year (those who were in a home arrangement in the first year and a center arrangement the second) and those who had been in a center more than a year (those who were in centers both years). In this comparison, consistent with the overall findings, in Year 1, children who were in centers were more independent, knowledgeable, and competent than children who were in homes. On gain scores, the late day-care center starters were again higher (significantly so on cognitive gains for children who were in either parent care or home day care in Year 1 and on social competence with the adult stranger for children who were in parent care in Year 1). On the second-year assessment, when both groups were in centers, the only significant difference, favoring two-year day-care center attendees, was in social competence with mother. This variable, as we have just seen, does not seem to fit with the other measures of competence, and is one that seems unlikely to demonstrate an effect of longer day-care center attendance. The weight of evidence from these analyses, then, is against a cumulative effect of day-care center attendance.

In brief, the results of all the analyses of variance comparing groups of children in different child-care arrangements suggest that day care, and particularly day care in center programs, is linked to advanced development of social, emotional, and intellectual competence in 2- to 5-year-old children, though not in a simple cumulative way. The next step was to investigate what it was about the day-care arrangements that might be responsible for the observed differences. Recall that our continuum of day-care arrangements was multidimensional, involving hours, people, settings, and activities.

Describing the Care Arrangements

Table 3.6 summarizes the characteristics of the five day-care arrangements and the analyses of variance comparing them. There were few differences between part-time center programs and full-time center programs (Group 5 vs. Group 6). Not surprisingly, full-time programs cost twice as much as part-time, but otherwise the only differences were in staff stability (caregivers in full-time day-care centers had been there longer: 3½ vs. 2½ years on the average) and the staff-child ratio, which was 1-to-4 in full-time programs and 1-to-6 in part-time programs. Since there was no *observed* differences between the two kinds of programs in class size (17) or number of adults in class or interacting with the child (3 or 4) during a given observation period, this difference in ratio as reported by the caregivers may be more one of form than of function. In full-time day-care centers additional staff such as cook and nurse and a second shift of teachers and aides would have been counted into the caregiver's statement of the number of adults regularly in the setting, which was used in calculating the ratio. At any given time, for the child, the adult-child ratio and all other assessed variables in part-time and full-time programs are probably functionally the same.

In comparing the two home day-care arrangements—babysitters and day-care homes—there also were relatively few significant differences. On the average, day-care home providers had been working in their present day-care settings twice as long as babysitters (3 vs. 1½ yrs), but this was a necessary result of our having limited the length of time children were in their day-care arrangements. They also were younger (36 vs. 47 years), more highly educated (some college

TABLE 3.5

Analyses of Variance for Child-Care Arrangements Over Time

Means

Variables	HOME-HOME		HOME-CENTER		CENTER-CENTER	*Contrasts*		
Year / *Year.*	1 P	2 P	P	BS, DCH	NS, DCC	HO-HO vs. CN-CN	HO-HO vs. HO-CN	HO-CN vs. CN-CN
	BS, DCH	BS, DCH	NS, DCC	NS, DCC	NS, DCC			
n	*19*	*9*	*22*	*20*	*51*			
PROX M 1	0.82	1.29	0.59	0.02	−0.85	.01√²		.09√
PROX M 2	0.50	−0.51	0.77	−0.31	−0.54			
SOC M 1	1.04	1.42	−1.44	−1.66	1.02		.05√	.05∧
SOC M 2	0.48	−0.86	0.14	−3.41	1.02			.02∧
SOC COG 1	0.02	−0.45	−1.13	−0.59	0.86	.07∧		
SOC COG 2	−0.24	−1.07	−0.24	−0.52	0.76			

	11.3	12.5	22.3	16.2	11.0		
COG GAIN						.07∧	.05∨ +
SOC STR 1	-0.46	-0.61	-1.81	0.12	1.57		.02∧
SOC STR 2	-0.74	-2.26	0.70	-1.22	1.10	.09∧	
STR GAIN	9.3	3.0	20.6	8.9	10.0		
SOC PEER 1	-0.57	-0.17	-1.37	-0.93	0.95		
SOC PEER 2	-1.32	-1.44	-0.05	-1.45	1.28	.03∧	
PEER GAIN	4.02	1.53	4.75	2.17	4.34		
COG	0.06	-0.51	-0.38	-0.48	0.44		
SOC HOM 1	62.2	66.6	63.1	63.9	66.2		
SOC HOM 2	64.4	68.6	67.5	65.1	68.4		
NEG PEER 1	-0.81	0.46	-0.01	0.40	-0.30		
NEG PEER 2	0.30	-0.81	0.57	-0.26	-0.32		

[1]Significance levels for MANCOVA with age controlled.
[2]Direction of difference.

83

TABLE 3.6
Characteristics of Care Arrangements

	MEANS							ANOVA SIGNIFICANCE LEVELS CONTRASTS			
	1-2 P	3 BS	4 DCH	5 NS	6 DCC	7[1] NS + BS	OVERALL	3 / 4	5 / 6	3-4 / 5-6
COST										
MONEY DC		120	140	60	120	170	.001		.000<[4]	
COST TO CG				75	156		.000		.000<	
DEMOGRAPHICS										
CG AGE		47	36	37	30		.001	.05 >		.01 >
CG TIME IN SETTING		1.5	2.9	3.7	2.6		.01	.05 <	.05 >	.05 <
CG EDN²		1.5	3.4	5.4	5.7		.000	.000<		.000<
CG % WITH GRAD EDN		0	5	37	48		.000			.000<
CG % WITH PROF EXP		8	15	72	62		.000			.000<
CG TRAINING (SOME/>6)		14/7	55/10	91/51	96/52		.000	.01 <		.000<
CG ATTITUDES										
CG GOOD CD										
CG TRAD										
CG POS EXP										
PHYSICAL ENVT										
ALL TOYS	12.2	19.0	17.0	28.0	28.0		.001			.001<

84

						F	p	comp	p (dir)
DC TOYS	12.2[3]	12.0	12.4	18.7	18.7		.001		.001 <
DC DECO	20.8[3]	20.0	18.0	11.2	13.2		.001		.001 >
DC MESS	4.80[3]	5.07	4.50	1.99	2.16		.001		.001 >
DC DANGER	1.58[3]	2.03	1.65	1.11	1.00		.01		.01 >
PROGRAM									
STRUCTURE	0.40	0.60	0.98	3.40	3.25		.001		.001 <
CG EVAL (YR1)		37.6	37.7	72.8	76.2		.000		.000 <
PEOPLE									
HETERO		5.38	9.85	14.20	14.30	14.28	.000	.05 <	.000 <
MATCH ETH	1.73	11.3	11.1	8.7	9.0	11.20	.000		.000 >
CHILDREN		1.85	3.07	10.50	10.00		.000	.05 <	.000 <
CH-CCA		2.34	6.00	67.30	72.03		.000	.01 <	.000 <
CH-CLASS		2.20	5.40	17.70	17.41		.000	.05 <	.000 <
YOUNG CH (% c̄ any)		40	50	10	15		.000		.001 >
OLD CH (% c̄ none)								.01 >	
CH/CG		1.7	3.4	5.8	4.0		.001	.01 <	.000 <
ADULTS	2.09	2.39	1.73	4.50	3.80		.000		.000 <
AD-CCA		2.32	2.50	6.31	6.05	4.80	.01		.01 <
AD-CLASS		1.25	1.60	3.30	3.35	7.42	.01		.01 <
DC MESH									

[1] Data for Group 7 are combined with those of Gp 5 or 3 where applicable.

[2] Edn 1 = <HS, 2 = HS grad, 3–4 = some college, 5 = college grad, 6 = graduate training.

[3] Comparison figures for HOME/FAMILY variables.

[4] Direction of difference.

Unless otherwise noted, figures apply to Year 1 and Year 2 data. Shows all means with a significant F value.

vs. some high school), and more likely to have had training in child development (55% vs. 14%). The day-care homes had more children (5 vs. 2), more children per adult (3½ vs. 1½) and, not unrelatedly, had more heterogeneous groups of children (in terms of age, sex, ethnicity, and SES).

The most numerous differences found were between home day-care arrangements and center-care arrangements. The center caregivers interviewed were younger, but had been in their day-care settings longer, had more professional experience, more training in child development, and were more highly educated than the home day-caregivers. They were not different, however, in their expectations for children, their traditional versus "liberated" family values, or their knowledge of what "experts" suggest is good for children's development (educational toys, learning opportunities, nonauthoritarian discipline). Centers had more toys, more structured programs, more children in the class (17 vs. 2 to 5) and in the setting (70 vs. 2 to 6), more adults in the class (3 vs. 1) and in the setting (6 vs. 2), more children per adult, and more people not of the child's ethnic group, but were less likely to have children younger than the target child in the class. They got lower scores on our checklist inventories for messiness and danger in the physical environment, and they were higher, according to the caregiver's overall evaluation, in providing opportunities for the children's learning, play, education, discipline, socialization, and experiences with people of other backgrounds.

Since there were these marked differences between centers and homes, we may be encouraged to think that they account for the observed differences in performance between center and home children. But what about the families of these children? Perhaps it was not the day-care programs themselves but the parents who selected them that account for differences in the children's development.

Describing the Families

Table 3.7 presents the results of analyses comparing the families who chose different care arrangements. As one would expect, there were many differences between families using parent care (Group 1–2) and those using day care (Groups 3–7). Demographically, day-care families were of higher socioeconomic status and more mobile (had spent less time in Chicago, in their present residence, etc.). The mothers using day care were more likely to have been in day care or nursery school themselves as children, and to have had professional experience with children. They claimed to be more satisfied with their current roles, including, in the second year, their maternal role. This was not just because these women were more satisfied with life in general: They were not different from mothers at home with their children on an index of overall alienation. Mothers using day care were more likely to spend their time on work and less likely to spend it on housework or on themselves. However, as a group they did *not* spend less time involved with their families: with their parents, with their husbands, or in active interaction with their children. (Teaching and playing with their children was related to the mother's work status, however; the median length of time spent daily playing and teaching was 3 hours for nonworking mothers, 2½ hours for part-time workers, and 1 hour for full-time workers.) Nor did they differ in their knowledge or attitudes about childrearing. Fathers in day-care families participated more fully in child care and spent more time involved with their children than fathers in families not using day care. They also scored higher on agreement with experts about good childrearing. Both mothers and fathers in day-care families had higher expectations and positive ratings of their children—perhaps because their children really were more developmentally advanced—and not surprisingly held less traditional family-oriented values. Finally, children who were in day care participated in fewer non–day-care social activities with friends (possibly because mothers at home deliberately arranged for their children to have such enriching social experiences). There were no differences in the physical home environments of day-care and non–day-care families (toys, decorations, mess, danger, organization), in the number of people in the family or the household, or in the frequency of activities within the extended family.

The two groups of families choosing either to use day care or to provide care for their children themselves were different, thus, in ways that would be expected or necessitated simply on the basis of that choice (e.g., day-care mothers spent time on their work, not on the house). In ways that we might expect would be directly related to advanced child development, however, (like playing with the child or having educational toys around) they were not different. It seems unlikely, therefore, that family differences alone account for the observed advance in the development of day-care children.

More critical disconfirmation of this hypothesis comes from an examination of differences between families choosing center day care (Groups 5–7) or home day care (Groups 3–4). Only one significant difference was found in these analyses. Parents choosing center day care in the second year were of higher SES. However, since SES was statistically controlled (covaried) in our analyses showing higher scores for day-care center children, it is not likely that this family variable could be responsible for the observed differences in children's performance. The group differences observed between center- and home-care children, thus, seem likely to be the result of differences in their day-care experiences. To test this hypothesis, predictions from variations in children's day-care experience were examined more directly.

Predicting Outcomes for Individuals

Thus far we have discussed only mean differences between groups. Our next task was to look at whether the variables that differentiate groups predict developmental scores at the individual level. Analyses correlating environmental predictors with child development outcomes appear in Table 3.8.

TABLE 3.7
Characteristics of the Families

	MEANS						ANOVA SIGNIFICANCE LEVELS CONTRASTS		
	1-2 P	3 BS	4 DCH	5 NS	6 DCC	7 NS + BS	OVERALL	1-2 / 3-7	3-4 / 5-7
DEMOGRAPHICS									
SES Yr 1	38	50	48	48	45	57	.000	.000 <	
Yr 2	34	44	35	48	45	54	.000	.000 <	.001 <
STABLE	45	42	36	38	38	42	.001	.05 >	
PHYSICAL ENVT									
HOM TOY									
HOM DANGER									
HOM STRUCTURE									
HOM DECO									
HOM MESS									
BACKGROUND									
M IN DC	16	18	18	17	18	18	.05	.05 <	
F IN DC									
M EXPER	3.9	5.6	3.6	3.9	4.5	5.6	.01	.05 <	
ATTITUDES									
M CAREER	-.82	.80	.57	-1.13	.63	1.22	.001	.05 <	

88

M ROLSAT (Yr2)	50	64	61	56	60	59	.10	.003<
M MROL SAT (Yr2)	59	72	58	66	68	58	.001	.05<
M ALIEN								
M GOOD CD	104	116	116	113	114	115	.01	.01<
F GOOD CD								
M POS EXP (Yr1)	70.4	72.7	72.9	76.0	77.3	78.0	.002	.01<
F POS EXP	82.7	88.0	89.0	86.0	87.0	89.0	.01	.01<
P TRAD	3.12	0.40	-0.80	0.00	0.30	-0.30	.000	.000>
PEOPLE								
FAM SIZE								
NIT PEOPLE								
ACTIVITIES								
FAMILY	84	87	59	71	67	70	.01	.001<
F INVOL C	-.60	.82	.15	-.15	.84	.32	.001	.000>
C SOC ACT	37.0	27.0	13.3	25.3	13.3	17.6	.001	
M TIME: HUSBAND								
(median hrs PARENTS								
per day) FRIENDS (Yr2)	1.0	0.0	1.0	1.0	0.0	0.5	.01	.000<
WORK	0	8	8	0	8	6	.000	.001>
HOUSE	3.5	1.5	1.5	3.0	1.5	2.0	.001	
SELF (Yr2)	1.0	0.0	0.8	1.0	0.8	0.5	.03	.03>
CHILD CARE								
TEACH/PLAY (Yr1)								
C SOC M	2	3	1	2	1	2	.01	

Shows all means with a significant F value.

TABLE 3.8
Correlations Between Outcomes and Environment

Environmental Variables	COGS		PROX M		SOC M		SOC PEER		NEG PEER		SOC STR	
	1	2	1	2	1	2	1	2	1	2	1	2
Child Care Arrangement (all subjects)												
1 CCA	.27	.16	-.26	-.19					.16	-.20	.26	
2 AMT BS	.16	.35			.22		.20	.33	.24		.17	.21
3 AMT DCH			-.35					.20		-.19		-.22
4 AMT DCC												
Daycare Variables (daycare subjects)												
5 ADULTS					.21							-.21
6 CHILDREN												
7 OLD CH	.25	.25										
8 YOUNG CH												
9 CH/CG						.22						
10 CG GOOD CD	.20	.17										
11 VARIETY								-.28				
12 PROGRAM		.21					-.29					
13 MESS	-.24									-.24		
14 MC PROP	.22	.26					-.22	-.20		-.29		
15 CG TIME												
16 MESH		.24										

17 LENG BS(Gp 3,7)
18 LENG DCH (Gp4)
19 LENG DCC (Gp 5–7) −.48

Family Variables (all subjects)

	17	18	19
20 FAM TRAD	.22	.23	
21 M, F POS EXPECT	−.24 / −.22		.19
22 M SAT ROL			
23 NEG HOM	−.21		
24 STIM HOM	.31		.18
25 F GOOD CD	.21		.26
26 F INVOLV		−.43	
27 M CAREER		.16	
28 SES	−.19		
29 HOM STRUC			
30 NIT PEOP			
31 C SOC M	.23		
32 M WORK	−.17	−.20	
33 M GOOD CD	.17		.18
34 M EXPER	.18	.25	.18
35 C SOC ACT		−.18	.19

Daycare + Family Variables (daycare subjects)

	36	37	38
36 ALL TOYS	.24	.30	.25
37 ALL CHILDREN		.28	.22
38 ALL ADULTS	.22	.20	.22

Shows all *r*'s significant at p ≤ .06.

The correlations of outcome variables with the child-care arrangement itself, from 1 (home with parents alone) to 7 (nursery school plus babysitter) were most consistently significant. Significant positive correlations were found with cognition, independence, sociability with mother, and social competence with peer and adult strangers. The correlation with negative behavior toward the peer was positive in the first-year assessment and negative in the second year. These correlations of outcomes with child-care arrangement replicate the results of the analyses of variance already discussed and serve to confirm the reasonableness of our a priori continuum of day-care arrangements. They are higher in the first year than in the second; most likely because there was a more balanced distribution of children across child-care arrangements in the first year and these child-care groupings were "pure," i.e., the children's first and only day-care arrangements. Similarly confirmatory of our child-care analyses of variance were correlations with the next three variables in Table 3.8: measures of the amount of time the child had spent with a babysitter, in a day-care home, or in a day-care center. The amount of time at home with a babysitter was correlated with cognition and social competence with peer and stranger; the amount of time in a day-care center predicted independence from mother; and the amount of time in a day-care home predicted less negative behavior to the peer and less social competence with the adult.

These correlations support the suggestion that supplementary experience in a day-care center or with a sitter advances children's development, but they tell us little beyond what we could already infer from our analyses of group differences. What can we say about the kind or quality of children's experiences in these day-care arrangements that would account for the results favoring children in day-care centers? The day-care variables that were available for analysis are of three types: those related to the number of people in the day-care setting, those having to do with the quality of the program, and those reflecting the intensity of the day-care experience. The next set of correlations in Table 3.8 (variables 5–19) are those between outcomes and these day-care variables for the sample of children who were in day care (Groups 3–7). Of the "people" variables (5–9), only the number of older children in the setting predicted an outcome—cognitive ability—in a significant and consistent way. Otherwise the correlations with people variables (number of adults in the day-care setting, number of children in the setting, number of younger children, and the adult-child ratio) did not present a meaningful pattern. This is somewhat surprising, since adult-child ratio and class size have often been suggested as indexes of day-care quality. Perhaps results would be different if we looked at predictors of development for the children in center care alone. Separate analyses were done for children in home day care (Groups 3–4) and center care (Groups 5–7). The same pattern of correlations appeared for children in center care as for the total day-care group. For the children in home day care a different, but equivalent, pattern of correlations with these variables appeared: outcomes were predicted not by the number of older children in the setting, but, negatively, by the number of younger children (significant negative correlations were found with cognition Year 2, independence Year 2, sociability to mother Years 1 and 2, and social competence with adult stranger Year 2).

The next set of variables (10–16) estimates some dimensions of program quality. The clearest finding in the correlational analyses of these variables is that the most significantly predicted outcome is cognitive development. This outcome was significantly correlated with caregiver training, knowledge, and stability; with structure, materials, and order in the program; and with the proportion of children in the class who were of high SES. It was not correlated with the heterogeneity or diversity of classmates offered in the program, or the mesh of the caregiver's and parents' attitudes. Separate analyses for home (Groups 3–4) and center (Groups 5–7) children served to confirm these results for the center children. For home day-care children no program variables analyzed predicted cognitive performance, probably because these day-care situations had no formal "program" as such.

The outcomes proximity to mother, sociability to mother, and social competence with an adult stranger were not related to any of the program quality variables analyzed. Positive social behavior with an unfamiliar peer was related to being in a day-care program that was not highly cognitive in orientation and had a high proportion of lower- or working-class children. Negative behavior toward the unfamiliar peer (in the second year) was also related to having a higher proportion of low SES classmates, and in this case the correlation was significant for home day-care children as well as center day-care children. Children with more opportunity to interact with low SES children, thus, seemed to be more socially outgoing in both positive and negative ways.

The third set of day-care variables (17–19) reflects the length and intensity of the child's day-care experience; that is, for children who were in a day-care home or center or with a babysitter, how many hours they had spent there. The results of these analyses, showing only one significant correlation, support our earlier suggestion that the effect of day-care attendance is not a simple continuing cumulation.

We may conclude from these correlational analyses that day-care variables do bear some relation to developmental outcomes, especially to cognitive development, but do these correlations replace those traditionally found with family variables? The next set of variables in Table 3.8 (20–35) reflects aspects of the child's family environment. Many significant correlations with these variables were found for the total sample and for the day-care sample analyzed separately. The first outcome, cognition, was most significantly predicted by the parents' SES, and, backing up this relation, children scoring high on cognitive tasks were found to live in more stimulating homes (in terms of toys and decorations), to have mothers who were more career oriented but worked fewer hours, and to have fathers who were more knowledgeable about child development and good child-rearing practices. Measures of maternal knowledge of good child-rearing practices, professional experience with young children, and role satisfaction were not related to children's cognitive scores. Significant correlations were generally so for both parent-care and day-care samples when analyzed separately, except that the amount the mother worked was not significantly correlated for parent-care children (since these mothers were working very little or not at all), and the correlation with paternal knowledge of child development was significant only for the day-care sample (perhaps because day-care fathers, on average, were more involved in child care than were parent-care fathers).

The second and third outcomes, which reflect the child's relationship with the mother, were, as one might expect, much more closely associated with family variables than with day-care variables. Children who maintained greater distance from mother in the Year 1 assessment were expected by their parents to perform developmental tasks earlier, and their mothers were more satisfied with their own roles in life. This was true for both parent-care and day-care children. In the Year 2 assessment, however, different patterns were found for day-care and parent-care children. More independent children in the day-care sample had parents with less traditional family-oriented values and spent less time in social interaction with their mothers; more independent children in the parent-care sample had parents (both mothers and fathers) who scored low on knowledge of child development and child rearing. This difference in correlational patterns for proximity (attachment) to mother suggests the possibility that independence from mother may reflect different things and develop along different routes in children being raised exclusively by their parents and those who are separated from their parents for large parts of each day. On the basis of studies of parent-reared children, it has been suggested that a pattern of behavior that appears to be precocious independence from mother is actually avoidance of mother, the child's response to maternal rejection of physical and emotional contact (e.g., Main, 1977). There is some hint of a suggestion in the different correlational patterns found in this study that a very high level of independence from mother is indeed related to parental rejection, but that the ''rejection'' takes different forms depending on the child's care arrangement. Parents of more independent day-care children did not value frequent activities involving the whole family—their ''rejection'' would be in terms of spending little time with the child; parents of more independent parent-care children did not value teaching and playing with the child and were likely to express a harsh attitude toward discipline—their rejection could be in terms of the quality of their interaction with the child.

Positive interactions with an unfamiliar peer and with an unfamiliar adult were also related to different constellations of variables for parent-care and day-care children. For day-care children, social competence with a peer related to parents' high SES and traditional family-oriented values, to a stimulating home environment, and to frequent social activities for the child outside of day care; for parent-care children it was related to a messy though also stimulating physical environment and to a mother who had professional experience with young children. Social competence with an unfamiliar adult was related to parents having higher SES and more knowledge about child development for parent-care children; for day-care children, those who were most socially skilled with the unfamiliar adult had been involved in more social activities outside of day care and had parents who expected them to achieve developmental milestones earlier.

Substantially overlapping correlational patterns appeared for children's sociability to mother. Among day-care children, those who were more reciprocally interactive and cooperative with their mothers had mothers who were knowledgeable about child development, had high expectations for the child, were not particularly career oriented, and lived in stimulating, neat, and safe homes. Among parent-care children, those who were more sociable with mother had mothers who had high expectations for the child, were not career oriented but rather valued family activities, and lived in orderly homes.

For negative interaction with the unfamiliar peer, the pattern of correlations was most distinctly different for the two assessments a year apart. In the first assessment, for both day-care and parent-care children, children who were more aggressive had mothers with more professional experience with young children. For day-care children, these mothers were, as well, more career oriented. Perhaps it is these mothers who are more likely to permit "aggressive" (or assertive) behavior in 2- and 3-year-old children. In Year 2, however, when children were 3 to 5 years old, children who were more aggressive toward an unfamiliar peer came from families in which parents held traditional family-oriented values, the father was not involved in child care, and the mother had no professional experience with children and did not work.

If we can overlook the problem of the instability of correlation coefficients for small samples (see Clarke-Stewart, VanderStoep, & Killian, 1979), these patterns of correlations do suggest that there are some differences, as well as substantial similarities, in environmental predictors of child development depending on children's care arrangements. Our next step was to investigate how home and day-care variables work together in predicting development for day-care children. This was done in two ways: by correlating outcomes with combined variables that reflected the "sum" of family and day-care experiences, and by including both family and day-care variables in regression analyses for each outcome.

The last three variables (36–38) in Table 3.8 represent combined family and day-care factors: the number of toys of different types available to the child in both home and day-care settings; the number of children the child interacted with in both home- and day-care settings; and the number of adults in both settings. Correlations of these three variables with the outcome measures revealed significant relations for number of toys and number of children with cognitive level and social competence with the peer, and for number of adults with social competence with peer and adult. These correlations were somewhat higher than those with equivalent home or day-care variables alone (variables 5, 6, 12, 24, 30), suggesting that home and day-care experiences may be additive.

A better probe of this suggestion occurred through regression analysis. Multiple regression analyses were performed for each outcome variable, entering variables from the pool of day-care and family variables plus the child's age and sex, stepwise, until no further variable entered at a level of significance $p < .08$. In these analyses, cognition was predicted by a combination of both day-care and family variables: In the first year significant day-care predictors were the number of older children, the level of the caregiver's training, education, and knowledge of good childrearing practices, and the structure and physical materials in the program; the significant family predictor was the stimulation of the home's physical environment. Each of these variables was positively related to the dependent variable cognition. In the second year, day-care predictors positively related to cognition were the number of older children in the class and the proportion of children who were middle or upper-middle class. Family predictors included the amount of time the child spent interacting with mother and the amount of time mother worked; both these predictors were negatively related to cognition. SES was the last family variable to enter the equation and was marginally significant at $p = .07$. This outcome offers perhaps the best illustration of predictability from the combination of home and day-care factors, and was predicted at the highest level of significance (R^2 for year 1 $= .72, p \leq .0001; R^2$ for year 2 $= .57, p \leq .0001$).

Other outcomes were also related to both day-care and family variables. Social competence with the adult stranger in Year 1 was predicted by a higher level of caregiver training and knowledge in day care and by more people, fewer hours of maternal employment, and earlier expectation of developmental achievements in the family, ($R^2 = .43, p \leq .0001$). In Year 2 it was predicted by a stimulating physical environment at home and more frequent social activities for the child outside day care ($R^2 = .24\ p \leq .001$). Social competence with a peer in Year 1 was predicted by a higher level of caregiver training and knowledge and a more favorable adult-child ratio in day care, and by more traditional family-oriented values, more social activities outside day care, less parental knowledge about good childrearing and more time with mother in the family ($R^2 = .31\ p \leq .001$). In Year 2 it was predicted by a higher proportion of lower- or working-class classmates in day care and a more stimulating physical environment at home ($R^2 = .30, p \leq .001$). Negative behavior to the unfamiliar peer in Year 1 was predicted by more and older children in day care and by more frequent social activities outside day care ($R^2 = .26, p \leq .001$). In Year 2 it was predicted by less father involvement in child care ($R^2 = .14, p \leq .001$). Only proximity and sociability to mother were, as in the correlational analyses, not related to any day-care variables. Otherwise, across outcomes reflecting children's social and intellectual competence there was some consistency in predictability from the day-care variable caregiver training in child development and

knowledge of childrearing and the family variable stimulating physical environment in the home.

Although the results of these regression analyses should be regarded as preliminary only, since this is not the final or definitive set of (statistically independent) variables reflecting children's experiences at home and in day care, they
clearly support the suggestion that the development of competence in children
who are in day care is influenced by factors in both environments.

Cause and Effect

Unfortunately, however, they do not prove it. We cannot be sure from correlational or regression analyses that either home or day-care factors are *causing* the
observed differences in children's performances. Establishing causal direction is
perhaps the greatest challenge of design and interpretation for the researcher in
this area. To explore the likelihood that day-care factors caused developmental
increments, our plan in the present study had been to observe children near the
beginning of their day care-experience and then to analyze gains in their development after a year of such experience, thinking that such might reasonably be
attributed to the day-care experience. Unfortunately this plan ran into several
unforeseen problems. First, as we have mentioned, children's care arrangements
turned out to be unstable from one assessment to the next; and, second, by the
time all the children had been tested in our first-year standard assessment they
had been in day care for an average of 7 months and the developmental differences were (already) apparent. Our attempts to tease apart cause and effect,
therefore, have been even more limited than we had hoped.

One attempt was the examination of gains in children's scores between the
first and second assessments for those children's scores between the first and
second assessments for those children who had shifted from a home arrangement
to a center between the two assessments ($n = 39$). In these analyses we looked
for environmental variables in the second year that were related to the relative
gains in child development scores. The following factors were significant predictors of cognitive gain: a greater number of older children in the child's day-care
class, more demographic homogeneity among the children in the class, greater
stability of the caregiver in the day-care setting, greater maternal knowledge
about good childrearing, and fewer hours of maternal employment. These variables are suggested by this analysis to be likely candidates for influencing children's development. They include, again, variables from both day-care and
family environments.

A second attempt to explore the issue of cause and effect was to compare
correlations between environmental variables at the time of the first assessment
and child development scores at the second assessment with correlations between
child development scores at the first assessment and environmental variables at
the second. For cognition, temporally preceding environmental variables predict-

ing Year 2 scores were number of older children, amount of caregiver training, and stimulation of the home environment. It may be reasonable to think of these as environmental "influences" on children's development. Disconcertingly, however, using this kind of reasoning and analysis, one result suggested that self-selection is also operating: children scoring at a high cognitive level in the first assessment (as well as in the second) were found to be in more structured and stimulating day-care programs at assessment 2. Thus it is not possible to conclude from these analyses that the differences we observed between children in day-care centers and children in homes are simply the consequence of their experiences in a more stimulating milieu or an educational program.

CONCLUSION

We have presented a variety of analyses here in our attempt to explore how the development of young children is affected by nonparental care and how it differs from the development of children being raised exclusively by their parents. One thing that is clear from these analyses is that there is no simple answer to those questions.

Children attending day-care centers, full-time or part-time, were found to score consistently higher on our measures of social, emotional and intellectual maturity than children in homes—with parents or other caregivers. The differences appeared to reflect advanced development rather than qualitative discrepancies, and in fact there was some suggestion for independence and cognitive development that the gap closed when children got older. There were also documented significant and systematic differences between the environments in which these children spent their days and those of children cared for at home in physical facilities, educational emphases, and the composition and characteristics of people with whom the children interacted. Moreover, at the level of individual children and programs, significant relations were found between children's performance on tests of social and intellectual competence and variation in qualities of the program and the composition of its participants.

Significant relations were also found, however, with variation in children's *home* environments; for indices of the child's relationship with mother, in fact, these were the only associations that were statistically significant. Being in day care, even in an educational center-based program, did not eliminate associations between child development and family factors, and we cannot say that the day-care experience *alone* was responsible for the advanced development observed in day-care children. More competent parents were likely to provide better environments for their children—both at home and in day care. Parents of higher SES, for example, chose day-care arrangements that were in centers, had more older children and better trained teachers; they also provided more stimulating physical environments at home. The provision of stimulating toys and interactions at home is also likely to have contributed to day-care children's advanced development. It is unlikely, however, that these home interactions, *alone,* account for the differences in development we observed: Combining both family and day-care variables increased the predictability of competence scores over either alone, and day-care variables continued to predict developmental scores even when family variables such as SES were statistically controlled. Moreover, although family variables, in general, predicted child development outcomes for children in day care as well as those at home. there was, as we discussed, some evidence that some of the particulars of those relations were different. While these differences may have been inflated by the instability of correlation coefficients for small samples, the suggestion is one worth pursuing in further analyses and research.

The evidence is clear, then, that in many ways day care does provide a new context for child development, a context that builds on the "traditional" one of parental care, adding dimensions, modifying dimensions, perhaps interacting with dimensions, but not eliminating the impact of the family.

For the researcher, too, day care provides a new context for development, a context that builds from the traditional model of parent-child interaction and influences, but adds a dimension of complexity. It is subject to the same problems of interpretation that these studies are, and it needs even more effort to untangle the strands of the causal net linking children's development with environmental "influences." Studies like this one are basically descriptive. They are indirect and inferential. They can only suggest, not confirm, causal direction. To crack the causal conundrum in this, as in studies of parent-child interaction, needs more sophisticated analysis and attempts at true experimentation. Only real experiments can establish, for example, whether the same "effects" of day-care center attendance can be achieved if children from unstimulating homes are placed in day-care center programs. One experimental study to test this (Ramey & Mills 1977) suggests that such effects are possible if the families are very poor and the day-care program is very good. But the limits of both family circumstances and day-care quality have not been explored. It may be that children from any family would benefit from even a quite ordinary community day-care center program. While randomly assigning children to care arrangements on a large scale may be on a par with randomly assigning children to mothers, it may be possible to test more narrowly conceived hypotheses within the general area of research on day-care effects. This strategy should be followed if we want ever to understand the processes of child development in a contemporary world of increasing complexity.

ACKNOWLEDGMENT

The research reported in this chapter was supported by the Bush Foundation, supplemented by funds from the Spencer Foundation. It was written during the author's year at the Center for Advanced Study in the Behavioral Sciences, on a fellowship from the

MacArthur Foundation. The assistance of these three Foundations is most gratefully acknowledged. Appreciated, too, is the assistance provided by various graduate students at the University of Chicago who collected, coded, and helped in the analyses of data. Particularly helpful for this report were the efforts of Chris Gruber, Linda Fitzgerald, Saba Ayman-Nolley, and Richard Rogers.

REFERENCES

Blehar, M. C. Anxious attachment and defensive reactions associated with day care. *Child Development,* 1974, *45.* 683–692.
Clarke-Stewart, K. A., VanderStoep, L. P., & Killian, G. A. Analysis and replication of mother-child relations at two years of age. *Child Development,* 1979, *50,* 777–793.
Cochran, M. M. A comparison of group day and family child-rearing patterns in Sweden. *Child Development,* 1977, *48,* 702–707.
Fraiberg, S. *Every child's birthright: In defense of mothering.* New York: Basic Books, 1977.
Heber, F. R. Sociocultural mental retardation—A longitudinal study. In D. Forgay (Ed.), *Primary prevention of psychopathology* (Vol. 2). *Environmental influences.* Hanover, N.H.: University Press of New England, 1978.
Main, M. B. Analysis of a peculiar form of reunion behavior seen in some day care children: Its history and sequelae in children who are home-reared. In R. A. Webb (Ed.), *Social development in childhood: Day care programs and research.* Baltimore: Johns Hopkins University Press, 1977.
Ramey, C. T., & Mills, P. J. Social and intellectual consequences of day care for high-risk infants. In R. A. Webb (Ed.). *Social development in childhood: Day care programs and research.* Baltimore: Johns Hopkins University Press, 1977.
Roopnarine, J. L., & Lamb, M. E. Peer and parent-child interaction before and after enrollment in nursery school. *Journal of Applied Developmental Psychology,* 1980, *1,* 77–81.
Ruopp, R., Travers, J., Glantz, F., & Coelen, C. *Children at the center.* Cambridge, Mass.: Abt Associates, 1979.
Scarr, S. W. *On the development of competence and the indeterminate boundaries between cognition and motivation: A genotype-environment correlation theory.* Paper prepared for Conference on Home Influences on School Achievement, Wisconsin Research and Development Center, Madison, Wisconsin, October, 1981.
Vaughn, B. E., Gove, F. L., & Egeland. B. The relationship between out-of-home care and the quality of infant-mother attachment in an economically disadvantaged population. *Child Development,* 1980, *51,* 1203–1214.

4 Maternal Employment and the Young Child

Lois Wladis Hoffman
University of Michigan

Any list of the recent social changes that have significance for parent-child interaction patterns would include the increased employment of mothers. The steady rise in maternal employment rates over the years is clearly illustrated in Table 4.1. The pattern, rare in 1940, had become modal by 1978 and has been found to be more prevalent at each new reading.

A change as impressive as this increase in the employment of mothers cannot occur in isolation. It is part of a complex pattern. The increased employment rates are a response to some new events, accompanied by other responses to these events, and the cause of still other changes. Such is the nature of social systems. A change in one part involves a change in others. It is important to understand the total pattern to see how maternal employment fits into the picture.

American family life has undergone so many transformations in recent years that the context within which maternal employment is now occurring is different from in the past. Technological developments—including clothes dryers, no-iron fabrics, disposable diapers, home freezers, and processed foods of good quality—have enormously diminished the amount of work necessary for operating a household; family size is smaller; marital instability has increased the necessity for women to establish occupational competence; economic pressures in general have increased; women's educational levels have risen; the adult roles for which children are being socialized are different; the prevailing social values have changed (Hoffman, in press). Today full-time mothers as well as employed mothers may feel a need to justify their role, and the role of full-time mother is a less satisfying one according to a number of recent studies (Gold & Andres, 1978; Kessler & McRae, 1982; Veroff, Douvan, & Kulka, 1981). The role of the present-day nonemployed mothers may be as new as the role of the majority of

101

TABLE 4.1
Labor Force Participation Rates
of Mothers With Children
Under 18, 1940–1980

Year	% of Mothers
1980	56.6
1978	53.0
1976	48.8
1974	45.7
1972	42.9
1970	42.0
1968	39.4
1966	35.8
1964	34.5
1962	32.9
1960	30.4
1958	29.5
1956	27.5
1954	25.6
1952	23.8
1950	21.6
1948	20.2
1946	18.2
1940	8.6

Source: U.S. Department of Labor, 1977; U.S. Department of Commerce, 1979; U.S. Department of Labor, 1981.

present-day mothers, who are employed. It is even difficult to know which represents more of a continuity with the nonemployed mother of the past. It is possible that the individual child in today's employed-mother household receives as much attention as the individual child in yesterday's nonemployed-mother household—work filling in the time previously spent on the extra household responsibilities and the additional children, while today's nonemployed mother represents the really new pattern. The nonemployed mother today may represent a more intense parent-child interaction than we have ever had before. There is no data base that would make testing that hypothesis possible, but it is important to keep in mind as employed-mother families are compared with nonemployed-mother families; neither one represents the traditional pattern.

Until recently there were very few studies of the effects of maternal employment on the infant and preschool child, largely because the pattern was unusual. But the pattern is no longer unusual. In 1982, over 48% of the mothers of preschoolers, with a husband present in the home, were employed; over 45% of the mothers of children under 3 (see Table 4.2). For mothers with no current husband, a rapidly increasing group, the comparable figures were 60% and 53%. In fact the rate of increase in employment has been greatest for mothers of preschoolers. The current figure of 48.7% employment among married mothers of preschoolers, for example, is more than double the rate in 1965.

The increase is hardly as dramatic, but there has also been a burgeoning of research on maternal employment and the preschool child in recent years. It is this research that is reviewed here. From one standpoint, this is a premature review: the data that have accumulated do not lend themselves to tidy conclusions. What does emerge, however, are interesting new questions and leads for future research. From another standpoint then, this may be exactly the time to undertake a review, now while new research is being launched. The goal of this review is not, then, to draw conclusions about how maternal employment affects the parents' relationships with their young children but rather to suggest paths that future research might take. As a first step, some of the methodological problems with this new work will be pointed out because they affect the interpretation of the results and also indicate concerns for subsequent investigators.

TABLE 4.2
Percentage of Mothers in the
Labor Force by Marital Status
and Age of Child 1982

Marital Status of Mother and Age of Child	Percentage
Mothers with children 6–17 only	
Married, husband present	63.2[a]
Widowed, divorced, separated	75.3[b]
Mothers with children under 6	
Married, husband present	48.7[c]
Widowed, divorced, separated	60.7
Mothers with children under 3	
Married, husband present	45.3[d]
Widowed, divorced, separated	53.5

[a]Of these 62.4% were full time, 30.6% were part time, and 7.0% were "unemployed but looking."
[b]Of these 74.3% were full time, 14.9% were part time and 10.8% were "unemployed but looking."
[c]Of these, 55.6% were full time, 34.2% were part time, and 10.1% were "unemployed by looking."
[d]Of these, 54.6% were full time, 34.4% were part time, and 11.0% were "unemployed but looking."
Source: U.S. Department of Labor, Bureau of Labor Statistics, data supplied by E. Waldman, Senior Economist.

Methodological Problems

Studies of maternal employment effects with older children have had to deal with the fact that employed mothers are often different from nonemployed in other ways besides the sheer fact of employment status. They are more likely to be from lower income groups, but within their social class they are better educated. They are more likely to be divorced, to have fewer children, and to be somewhat less traditional in their outlooks. These variables need to be considered in any study lest the outcomes observed reflect these differences rather than employment status per se. Furthermore, effects of maternal employment have been shown to be different in different subgroups of the population. For example, effects are different in the middle class than in the blue-collar class, different for sons than for daughters. All of these problems also plague the studies of younger children. The studies of younger children, however, have additional problems, and the effort to cope with these has often led to a neglect of the more traditional methodological concerns in maternal employment research. Three problems that the work with young children is particularly likely to confront will be discussed—the choice of the dependent variables, sample size, and the location of subjects.

In studying maternal employment effects on infants and young children, what will the dependent variable be? The heavy use of the Stanford-Binet as an index of how the child fares when studying school-aged children has often been criticized, but at least it predicts school performance and adult Stanford Binet scores. Such measures of developmental status obtained with very young children do not even have that virtue. Thus, a study of the preschool child which examines the relationship between maternal employment and the Stanford-Binet or the Bayley may suggest an effect, though that outcome may have nothing to do with adult functioning. Furthermore, if no relationships are evident between maternal employment and early functioning, there may be an effect which can be tapped only later when the child is older.

A solution to the difficulties in measuring meaningful predictive behaviors in infants and very young children is to turn instead to longitudinal and retrospective studies. But there is also a problem here. As already indicated above, and as stressed in previous reviews (Hoffman, 1963, 1974a, 1979, 1980), the effects of maternal employment depend on the social milieu. The mother who works when the pattern is rare is different from those who work when it is common and the effects on the child will be different under different social conditions. So a danger of longitudinal research, particularly over a long period, is that we learn a great deal about a pattern that no longer exists and very little about the pattern that does exist.

If, on the other hand, the dependent variable is not a child characteristic but parent-child interaction, behavioral observation techniques are typically used. The data are rich in many ways, but so time-consuming and expensive to obtain and analyze that studies must settle for small N's that make it impossible to do the complex analyses necessary in studies of maternal employment where variables such as social class, education, attitudes, father's role, and the omnipresent sex differences must be considered. Under the best of circumstances, when the employed and nonemployed groups are adequately matched on these variables, the small sample limits the results to a very restricted population and makes it very difficult to do any subsample analysis although most of the studies require such analysis for adequate interpretation of the results.

A third difficulty in carrying out maternal employment research with infants and young children stems from the problem of locating subjects. Although there are more subjects available now than there were 20 years ago, where do you find them? If a researcher wants to do a study of third-graders, they can be located through the public schools, but it is not as easy to locate an appropriate sample of preschoolers in clusters, nor an appropriate sample of mothers of preschoolers. Subjects can be obtained through birth announcements in newspapers, birth registrations, maternity hospitals, or knocking on doors, but most researchers have shunned these more time-consuming methods and instead recruited subjects through childbirth preparation classes, day-care centers, or from subgroups of ongoing research projects. These procedures have introduced sample bias that could affect the validity of the results. For example, in one study of infants (Pederson, Cain, Zaslow, & Anderson, 1983) subjects were recruited through childbirth preparation classes that encouraged active participation of both parents in the birth process. In this study the fathers in the nonemployed-mother families were found to be very active in interactions with their 5-month-old infants. It seems possible that their high level of involvement was not typical of fathers in nonemployed-mother families but represented a selective factor, and not necessarily the same selective factor that characterized the fathers in the employed-mother families. The first group may have been particularly involved with their child even before birth since there was no objective pressure, such as anticipated maternal employment, to motivate their class enrollment. In two other infancy studies (Cohen, 1978; Vaughn, Gove, & Egeland, 1980), the subjects were part of a larger project dealing with troubled families, and it is difficult to know how the various stress factors—e.g., infant prematurity, father absence—interacted in affecting the results.

The studies of toddlers frequently recruit subjects through nursery schools and day-care centers. This procedure offers efficiency in locating subjects and enables the researcher to obtain observations of the children in a common group setting. The problem is again that it introduces a selective factor and one that may operate differently for the children of employed mothers than for the children of nonemployed. Participation in preschools, unlike public school attendance, is self-selected, and the reason an employed mother enrolls her child in the program may be different from the reason a nonemployed mother does. For example, if it is a full-time day-care center, the employed mother is likely to have her child there because she needs reliable substitute care during her working hours. But why does the nonemployed mother have her child there? The latter may have her child in full-time day care because of some disturbance in the home or because of the attitude of the mother toward the child. Comparisons between the children of employed and nonemployed mothers then, even when the two groups are matched on such variables as family size and ordinal position, may reveal differences that reflect not employment status but the contrasting self-selection process. There are few shortcuts to locating subjects for maternal employment studies of preschool children and careful attention to sampling procedures is essential.

Despite these problems, enough adequate research has been done recently that some patterns are beginning to emerge, at least enough to identify areas for future research. Although many of these studies are only exploratory, and they differ in their measures of the independent variable—the mother's employment status, in their choice of dependent variables, and in the populations sampled, the findings reveal some interesting commonalities across studies. It is fortunate that this work has been conducted at a time when researchers were sensitive to sex differences and to the fact that children have fathers as well as mothers because some of the most provocative results have to do with the role of the father and the different effects for boys and girls.

Studies of Day Care

The goal of this review is to integrate the research bearing on maternal employment and parent-child interaction. The recent investigations that have examined the effects of day-care experience on the preschool child are clearly relevant to understanding the effects of maternal employment on the preschool child, since employed mothers are more likely than nonemployed to utilize day-care facilities (Kamerman & Hayes, 1982). This body of research, however, is peripheral to the focus here. Though some of the day-care studies have considered the impact on the mother-child relationship, most have looked at the direct impact of the day-care experience on the child. Furthermore, not all children with day-care experience have employed mothers, and day care is not the most common form of substitute child care that employed mothers use. Among the preschool children of part-time employed mothers (employed 10 to 29 hours per week), 18.8% spend time in day-care centers, while 29.8% of the children of full-time employed mothers spend time there. Most employed mothers of pre-schoolers rely on care in their own homes or in the home of the caretaker, and the younger the child, the less likely the mother is to use center-based care (Kamer-man & Hayes, 1982).

In any case, the research on the effects of day care has been well reviewed already in several recent publications (Belsky & Sternberg, 1978; Clarke-Stewart & Fein, 1983; Etaugh, 1980; Rubinstein, 1984; Rubinstein & Howes, 1979).

The overall conclusions from these reviews indicate that there are not adverse effects for the mother-child relationship, that there are sometimes cognitive gains for children from disadvantaged backgrounds (particularly attenuation of IQ declines), and that day-care children tend to interact more with their peers in both positive and negative ways. A criticism often leveled against this work is that studies typically have examined the better quality centers, frequently those attached to a university. The question of how children fare in the less adequate day-care centers that are more prevalent has only recently been addressed. Two recent studies looked at children attending a wider range of day-care centers and both studies found patterns consistent with the previous results. An investigation of low-income children in publicly funded Infant Center and Family Day Care in New York City found that even in these centers, many far from ideal, the Center children had higher IQ scores (tested at 18 months and 3 years) than a comparable home-reared sample and no differences in social-emotional development (Golden, Rosenblith, Grossi, Policare, Freeman, & Brownlee, 1978). In a very recent study in Chicago by Clarke-Stewart, reported in this volume, a more middle-class sample was examined. Children from a broad spectrum of day-care centers were compared to children without day-care experience on a variety of cognitive and socio-emotional measures. The day-care children indicated more mature social development and intellectual competence.

On the other hand, in a study of public day-care effects in Bermuda by Schwartz and his colleagues (Schwartz, Scarr, Caparulo, Furrow, McCartney, Billington, Phillips, & Hindy, 1981), the results were quite different. In this study, children with extensive care in centers during the first 2 years of life showed significantly poorer adjustment on several cognitive and personality dimensions than children cared for at home or in nonparental home-based care. Furthermore, analysis showed that these results characterized particularly those centers where groups were large and where there were few adults per child. The effects were most pronounced when the child received such care during the first year of life. These results are not necessarily inconsistent with the previous studies. If the quality of child care is conceived of as a continuum, the Bermuda day care may represent a point where the quality of care is inadequate in comparison to the home-based care whereas this has not been true in the other day-care centers studied. Even in the Bermuda study, it is clear that the crucial variable is not absence from the mother per se, but the quality of the substitute care.

Increasingly the research in this area is moving toward defining what aspects of the child-care setting have particular effects rather than seeking global judgments of each of the different types of care. The advantages and disadvantages of center-based care, family-based out-of-home care, and full-time maternal care should be expected to vary depending on the quality of each. In the New York study, for example, the day-care centers not only showed cognitive advantages for children over full-time parental care, but also showed advantages over family day care. In the Bermuda study, exactly the opposite pattern prevailed: the day-care centers were inferior to home-based substitute care as well as parental care.

EFFECTS OF MATERNAL EMPLOYMENT

The dependent variables that have been examined in studies of maternal employment and the preschool child include the amount of parent-child interaction, the quality of parent-child interaction, the nature of the attachment between the infant and each parent, and various child characteristics such as the child's developmental level, peer behavior, and socio-emotional adjustment generally. Major emphasis here will be on the first three variables: the amount of interaction, the quality of interaction, and the attachment relationship and this research will be discussed first. To place some of the results of these investigations in context, however, it is necessary to range beyond the early childhood years. Some of the sex differences emerging in even the infancy work have parallels in the studies of school-aged children.

Following the discussion of the interaction and attachment studies, the research coverage will be completed by summarizing work that has focused mainly on child characteristics without examining directly the parent-child interactions. These studies include investigations of two distinct populations: middle-class children usually in nursery school settings and lower-class children from specially selected disadvantaged populations.

In the final section, some specific issues are considered: How are the relationships between variables affected by the timing of the mother's entry into the work force and by the stress factors in the home? Research directions and policy implications are also discussed.

Quantity of Mother-Child Interaction

National time-use studies in which subjects keep records reporting their activities have been conducted that compare the amount of time employed mothers spend with their children with the amount of time full-time homemakers spend. In general, as might be expected, employed mothers spend less time in child care than nonemployed but this differs by social class, and by the definition of child care. Hill and Stafford (1978), for example, included as child care physical care, teaching, reading, talking, playing, and providing medical care. They report that women employed more than 20 hours a week spend less time in child care whether the child is a baby, preschooler, grade-schooler, or high-schooler. They also note that the differences vary with the education of the mother; the employed-nonemployed difference is considerably less for college-educated women. Employed college-educated women reduce mainly sleep and television watching. These authors still report, however, a 25% deficit in child-care time for employed college-educated mothers of preschoolers. On the other hand, Goldberg (1977) differentiated child care into different types of interaction in a study of middle-class preschool children enrolled in a nursery school. She found no difference in the amount of direct one-to-one interaction between the mother and the child although the full-time employed mothers had less "available" time with the child (when the mother was within calling distance) and less "indirect" time (when the two were in the same room engaged in separate activities). The possibility that the "one-to-one" time the employed mother spends with her infant is particularly intense, at least with respect to social play and verbal stimulation, is suggested by some of the work of Pederson and his colleagues (1983) discussed below. A number of studies also indicate that the employed mother often sets aside special periods for uninterrupted time with the child (Hoffman, 1980).

Quantity of Father-Child Interaction

The question of whether or not fathers participate more in child care when mothers are employed has been a complicated one. In a recent national time-use study it was reported that husbands of employed women had more child contact time than husbands of nonemployed women, as well as higher participation in household tasks (Pleck & Rustad, 1980). It might be noted that this recent time-use study is one of the first to report a substantial effect of maternal employment on the husband's family role. This finding may reflect, as the investigators suggest, an increase in the fathers' responsiveness to maternal employment. However, my own analysis of time-use data as well as data based on a variety of other measurement procedures have consistently indicated over the years that fathers in working-mother households engage in more household tasks and child care when the number of children in the family and the age of the child are taken into account (Hoffman, 1983, in press). The problem is that many of the time-use studies fail to control for family size, and the working-mother families have fewer children and older ones. The new time-use studies then may be showing this effect more than the previous ones for three reasons: first, fathers may in fact be helping more; second, family size in America shows less variance, with the two-child norm increasingly prevalent, and thus the obscuring effect of a wide range in family size is diminished; and third, the new time-use studies are more sensitive to the family-size and age-of-child variables.

If it is true in general that fathers are more involved in child care when their wives are employed, is it true specifically for families with young children? There are two conflicting sets of data that are relevant; one set is based on parent reports, the other on behavioral observations.

On the one hand, the time-use data analyzed by Pleck and Rustad (1980), already cited, indicate the pattern holds when there are young children. In addition, several smaller studies of children between 1 and 4 (Baruch & Barnett, 1981; Gold & Andres, 1978) provide data, also based on parent reports, that fathers in dual-wage families spend more time in interaction with their children.

Some of the recent work with infants using behavioral observations, on the other hand, suggests that when mothers of infants work, the father may actually have less interaction with the infant than fathers in single-wage families. In a small exploratory study by Pederson and his associates (1983), the interaction between parents and their 5-month-old infants was observed during the early evening hours, comparing interaction patterns in mother-working and mother-not-working families. The employed mothers had more verbal interaction with their infants than their husbands or either parent in the single-wage family, as well as a high rate of social play. The dual-wage fathers, on the other hand, had the lowest amount of noncaregiving infant interaction. Pederson suggested that when both parents return from work the father helps by handling various household demands while the mother uses this time as a period of intense mother-child interaction. This is mother's special time when she compensates for her absence during the day. In the nonemployed-mother family, however, this period is the father's time with the baby and the mother turns to other activities. The after-work hours yielded a picture of intense mother-infant interaction in the dual-wage family that seemed to squeeze fathers out, while this time was a period for father-child interaction in single-wage families. In a second study by this same research group (Zaslow et al., in press), the more intense father-infant interaction pattern in families with nonemployed mothers was again borne out, although the mother-infant interaction differences were not found.

The first of the two studies by Pederson and his colleagues is also interesting in that much of the parent-infant interaction that has typically been found to characterize fathers, social play and physically robust handling of the infant, was more characteristic of the employed mothers and less true of their husbands, leading the authors to suggest that sex differences in parenting style may be partly a function of work roles. This pattern, however, did not show up in the second study.

The difference between the data from studies relying on parent reports and those relying on coded observations is not that one method is more valid than the other. Rather, the two kinds of studies are tapping different dimensions. The observation studies measure the number of interactions during a specific time period, such as one hour. In a sense, they are measuring the intensity of the interaction, not the total amount. During two 1-hour periods in the early part of a weekday evening, the fathers in the nonemployed-mother families had more interactions with their infants than did fathers in the employed-mother families (Pederson et al., 1983) but that does not mean they spent more time with their infants over the course of a week. The parent-report studies, on the other hand, covered the time the father spent with the child over the week. It is possible that both sets of results are valid and the question is which kind of interaction, if either, is more meaningful.

Quality of Mother-Child Interaction

The distinction between the quantity of interaction and the quality is not always easy to maintain for, as already indicated, quantity can be conceptualized in different ways. Nevertheless, there are several recent studies using behavioral observations that seem to focus primarily on the quality of the mother-infant interaction. These studies have produced a confusing array of results.

Two of the studies, one by Hock (1980) and the other by Cohen (1978), found no differences between the interaction patterns of employed and nonemployed mothers during the infant's first year. The Cohen study did find differences during the second year, not in the mother's behavior but in the baby's responses: the infants of nonemployed mothers engaged in more "non-distress vocalization." They also performed better on standard developmental tests, the Bayley Scales at 18 and 25 months and the Gesell Developmental Schedules at 24 months. This study, however, is very limited. All of the infants in the sample were preterm, but the infants with employed mothers weighed significantly less at birth and were more likely to have absent fathers. Although the researcher attempted to control on these factors, the sample size was too small for a simultaneous control and it is quite possible that the results reflect the interaction of these rather than maternal employment per se. Findings from studies of full-term infants in two-parent families, by and large, do not seem consistent with Cohen's result. For example, in their first study of 5-month-olds, Pederson and his colleagues (1983) found no differences in Bayley scores, and the infants in the employed-mother families showed higher rates of exploration and accompanying verbalization. Although the infants in this study were not tested in their second year, the pattern of differences seems counter-indicative to the Cohen results. On the other hand there is one recent indication of support: In a follow-up analysis of the second study by the Pederson group, comparisons at 12 months revealed that the infants with employed mothers smiled and laughed less than the infants with nonemployed mothers (Zaslow, Pederson, Suwalsky, & Rabinovich, 1983).

Several investigations of maternal employment and the quality of mother-infant interaction have looked at the mother's verbal behavior. As already indicated, in the two studies by Pederson and his colleagues (Pederson et al., 1983; Zaslow, Pederson, Suwalsky, Cain, Anderson, & Fivel, in press) employed mothers were higher in verbal interaction and social play in the first study, but there were no differences in the second. In an investigation by Schubert, Bradley-Johnson, and Nuttal (1980), the finding that employed mothers were higher in verbal stimulation was repeated, at least during the first 8 minutes of a

12-minute observation, but to add to the mixed picture, data by Stuckey, McGhee, and Bell (1982) showed employed mothers more verbal in observations in an unstructured situation and less verbal in a structured play situation.[1] A study by Schwartz (1983) found that the employed mothers of 18-month-olds displayed significantly more positive emotional behavior toward their children than did the nonemployed mothers.

In these studies, all of which used behavioral observations to compare employed and nonemployed mothers with respect to the quality of their interaction with the child, the major impression is that maternal employment is not a robust variable. Though most of the differences seem to suggest the employed mother was the more attentive, particularly verbally, no clear-cut pattern has yet emerged. Variations in the sampling and the situation observed seem to affect the result in ways not yet understood.[2]

Several of these researchers tried to demonstrate that congruence between employment status and attitude was the really potent variable in predicting mother-infant interaction (Hock, 1980; Schubert et al., 1980; Stuckey et al., 1982). A major reason for predicting that employment status will affect the quality of the mother's interaction with the child is that her morale is affected. If employment provides satisfaction and increases the mother's morale, the quality of her interaction with the child should be enhanced. If on the other hand, the dual role of mother and employee involves strain, her interaction will be adversely affected. Similarly, if the full-time homemaker would prefer to be employed, her resentment and discontent may be expressed in her interaction with the child. Thus, a reasonable hypothesis is that congruence between one's employment status and one's attitudes, or satisfaction with one's employment status, will be related to higher quality mother-child interaction. The data are consistent with this hypothesis, but it is not an easy one to prove empirically. Studies with infants, as well as with older children, have consistently demonstrated that the mother's satisfaction with her employment status relates positively to the quality of mother-child interaction and also to various indices of the child's adjustment and abilities

---

[1]In all the studies of mother-infant behavioral observations reviewed here except Stuckey et al. (1982) the infants were not more than 18 months old. In the study by Stuckey et al. the children ranged in age from 32 to 72 months.

[2]In addition, a study of children between 3 and 6 years by MacKinnon, Brody, and Stoneman (1982) examined the amount of cognitive and social stimulation in the home and the amount of sex-typed toys and furnishings comparing employed-mother intact families, nonemployed-mother intact families, and employed-mother single-parent families. There were no employed-nonemployed differences in stimulation in the intact families but the single-parent families were less stimulating than either of the intact families. It is not possible to determine whether this stimulation difference was a function of the combination of single-parent status *and* employment status or of single-parent status alone since there were no single-parent families where mothers were not employed. The employed mother families, intact and nonintact, showed less sex-role stereotyping in the children's room furnishings and toys.

(Farel, 1980; Hock, 1980; Schubert et al., 1980; Stuckey et al., 1982; Yarrow, Scott, DeLeeuw, & Heinig, 1962). The difficulty lies in demonstrating the direction of causality. While maternal satisfaction may be the reason for the positive mother-child interaction, it may also reflect the relationship with the child and the mother's awareness that the child is faring well. Difficulties with the child, on the other hand, could cause the mother's discontent. Attempts to prove this hypothesis over the years have shown improvements in design and measures, but none has succeeded in demonstrating the direction of causality.

ATTACHMENT STUDIES

There are several studies in which the quality of the mother-infant attachment has been investigated using Ainsworth's Strange Situation measure (Ainsworth, Blehar, Waters, & Wall, 1978). The first of these was Hock's (1980), which compared mothers who returned to work by 3 months after the child's birth to a matched nonemployed group and found no differences. The second was a study of attachment in an economically disadvantaged group (Vaughn et al., 1980). This study examined the security of attachment between infants and mothers who returned to work during the first year after the child's birth, mothers who returned to work between 12 and 18 months after the birth, and mothers who did not return to work. There were no differences in the security of attachment among these three groups.

In the second study, the investigators also looked at the type of insecure attachment. Ainsworth differentiated two types of insecure attachment. In one type, called anxious-avoidant, the infants seem to show more avoidance of the mother when she returns after a brief separation in the laboratory, but the infants' exploratory behavior continues throughout, even when the infant is distressed. In the other, called anxious-resistant, the infant shows impoverished exploration— even prior to separation. Although there was no relationship between security of attachment and employment status, and no significant relationship at all for the intact families, there was one statistically significant relationship in nonintact families: the *kind* of insecure attachment shown by the infants whose mothers returned to work during the first year was the anxious-avoidant.[3]

The pattern of finding not more insecure attachment but more of one specific kind, anxious-avoidant, was reported again in a third study (Schwartz, 1983). Schwartz, in a study of intact, middle-class families, compared attachment patterns between infants whose mothers returned to work within 9 months of the birth to infants with nonemployed mothers. For those who returned to work full time, the same pattern noted in the disadvantaged, nonintact families was found: i.e., not more insecure attachment, but more of the anxious-avoidant type. There

---

[3]The statistics are not reported in the published article, but Exact Fisher Tests were performed using the data presented in the tables (with a printing error corrected).

were no attachment differences between the infants with part-time employed mothers and nonemployed.

In the earlier study with disadvantaged infants, the investigators had measured attachment by the method recommended by Ainsworth which involves a configural classification system. In the Schwartz study, a 7-point rating scale was used instead. Since few of the infants in the middle-class sample showed very clear-cut insecure attachment, scores of 3 or more were coded as insecure. This resulted in a rather liberal assignment of anxious-avoidant labels. Most of the infants classified as anxious-avoidant had only scores of 3 and it seems possible that this is tapping a coping style rather than a truly insecure attachment. It is possible that the results suggest that infants of full-time employed mothers in the middle class cope with maternal absence by continuing to explore their environment and are less disrupted in their activities, and not that they are anxious-avoidantly attached.

Perhaps the best designed study to date investigating the relationship between maternal employment and parent-child attachment was conducted by Chase-Lansdale and Owen (Chase-Lansdale, 1981). All infants were from intact middle-class homes; in addition all were firstborn. The employed mothers had returned to work full time before the infant was 3 months old, and thus were employed before attachment was established and the daily separations occurred throughout this period. The configural classification system suggested by Ainsworth (Ainsworth et al., 1978) was used. One hundred ten families were included in the sample, thus enabling the investigators to carry out important subgroup analyses. Particularly innovative was the inclusion of fathers in the study and attention to the sex of the infant; these two aspects yielded the most interesting results.[4]

In the Chase-Lansdale and Owen study there were no relationships between the mother's employment status and the security of the mother-infant attachment nor between the mother's employment status and the type of attachment. This result was consistent with the earlier study by Hock and with the study by Vaughn, Gove, and Egeland. The Hock study found no differences in the quality of attachment. Hock did not look for differences in the type of attachment as defined by Ainsworth's configural classification, but she did examine other specific aspects of the infant's behavior in the Strange Situation. The only difference noted was that the children of employed mothers showed less resistance to the stranger. The study by Vaughn and his colleagues of disadvantaged families had found no significant differences for the intact families in either the security of the attachment or the type. On the other hand, the results obtained by Chase-Lansdale and Owen are not consistent with the results reported by Schwartz.

---

[4]Some interesting support for the father-infant attachment classification was provided in this research. Fathers who failed to return a mail-in questionnaire about their attitudes and behavior toward the child were more likely to have infants who were insecurely attached to them.

Although the results of three of these studies are similar, the measures and samples were different in several ways. (See Table 4.3). Hock and Chase-Lansdale and Owen included only employed mothers who had returned to work within 3 months of the child's birth, whereas the employed mothers in both of the other studies may have returned later during the first year. The Chase-Lansdale and Owen study is like the study by Vaughn, Gove, and Egeland in the measure of attachment used: both used the classification system and both used raters trained at the Minnesota Institute of Child Development. Very different populations, however, were sampled in these two investigations.

Comparability of sample was greatest between the Schwartz study and the Chase-Lansdale and Owen study. Both of these examined only middle-class, intact families living in or around Ann Arbor, Michigan. All infants were receiving home-based, as opposed to center-based, care. It is possible that the differences between the results of these two studies reflect other sample differences such as the fact that Chase-Lansdale and Owen included only firstborn infants, or that they reflect differences in the time of the mother's return to work (early in the first year rather than later). In view of the total pattern of results from all four studies, however, it seems most likely that the different results reflect differences in the measuring techniques. As suggested above, it is possible that the rating scale, as employed by Schwartz, though intended to approximate the classification coding, may have resulted in an overly liberal assignment of anxious-avoidant attachment.

Father-Infant Attachment.   The study by Chase-Lansdale and Owen investigated the effect of maternal employment on father-infant attachment as well as on mother-infant attachment. From the discussion above of the effects of mater-

TABLE 4.3
Studies of Attachment

	Sample	*Return to Work*	*Measure of Attachment*
Hock (1980)	Mixed social class 1- and 2-parent families	Within 3 months	7-point scale
Vaughn, Gove, & Egeland (1980)	Disadvantaged, lower-class 1- and 2-parent families	Within 12 months and 12–18 months	Configural classification
Schwartz (1983)	Middle-class 2-parent families	Within 9 months	7-point scale (3 points and above = insecure)
Chase-Lansdale (1981)	Middle-class 2-parent families firstborn only	Within 3 months	Configural classification

nal employment on father-child interaction it is apparent that maternal employment might be viewed as increasing the father's interaction with the infant, since he helps his wife with the parenting activities, or as decreasing the father's interaction, since the mother is given priority with the infant during the after-work hours, the time fathers in single-wage families are most likely to spend playing with and caring for their infants. The effects of maternal employment on father-infant attachment might be expected to depend on which of these patterns predominates. This research was poised for either outcome, but the actual results were unexpected. There was no relationship between maternal employment and father-infant attachment for daughters, not even a trend. There was, however, a significant relationship between maternal employment status and father-infant attachment for sons: Fathers in dual-wage families had significantly less secure attachments with their sons. (The type of insecure attachment was not related.)

This result was unexpected, but it was consistent with the accumulated research on older children that any relationship suggesting a negative effect of maternal employment was found for sons but not daughters. The Chase-Lansdale and Owen study was the first investigation of infants, however, that examined the correlates of maternal employment separately by sex of child. To interpret the finding that father-son attachment was less secure in the employed-mother family, it is useful to review briefly the previous research with older children.

Sex Differences

Many of the studies of the effects of maternal employment on older children have found no effects, or patterns that were revealed only when specific subgroups of the population were examined. By and large, however, when significant relationships did emerge, they suggested positive effects for girls. Daughters of working mothers, compared to daughters of nonworking mothers, generally appear to be more independent, outgoing, higher achievers, to admire their mothers more, to have more respect for women's competence, and to show better social and personal adjustment. While sons also usually show better social and personal adjustment, and sometimes no difference in cognitive performance, there is a reoccurring finding that middle-class sons of employed mothers show lower academic performance in grade school and sometimes lower IQs. This finding does not occur among lower-class boys where, if there are academic differences, they tend to favor the employed-mothers' sons. On the other hand, for the blue-collar class, while the data do not suggest lower academic performance, there are indications of a strain in the father-son relationship. This result does not show up in the middle class (Hoffman, 1979, 1980).

In a recent review (Hoffman, 1980), several different hypotheses were proposed to explain these results. The positive effects for daughters seem almost over-determined. The employed mother provides a model that is associated with competence and accorded higher status in the family. The children of employed mothers receive more independence training, a pattern that is particularly valuable for daughters since they often receive too little in the traditional nonemployed-mother family. Other aspects of the employed-mother family—the involvement of the father, the greater participation of children in household responsibilities, and the more equalitarian sex role attitudes—have all been linked to greater self-confidence and competence in girls.

The pattern for boys in the blue-collar class was seen as reflecting the fact that here maternal employment, though very prevalent, is still not seen as socially desirable or normative and may be viewed as a failure on the part of the father. In fact, the mother often enters the labor force at a point of financial need. It might be expected, if this interpretation is correct, that as the acceptability of maternal employment, and awareness of its prevalence, extend to the blue-collar class, the father-son strain may disappear.

For the middle-class pattern of lower academic performance by sons of employed mothers, two hypotheses were discussed: One is that in the modern middle-class family, with its two children, streamlined household operations, and need to justify full-time mothering, nonemployed mothers may have an intense interaction with the child, a pattern which results in a heavy dose of socialization and conformity. This interaction would lead to higher academic performance in grade school, though not necessarily at higher levels where conformity is less relevant. There are data suggesting these boys with non-employed mothers are also inhibited and over-conforming which seems consistent with this interpretation (Moore, 1975). What this hypothesis is suggesting is that sons of full-time housewives in the present social milieu show a pattern formerly seen as typical for girls, a pattern of intense socialization—perhaps smother-love—that results in high performance in grade school but dependency and achievement difficulties at the older ages (Hoffman, 1972).

An alternate hypothesis was that the greater independence training that is offered by employed mothers brings girls up to the optimum level since they otherwise suffer from too little, but it pushes boys over the top. That is, previous research has shown that American parents encourage their sons' independence more than their daughters'. If maternal employment increases the independence training for both sons and daughters, as indeed the data indicate, it might have a positive effect on daughters, but may involve a push toward independence in sons that is too early or too much.

Chase-Lansdale and Owen (Chase-Lansdale, 1981) used the second hypothesis to explain their finding that in dual-wage families, father-son attachment was less likely to be secure. They argued that the pattern showed up for fathers and not mothers since fathers are the main independence encouragers for sons. Thus, if independence is encouraged in sons more than daughters, by fathers more than mothers, and in dual-wage more than single-wage families, it is exactly in the dual-wage, father-son relationship that attachment would be most strained.

There are, however, other possible explanations for why father-son attachment might be less secure in the employed-mother family. One, for example, builds on the findings of Pederson and his colleagues that suggest a diminished intensity in the father-infant interaction in the dual-wage family. This would explain why father attachment but not mother attachment was affected. But why the effect for boys and not girls? A relevant finding comes from the recent investigation by Stuckey et al. (1982). In this study of children between 2 and 6, the researchers found that in the employed-mother family, girls received more attention from parents, while in the nonemployed-mother family, boys received more attention. This same result was obtained in the behavioral observation study of 1-year-olds by Zaslow and her associates (1983). These interesting findings receive additional confirmation from a study of 3-year-olds being conducted by Alvarez, Henderson, and Bronfenbrenner (1982; Bronfenbrenner & Crouter, 1982). In this study it was found that full-time employed mothers described their daughters in the most positive terms—more positively than either part-time employed or nonemployed mothers; they indicated, however, the *least* positive view of sons. The nonemployed mothers, on the other hand, were more enthusiastic about sons than daughters.

Thus, three studies of preschoolers seem to show that maternal employment is associated with a more positive orientation toward daughters while nonemployment goes with a more positive orientation toward sons. Consistent with this picture, the Chase-Lansdale and Owen data indicated that while the mother's employment status was not at all related to the security of the infant-mother attachment for either sex child, nonemployed mothers were more likely to have securely attached sons than securely attached daughters ($p < .10$), but this was not the case for the employed mothers.[5]

But why would dual-wage parents respond differently than single-wage to sons and daughters? There are several possible explanations: First, the traditional pattern is for parents to favor boys (Hoffman, 1979) and to interact more with sons than daughters (Block, in press). Thus, the findings for the nonemployed-mother families are simply replications of previous results from studies where the mother's employment status was not considered. Since employed-mother families are less likely to hold traditionalistic sex role attitudes (Hoffman, 1974a), the prevalent son preference also might be expected to be less. Second, an additional explanation has to do with possible differences in the stimulus qualities of male and female children. There are data on sex differences that suggest that boys are more active and less compliant than girls (Block, in press). In the employed-mother home, this may provide a considerable inconvenience because of the stress of the dual roles, making sons more of a strain than daughters. Furthermore, as a third factor, preschool group experience has been noted to increase the activity level and noncompliance of children (Rubinstein, 1983), so the experiences that employed-mothers' children are particularly likely to have may exacerbate this strain.

---

[5]Sex of child was not related to security of attachment for employed mothers. However, avoidance of mother in the second reunion was higher for boys in the employed-mother families and girls in the nonemployed-mother families ($p < .06$).

Whatever the explanation behind it, subsequent confirmation of more positive attitudes and interaction patterns with daughters in the employed-mother family and with sons in the nonemployed-mother family would provide an additional link to the generally positive picture of the effects of maternal employment on daughters' development in contrast to the more mixed picture found for sons.

However, one final point must be made here and that is that there is an accumulation of research from various quarters—Hetherington's (1979) research on divorce, the Blocks' research on stress (Block & Block, in press), as well as the work on maternal employment—that suggests the vulnerabilities of sons, and not daughters. Indeed, the Blocks' data suggest that girls blossom under disruption. It may be that for reasons discussed elsewhere (Hoffman, 1972), the parent-daughter tie is so close, with its person-dependent aspects, that any break in this tie—maternal employment, divorce, or minor stress—may be beneficial to daughters but not to sons.

While these various findings require replication and further research, they clearly imply that sex differences must be considered in all future research on maternal employment even if the children are neonates.

Children in Middle-Class Preschools

There are a small group of studies in which working-nonworking differences have been investigated among children attending middle-class nursery schools. Gold and her colleagues in Canada carried out two studies of 4-year-olds comparing children whose mothers had been employed since birth with 4-year-olds whose mothers had not been employed at all. One study was of English-speaking children (Gold & Andres, 1978), one of French (Gold, Andres, & Glorieux, 1979). Their findings parallel the results reported with older children: Both sons and daughters of employed mothers showed better social adjustment in the nursery school setting, but in the English-speaking sample, the sons had lower scores on the Wechsler Preschool and Primary Scale of Intelligence. There were no differences on the Wechsler Scale for girls or French-speaking boys. It is Gold's theory that the French-English difference reflects the greater participation of the French father in childrearing but her data lend only partial support to this interpretation (Hoffman, 1980).

A somewhat comparable study was carried out in New York City with toddlers between 2 and 3 years of age. The investigator (Schachter, 1981) reported no interaction for sex and so combined boys and girls. She found the children of employed mothers to be more independent and peer oriented but to have lower Standford-Binet IQ scores. The interpretation of this result requires longitudinal follow-up because Stanford-Binet scores at the age studied do not predict well to later ones, and the personality traits attributed to the employed-mothers' children are those previously found to be associated with rising IQs (Kagan & Moss, 1962).

Economically Disadvantaged Children

Studies that have examined maternal employment and the characteristics of children from economically disadvantaged populations have typically found that the children with employed mothers score higher on various indices of cognitive performance and social adjustment (Hoffman, 1980). For example, in one of the better studies, Cherry and Eaton (1977) examined, in a longitudinal design, the relationship between maternal employment during the first 3 years of the child's life and the child's cognitive development at 4, 7, and 8 years of age in a sample of 200 lower-class black families. The correlations between maternal employment and the several measures of cognitive development including Wechsler IQ scores were predominantly positive at each of the ages tested.

This pattern, however, needs to be interpreted cautiously. It is possible that there are selective factors involved. In the Cherry and Eaton study, for example, the employed-mother homes included fewer children and more adults per child, factors that have themselves been linked to higher IQ scores (Zajonc & Markus, 1975). Furthermore, although the data did not show it, the employed mothers might be better educated, more stable, and better organized. That is, in economic circumstances where the mother's employment is needed, the women who do not seek work may be particularly handicapped by circumstances or personal qualities, and the positive effects of employment may reflect this selective factor rather than employment itself. This background information is important to establish before policy conclusions can be drawn about such programs as the federal Aid to Families with Dependent Children (AFDC). If employment has a positive effect, the receivers of AFDC money might be encouraged to work, rather than discouraged. If selective factors. on the other hand, explain these correlations, forcing the nonemployed mothers into employment might aggravate an already difficult situation. In the Cherry and Eaton study, the higher IQ scores for the children of employed mothers did survive a number of the controls introduced, but it is interesting to note that when there were extra strains in the family, such as when there were more than five children, relationships were not positive, but showed a negative trend.

It should be pointed out also that for this economically disadvantaged population, maternal employment offers more than a psychological advantage for the mothers. It makes a considerable difference in the per capita income, and per capita income under these circumstances is itself related to the child's cognitive performance (Cherry & Eaton, 1977).

SUMMARY AND DISCUSSION

A summary of the research findings presented here yields a picture that is far from clear. It would appear that employed mothers spend less time with their preschool children, but the time spent with them is more likely to include direct or intense interaction. Either because of intrinsic motivation or conscious effort, employed mothers, and particularly the more educated, compensate to some extent for their absence. There is no evidence for diminished quality of interaction between employed mothers and their young children and some evidence for the opposite pattern; however, most of these studies, which involve behavioral observations, have been carried out with middle-class samples. Data support the idea that the mother's morale is an important mediating factor, but the direction of causality is difficult to prove. The husbands of employed women spend more time with their children, though they may have less after-work interaction with their infants—priority being given to the mothers who have also just returned from work. There is no indication of less secure mother-infant attachment when the mother is employed, although there is some tentative evidence that under certain conditions any insecure attachment that does occur will be of the avoidant rather than the resistant type, and there is some evidence for less secure father-son attachment.

In middle-class preschool populations there is evidence for lower scores on the Wechsler or Stanford-Binet, particularly for boys, though it is not clear that these will predict to later IQ scores. In disadvantaged populations, on the other hand, early maternal employment is associated with higher IQ scores even in longitudinal research. Some of the most interesting research results suggest that employment may have different effects for sons and daughters—involving different parent-child interaction patterns, attitudes, and child effects.

It has been noted in this review that the effects of maternal employment may be different depending on a number of other aspects of the situation. The sex of the child, social class, and the mother's attitude were discussed in some detail. The data are still inadequate but there have been some efforts to investigate how these variables affect the relationship between maternal employment and parent-child interaction. Other important considerations are the timing of the mother's entry into the labor market, both with respect to the child's age and with respect to other significant family events, and the degree of stress or support in the family. The impact of these variables, timing and stress, have not only been inadequately studied, they have barely been studied at all, and yet variations in the timing of the mother's beginning employment and in the stress level of the family may explain some of the apparent incongruities between different studies.

Timing

The timing of the mother's reentry into the labor force is an important issue to investigate particularly with respect to the infant or young child. Although Vaughn et al. (1980) differentiated mothers who returned during the first year of the child's life and those who returned between 1 year and 18 months, no one has systematically examined whether early in the first year, before attachment begins, is a more or less advantageous time than later while attachment is forming. The two studies that measured employment as a return to work during the first 3 months (Chase-Lansdale, 1981; Hock, 1980) found no difference in mother-infant attachment from a nonemployed sample and it is possible that a change in the mother's availability at a later point in the first year would be more disruptive for the infant. More equivocal results were obtained in the two studies that included employed mothers who returned later, during the time attachment is forming (Schwartz, 1983; Vaughn et al.. 1980). A more systematic investigation of the time of the mother's return to the labor force—before attachment, during attachment formation, and after the attachment has been established—later in the second and third year—would be valuable.

Another aspect of the timing of the mother's return to work has to do with what else is happening in the family. Mothers often enter the labor force at a point when there is an increased need for their employment. This can involve an increase in expenses, a decrease in alternative sources of family income, or a time of emotional stress at home (Hoffman, 1974b). It is likely to occur if the husband is unemployed, during a period of marital difficulty, or in the face of divorce. The significance of the mother's return to work may thus be compounded by family stress that accompanies it. Although the mother's employment may in some ways ameliorate the stress, either economically or psychologically, it may also augment the disruption for the child. This pattern was empirically demonstrated in the research by Hetherington (1979) examining the impact of divorce on 4-year-olds. In this study it was found that adverse effects of the divorce were diminished when the mother had been employed before the divorce. The mother's job helped her to cope more effectively psychologically and economically and her interaction with the child was less distressed. On the other hand, a particularly difficult situation for the child occurred when the mother started work at the time of the divorce. While the new job helped the mother in some ways, such as providing self-esteem and new social contact, it was difficult for the child because it increased the disruption in routines that was already occurring because of the divorce and added to the child's losses. Thus, in this study, the timing of the mother's employment made a crucial difference in its effects.

No one has examined the impact on the child of the mother's employment when it is a response to the father's job loss. Under some conditions it might provide a stabilizing influence; the mother's wages could fill the economic gap and the father's availability could provide supplementary child care. But the father's job loss often involves considerable psychological stress for the father and strain in the family, so the shift in the parents' roles might actually diminish the quality of the child's interaction with both parents (Hoffman, in press; Parke & Collmer, 1975).

Stress

Obviously the existence of good supports—other adults in the household, available family and friends, good day-care programs—facilitate maternal employment and increase the likelihood of its having a positive effect on the parent-child interaction. Similarly, extra stress in the family can make the mother's dual role more difficult with possible adverse consequences for the parent-child relationship. The interaction between stress and maternal employment emerges in a number of the studies reviewed here. Thus, Cherry and Eaton (1977) found that the positive correlation between maternal employment and scores on cognitive scales found in their sample of disadvantaged families became a negative one if there were more than five children. Vaughn et al. (1980) found no relationship between maternal employment and the type of mother-infant attachment except when there was only one parent in the family. Cohen's data (1978) are difficult to interpret because it is not clear that the mother's employment status was a causal factor at all, but it is possible that the combination of infant prematurity, very low birth weight, and father absence made maternal employment more problematic. The possibility has even been raised in the discussion of sex differences that sons may be more of a strain than daughters, and thus some of the findings of possible negative effects of maternal employment that occur only with sons may reflect this. Twins, a handicapped child, the chronic illness of either parent might also affect the relationship between the mother's employment status and parent-child interaction.

But while it seems clear that the existence of stressful conditions in the family can have an impact on the relationship between employment and parent-child interaction, the nature of the impact is complicated. This has already been indicated in the preceding discussions of divorce and the father's unemployment. Although stress may make the mother's dual role more difficult, it may also make it more necessary. Many of these situations increase the economic need for employment; and many increase the psychological need. Outside employment at all socio-economic levels can provide a considerable boost for a mother (Cherry & Eaton, 1977; Gold & Andres, 1978; Walshok, 1978) and enable her to have a more positive interaction with her child than if she were at home with the child full time.

The research on part-time employment may be relevant here. In the Schwartz (1983) study of attachment, the effects of part-time employment were like those of full-time in the higher expression of positive affect by mothers, and like those of nonemployment in the type of attachment. In the study of 3-year-olds by Alvarez et al. (1982), the part-time employed mothers were more positive than the nonemployed in their descriptions of both sons and daughters. Research with older children also suggests that part-time employment may be different from either full-time employment or nonemployment in its effects (Kappel & Lambert, 1972), and it may be particularly appropriate as a compromise solution when there is noneconomic stress that makes full-time child care emotionally difficult, and full-time employment too much of a strain.

Research Needs

Many questions for future research have emerged here, and all of them go beyond the simple correlations that characterize so much of the existing work. Research is needed to examine the timing of the mother's entry into the labor force, and the conditions of stress or support that prevail in the family. More attention should be given to the father's role. The presence or absence of the father is clearly important, and so is the nature of his participation in the family, particularly in childcare. No one has studied sibling interaction either as a dependent variable or as a mediator of other employment effects. A program of research in which procedures were standardized but specific conditions were systematically varied would help answer many of the questions raised here.

Short-term longitudinal research is needed. In infancy studies, it is needed to see if effects observed are temporary, or if there are delayed effects that are not observed. In studies of older preschool children, it is needed to see how the pattern of independence, peer orientation, and social competence on the part of employed-mothers' children manifests itself at later ages. And how do the Wechsler and Stanford-Binet scores look for these children during their school years when the scores stabilize more?

Is it true that parents respond differently to sons and daughters depending on what are the alternative demands on their time? Does stress diminish the satisfaction of parenting young sons and increase the satisfactions provided by daughters? That question has significance for a number of different situations—twins, large families, divorce. and single parenthood, for example. The emergence of data suggesting that the mother's employment status affects parent-child interaction differently for sons and daughters opens an important new line of inquiry.

It is necessary that research in this area be cast in a theoretically meaningful framework. The vulnerability of research findings to social change is exacerbated by the atheoretical approach. The importance of the social context needs to be built into the investigation and the interpretation of results. This is essential not only for sound social science but also for action conclusions.

Policy Implications

The implications of this research for individual decisions and social policy cannot be cast in simplistic terms. It is not that maternal employment status does not have an effect on parent-child interaction but rather that the effects will be different under different circumstances. The wisdom of an individual decision depends on the particular mother, the particular child, the particular child-care arrangements, and the family situation. Although some mothers do very well with the full-time exclusive care of their infants, some may require the stimulation and variety of outside employment for optimal performance as mothers. Though some substitute care arrangements are inadequate, some substitute care provides a stimulating environment that augments the mother's care. The data sensitize us to the aspects that must be considered and the vulnerabilities in either the employed-mother or the nonemployed-mother situation—but even here the action conclusions need to be drawn with caution. For example. the data seem to indicate that full-time maternal employment works best when there are a minimum of extra strains in the family, but these strains also may put the mother under stress to which outside employment can provide a necessary relief. Support systems and part-time employment may be the most appropriate answer under such conditions, rather than admonishments against employment.

From a social policy standpoint, one thing is clear: mothers of preschoolers are moving increasingly into the labor force and will continue to do so. There are both economic and social needs pushing in this direction reflecting a whole complex of social changes. Social institutions, community services, government policies, and family educational services all lag behind the facts in their recognition of the prevalence of maternal employment and in their response to these new needs. Quality day-care programs are very much needed. Maternal employment under adverse circumstances can put excess pressure on the mother, and instead of the positive effects mediated by higher morale, there may be negative effects mediated by the strain of the double role.

If the data at this point in time seem inadequate, it must be remembered that, until recently, there were no data on maternal employment and the young child. All of this research has been done in the last 5 years, and even if there were older data, they might be quite limited in relevance because the meaning of both employment and nonemployment has changed as maternal employment in preschool families has moved from a rare to a common occurrence. There is a great deal to learn about both employed-mother and nonemployed-mother families because, in the context of other social changes, both patterns are new.

REFERENCES

Ainsworth, M., Blehar, M., Waters, E., & Wall, S. *Patterns of attachment.* Hillsdale, N.J.: Lawrence Erlbaum Associates, 1978.

Alvarez, W., Henderson, C., & Bronfenbrenner, R. Maternal employment and mothers' descriptions of their three year old children. In M. Cochran & C. R. Henderson, Jr. (Eds.), *The ecology of urban family life: A summary report to the National Institute of Education.* Unpublished manuscript, Cornell University, 1982.

Baruch, G. K., & Barnett, R. C. Fathers' participation in the care of their preschool children. *Sex Roles,* 1981, *7,* 1043–1055.

Belsky, J., & Sternberg, L. D. The effects of day care: A critical review. *Child Development,* 1978, *49,* 929–949.

Block, J. H. Personality development in males and females: The influence of differential socialization. *Child Development,* in press.

Block, J., & Block, J. H. A longitudinal study of personality and cognitive development. In S. Mednick & M. Harway (Eds.), *Longitudinal research in the United States,* in press.

Bronfenbrenner, U., & Crouter, A. *Work and family through time and space.* In S. B. Kamerman & C. D. Hayes (Ed.), *Families that work: Children in a changing world.* Washington: National Academy Press, 1982.

Chase-Lansdale, P. L. *Effects of maternal employment on mother-infant and father-infant attachment* (Unpublished doctoral dissertation, University of Michigan, 1981). *Dissertation Abstracts International, 42* (6), p. 2562, DEN81–25083.

Cherry, R. R.. & Eaton, E. L. Physical and cognitive development in children of low-income mothers working in the child's early years. *Child Development,* 1977, *48,* 158–166.

Clarke-Stewart, K. A., & Fein, G. G. Early childhood programs. In P. Mussen (Ed.), *Manual of child psychology* (4th ed.). New York: Wiley, 1983.

Cohen, S. E. Maternal employment and mother-child interaction. *Merrill-Palmer Quarterly,* 1978, *24,* 189–197.

Etaugh, C. Effects of nonmaternal care on children. *American Psychologist,* 1980, *35,* 309–319.

Farel, A. N. Effects of preferred maternal roles, maternal employment, and sociographic status on school adjustment and competence. *Child Development,* 1980, *50,* 1179–1186.

Gold, D., & Andres, D. Relations between maternal employment and development of nursery school children. *Canadian Journal of Behavioral Science,* 1978, *10,* 116–129.

Gold, D., Andres, D., & Glorieux, J. The development of Francophone nursery school children with employed and nonemployed mothers. *Canadian Journal of Behavioral Science,* 1979, *11,* 169–173.

Goldberg, R. J. *Maternal time use and preschool performance.* Paper presented at the meeting of the Society for Research in Child Development, New Orleans, March, 1977.

Golden, M., Rosenblith, L., Grossi, M. T., Policare. H. J., Freeman, H., & Brownlee, E. M. *The New York City infant day care study.* New York: Medical and Health Research Association of New York City, 1978.

Hetherington, E. M. Divorce: A child's perspective. *American Psychologist,* 1979, *34,* 851–858.

Hill, C. R., & Stafford, F. P. *Parental care of children: Time diary estimates of quantity predictability and variety.* Working paper series, Institute for Social Research, University of Michigan, Ann Arbor, 1978.

Hock, E. Working and nonworking mothers and their infants: A comparative study of maternal caregiving characteristics and infant social behavior. *Merrill-Palmer Quarterly,* 1980, *46,* 79–101.

Hoffman, L. W. Effects on children: Summary and discussion. In F. I. Nye & L. W. Hoffman (Eds.), *The employed mother in America.* Chicago: Rand McNally, 1963.

Hoffman, L. W. Early childhood experiences and women's achievement motives. Journal of Social Issues, 1972, *28,* 3, 129–156.

Hoffman, L. W. Effects of maternal employment on the child—A review of the research. *Developmental Psychology,* 1974, *10,* 2, 204–228. (a)

Hoffman, L. W. Psychological factors. In L. W. Hoffman & F. I. Nye (Eds.), *Working mothers.* San Francisco, Calif.: Jossey Bass, 1974. (b)

Hoffman, L. W. Maternal employment: 1979. *American Psychologist,* 1979, *34,* 10, 859–865.

Hoffman, L. A. The effects of maternal employment on the academic attitudes and performance of school-aged children. *School Psychology Review,* 1980, *9,* 4, 319–336.

Hoffman, L. W. Increased fathering: Effects on the mother. In M. Lamb & A. Sagi (Eds.), *Fatherhood and Family Policy.* Hillsdale, N.J.: Lawrence Erlbaum Associates, 1983.

Hoffman, L. W. Work, family, and the socialization of the child. In R. D. Parke (Ed.), *The review of child development research* (Vol. 7). Chicago, Ill.: University of Chicago Press, in press.

Kagan, J., & Moss, H. A. *Birth to maturity.* New York: Wiley, 1962.

Kamerman, S. B., & Hayes, C. D. The direction of change: Trends and issues. In S. B. Kamerman & C. D. Hayes (Eds.), *Families that work: Children in a changing world.* Washington: National Academy Press, 1982.

Kappel, B. E., & Lambert, R. D. *Self-worth among the children of working mothers.* Unpublished manuscript, University of Waterloo, Ontario, Canada, 1972.

Kessler, R. C., & McRae, J. A., Jr. The effects of wives' employment on the mental health of married men and women. *American Sociological Review,* 1982, *47,* 216–227.

MacKinnon, C. E., Brody, G. H., & Stoneman, Z. The effects of divorce and maternal employment on the home environments of preschool children. *Child Development,* 1982, *53,* 1392–1399.

Moore, T. W. Exclusive early mothering and its alternatives. *Scandinavian Journal of Psychology,* 1975, *16,* 256–272.

Parke, R. D., & Collmer, C. W. Child abuse: An interdisciplinary analysis. In E. M. Hetherington (Ed.), *Review of child development research* (Vol. 5). Chicago: University of Chicago Press, 1975.

Pederson, F. A., Cain, R., Zaslow, M., & Anderson, B. Variation in infant experience associated with alternative family role organization. In L. Laosa & I. Sigel (Eds.), *Families as learning environment for children.* New York: Plenum, 1983.

Pleck, J., & Rustad, M. *Husbands' and wives' time in family work and paid work in the 1975–1976 study of time use.* Unpublished manuscript, Wellesley College Center for Research on Women, 1980.

Rubinstein, J. L. The effects of maternal employment on young children. In F. Morrison, C. Lord, & D. Keating (Eds.) *Advances in applied developmental psychology,* Vol. II, New York: Academic, 1984.

Rubinstein, J. L., & Howes, C. Caregiving and infant behavior in day care and in homes. *Developmental Psychology, 1979, 15,* 1–24.

Schachter, F. Toddlers with employed mothers. *Child Development,* 1981, *52,* 948–964.

Schubert, J. B., Bradley-Johnson, S., & Nuttal, J. Mother-infant communication and maternal employment. *Child Development,* 1980, *51,* 246–249.

Schwartz, J. C., Scarr, S. W., Caparulo, B., Furrow, D., McCartney, K., Billington, R., Phillips, D., & Hindy, C. *Center, sitter, and home day care before age two, A report on the first Bermuda infant care study.* Paper presented at the annual meeting of the American Psychological Association, Los Angeles, Calif., August, 1981.

Schwartz, P. Length of day care attendance and attachment behavior in 18-month-old infants. *Child Development,* 1983, *54,* 1073–1078.

Stuckey, M. F., McGhee, P. E., & Bell, N. J. Parent-child interaction: The influence of maternal employment. *Developmental Psychology,* 1982, *18,* 635–644.

U.S. Department of Commerce, Bureau of the Census. *Population profile of the United States, 1978, population characteristics* (Current Population Reports, Series P-20, No. 336). Washington, D.C.: U.S. Government Printing Office, April, 1979.

U.S. Department of Labor, Women's Bureau. *Working mothers and their children.* Washington, D.C.: U.S. Government Printing Office, 1977.

U.S. Department of Labor, Bureau of Labor Statistics. *Marital and family characteristics of labor force,* (Special Labor Force Report 237). 1981, 3–79.

Vaughn, B. E., Gove, F. L., & Egeland, B. The relationship between out-of-home care and the quality of infant-mother attachment in an economically disadvantaged population. *Child Development,* 1980, *51,* 1203–1214.

Veroff, J., Douvan, E., & Kulka, R. *The inner American: A self-portrait from 1957 to 1976.* New York: Basic Books, 1981.

Walshok, M. L. Occupational values and family roles. A descriptive study of women working in blue-collar and service occupations. *The Urban and Social Change Review,* 1978, *11,* 12–20.

Yarrow, M. R., Scott, P., De Leeuw, L., & Heinig, C. Childrearing in families of working and non-working mothers. *Sociometry,* 1962, *25,* 122–140.

Zajonc, R., & Markus, G. Birth order and intellectual development, *Psychological Review,* 1975, *82,* 74–88.

Zaslow, M., Pederson, F. A., Suwalsky, J., Cain, R., Anderson, B., & Fivel, M. The early resumption of employment by mothers: Implications for parent-infant interaction, *Journal of Applied Developmental Psychology,* in press.

Zaslow, M., Pederson, F. A., Suwalsky, J., & Rabinovich, B. *Maternal employment and parent-infant interaction.* Paper presented at the meeting of the Society for Research in Child Development, Detroit, April, 1983.

5

The Continuous Bond: A Dynamic, Multigenerational Perspective on Parent-Child Relations Between Adults

Gunhild O. Hagestad
College of Human Development,
The Pennsylvania State University

INTRODUCTION

The focus of this symposium is parent-child interaction. Our language is relatively unambiguous when it comes to defining a parent: one who has living offspring. Most of us would agree that this is a role which endures as long as there is at least one living child. There is no mandatory retirement from parenthood. and most likely not a voluntary one, either. However, the term child is considerably more ambiguous, because it is used to denote two different concepts. First, it may refer to a chronological category or age group. In that case, its upper age boundaries are likely to fall somewhere in the teens. Second, it refers to a role, one which is reciprocal to that of parent. In this instance, it has no age boundaries, but is contingent on having at least one living parent. If we start with this role definition of child, we may study parent-child interaction between a 90-year-old mother and her 70-year-old daughter, both of whom are retirees, widows, and great-grandmothers.

It should be clear from the title of this chapter that my definition of child is of the second type. I attempt to argue that even for scholars whose main interest centers on ''the chronological child'' and the early stages of parenting, it is necessary to consider the entire span of parent-child relations and the embeddedness of such ties in a set of multiple parent-child links, joined in vertical family connections.

The chapter first briefly outlines demographic changes which have reshaped parent-child ties and which, in my view, should push us to consider time as a factor in the study of such ties. Then, a framework for studying parents and children over time is presented. Finally, I seek to apply this framework to questions I have asked in my past research and some that I think need to be posed in the future.

DEMOGRAPHIC CHANGE AND PARENT-CHILD RELATIONSHIPS

Until quite recently in American society, young people wondered if their parents would survive to become grandparents. Today, many young parents have living grandparents—their children's great-grandparents. This contrast is but one example of how demographic change has altered the nature of family life in our society. Two aspects of such change are of particular interest here: the unprecedented duration of parent-child ties and the rise of multigenerational families. Demographers have shown that among individuals born around the turn of the century, a substantial number lost their parents before reaching adulthood. Uhlenberg (1980) estimates that in the 1900 birth cohort, one of four experienced the death of at least one parent before reaching the age of 15. The corresponding figure for children born in the 1970s is one of 200. In today's society, parents and children expect to spend several decades of shared lives after the children are adults and likely to be parents themselves. Winsborough (1980) suggests that when women born in 1930 reach the age of 60, more than one-fourth will still have their mothers living. These new realities are found in many industrialized societies. A Japanese poet wryly expressed reactions to his family's demographic composition in a *Haiku* titled "Filial Deception":

I have concealed for one more year today
From aging parents
That my hair is grey.

Not only do parents and children share more years than ever before, they also increasingly find themselves as part of an intergenerational context which include multiple parent-child links. Four-generation families are now common (Shanas, 1979); five or six generations in the same family are not unheard of. While we have long recognized that parent-child pairs represent vertical links in ongoing, evolving chains that make families continuous systems across historical time, our era is unique in the extent to which we frequently can observe multiple such links at one point in time. For example, in a four-generation family, we find three sets of parent-child relationships and two generations of members who simultaneously occupy the roles of parent and child.

   The new duration of parent-child relationships and the increasing number of multigenerational families stem from two sets of demographic changes: increased general life expectancy and altered rhythms of family formation. American women now live close to eight decades, but have their children earlier in life than did women in previous historical times. Thus, we have witnessed an "acceleration of generational wheels."

Because of the changes which I have sketched above, it is *imperative* that scholars interested in parents and children pay close attention to dimensions of time. Three such dimensions need to be considered: individual life time, family time, and historical time.

PARENTS, CHILDREN, AND DIMENSIONS OF TIME

Change and development in family relationships can be addressed on three levels: individual, family, and history (Aldous, 1978; Elder, in press; Hareven, 1977). As individuals, parents and children go through maturation and aging, as well as socially marked life transitions, changes which produce shifting constellations of needs, physical abilities, and available resources. Families also have their course of development and ways of marking time. There are two aspects of family time. First, nuclear families move through recognized phases of development, starting with early family building and childrearing and ending with the empty nest, retirement marriage, and widowhood (e.g., Hill & Rodgers, 1964; Rodgers, 1973). However, there is a second, commonly neglected aspect of family time. Family lineages have generational careers. Throughout their lifetime, nuclear families and individual members move across a series of generational locations or stations. Moreover, the number of such stations is not fixed. Through a process similar to that taking place on a societal level, family lineages go through what Ryder (1965) described as "demographic metabolism": the entry of new members and the departure of old. Thus, the generational structure within which family relationships evolve also changes, sometimes linking many "tiers" of lives, sometimes only two. A set of parents and children may start out their relationship career as the fourth and fifth generations in a family lineage. Sixty year later, the parents may be the oldest of three generations, while the children find themselves in a middle generation. It would seem reasonable to expect that the nature of parent-child bonds not only changes as a result of individual maturation and aging on both sides of the relationship and the amount of time they have spent together, but also as a consequence of their location in a generational structure. If we want to study parents and children over time, we not only need to consider their meshing life careers and phases of maturation and aging, but also need to pay attention to their location in a multilink vertical generational chain, which changes over time. Seen cross-sectionally, different parent-child pairs may have similar dyadic matches of ages and life stages, but may be in quite different generational locations. I would expect this difference in their contexts to be a significant one. To sum up: we have a set of *nested careers*. Individual life trajectories are shaped in developing nuclear families, and these nuclear families are embedded in a dynamic, shifting constellation of vertical relationships which connect members of different generations.

Finally, these careers unfold in the context of *historical time*. Generational linkages connect families and individuals to the movement of history, providing human bridges to known pasts and unknown futures. Historical changes bring shifts in cultural definitions of parenthood and historical events may influence the life course of individual parents and children, as well as the course of their relationship (Elder, 1974).

Parents and children not only represent different generational locations in family lineages, but they also have different anchorings in societal generations, what we now commonly call cohorts. Families represent unique meeting grounds for individuals with different historical backgrounds. Through cross-generational interaction, cohort contrasts in the wider society are softened and modified, and historical changes are seen and interpreted through family lenses. However, as I have stated in an earlier paper (Hagestad, 1981), it is important not to overlook the fact that *people do not file into generations by cohort*. We often forget that individuals from different families who are grouped into the same generational categories, such as "parent" or "grandparent," may represent quite different cohorts. Each family creates its own combinations of age and cohort member-ships, reflecting the timing of births in several generations. For example, in two families with three generations, one may have grandparents in their fifties, parents in their twenties, and children who are preschoolers. The other may also have a generation of young children, but parents in their thirties and grandparents in their seventies. Not only do these two lineages have contrasting age composi-tions, they also have biographies reflecting different slices of history and so-ciopolitical events. For instance, the grandparents in the first family were born in the Depression era and children during World War II. The second set of grand-parents were adults during the Depression and the war. These contrasting events quite possibly shaped individual expectations and outlooks, as well as patterns of intergenerational interaction.

The meaning of family events takes shape along all three dimensions of time outlined above. The birth of the first child, in individual life time, represents the assumption of a new and demanding role. It also signals the starting of a nuclear family and new significant, durable dyadic relationships. Furthermore, for the new parent it means a new generational location, with a link "down" genera-tional lines. Finally, the expectations new parents encounter, as well as the resources available to them, depend on generational context, both in the sense of lineage and cohort. Often, the financial situation of young couples results from the resources and needs of two older generations. Oppenheimer (1981) has provided an intriguing discussion of how we need to consider family financial resources from a multigenerational perspective and keep in mind the needs and resources of young adults, middle-age parents, and aging grandparents. On the macro, societal level, cohort membership shapes opportunity structures for young parents and the social supports available to them.

PAST RESEARCH ON PARENTS AND CHILDREN: ALPHA AND OMEGA

Scholarly work on parent-child relations has by no means kept up with demographic reality and has paid little attention to time. Past work has taken two distinct directions (Hagestad, 1982), representing two separate traditions and focusing on two extremes of the human life span. One tradition, the one with the most empirical work, has focused on young children and their parents. Here, "child" is defined choronologically and the parent is for the most part treated as "ageless." In a recent review of 1970s research on parent-child relationships (Walters & Walters, 1980), it is concluded that even in most recent work, the emphasis is overwhelmingly on young children and their parents. Even among authors who claim to take a life-span perspective, this typically means extending considerations of change in the child beyond childhood and into adolescence— still less than one-fourth of the span of the individual's life that is likely to include the *role* of child. Thus, the analytic focus is on the very beginning of a long relationship career, on the *alpha* of bonds. A second body of work has concentrated on aged parents and middle-aged offspring. This *omega* focus typically is not included in discussions of parent-child relations, but is found under such headings as "older families," "families in later life," and "kin relations." The *Journal of Marriage and the Family* has had two "decade review issues," summarizing research and theory development in the 1960s and 1970s. In both cases, the early and late phases of parent-child ties were addressed in separate articles. Yet, only the former was discussed under the heading "Parent-Child Relationships." Two students and I (Hagestad, Croft, & Waitsman, in progress) recently carried out a systematic content analysis of 18 family textbooks for college courses. All the books were published after 1978. We found the volumes' coverage of parent-child relations to reflect a strong alpha focus. Only one-half of the books had discussion of either young adults and their parents (which should have direct personal relevance for the students) or middle-aged individuals and their parents. One-third of the texts covered neither. Among the remaining two-thirds, there were typically several chapters devoted to the early years of parent-child relations, while only a few pages covered such relationships among adults.

Three basic shortcomings strike me in past work on parents and children. First, there is a great data gap between alpha and omega. We know very little about young adults and their parents, or about individuals in middle adulthood and their parents (Streib & Beck, 1980; Troll, 1971; Troll & Bengtson, 1979).

Little or no effort has been made to link our knowledge about the beginning and the end of parent-child relations, either through cross-sectional or longitudinal research. Such linkages could focus on individual time or family time. Second, there is a conceptual and theoretical void between the two bodies of empirical work. Attempts to integrate generalizations which have emerged from each are virtually nonexistent. Third, the generational context of parent-child relations has been greatly neglected. This weakness exists for generations in the sense of family lineage constellations, as well as generations on a macro-level (i.e., the family's linkages to history). In sum, most of our past work in this area has been highly *synchronic,* relying on a static and fragmented view of parent-child ties.

It is time that we seek to bridge the alpha and omega views of parents and children, both through conceptual and theoretical integration and by filling the great research void between two traditions of empirical work (Hagestad, 1982). In order to bridge the knowledge gap between the beginning and the last phases of parent-child relationships, we need to consider the entire span of their joint careers. A first step would involve cross-sectional research, in which dyads who are in different phases of their relationship and have contrasting parent-child combinations of individual development and generational contexts are compared. However, longitudinal work which follows parent-child units over time is also needed. Most longitudinal studies of parents and children have been over relatively short periods of time (e.g., 5 years). Very little work has traced individual parents and children or parent-child dyads across the life course. Even fewer attempts have been made to examine the impact of generational turnover. For example, a few authors have argued that the relationship between young adults and their parents changes when the children become parents (e.g., Fischer, 1981). This phenomenon has mostly been discussed as a result of changes in individual roles and orientations and has typically not been considered within a generational framework. Thus, we have not asked if more marked changes are observed if the new child is the first grandchild and therefore represents the addition of a new generation. Similarly, we have not asked if we see more closeness between the new parents and their own parents in lineages where there are no older generations (i.e., where the parents themselves no longer have a relationship "up" in vertical linkages in the role as child).

Conceptualizations and measurements have not been geared to cover the various phases of parent-child relationships. For example, while recent discussions of attachment portray it as a property of dyads rather than individuals (e.g., Hartup & Lempers, 1973), there have not been any concentrated efforts to implement such a view in research. Little work has been carried out to develop measures of attachment that can be used for young children and their parents as well as parent-child relations among adults (Block, vonderLippe, & Block, 1973; Bronson, 1967; Troll & Smith, 1976). Not until we have confronted such issues can we move on to questions addressing several parent-child linkages. For instance, is the attachment between a new mother and her infant related to the quality of the present attachment between the mother and her own mother?

There is an astonishing lack of research on parents and children over time. For example, nobody, to my knowledge, has examined "parenting styles" from a life-span perspective. We have not asked if the "authoritative" parent, in Baumrind's (1971) conceptual framework, ends up having an easy time developing an adult-adult relationship with a child who is about to become a parent. Are there early parenting styles which make "the role reversal of later life"—a situation in which the parent becomes increasingly dependent on the child— easier to accept? Do parent-child pairs display consistency in interaction patterns, affective closeness, and attitude similarities across the duration of their relationship? Are "relational styles" transmitted across generations? *Where* do we have the greatest similarity? Across the same units over time? Across units in the same developmental phases? Across units embedded in similar generational contexts? Across individuals who share historical-cultural definitions of parent and child roles?

As these brief remarks should illustrate, I believe there are distinct and important gaps in our knowledge of parents and offspring in today's society. Before we can begin to remedy such shortcomings, we need to develop conceptual frameworks which incorporate multiple dimensions of time.

TOWARDS A DYNAMIC, MULTIGENERATIONAL VIEW OF PARENTS AND CHILDREN

In recent work I have attempted to develop ways to conceptualize parent-child linkages within a diachronic, process-oriented framework. As a first step in bridging the alpha and omega of parent-child relations, we need to put them in a model which allows us to discuss time and change on an individual, a family, and a historical level (see Fig. 5.1). To begin, we need to recognize that a particular parent-child linkage is typically part of a multilink, vertical chain in which several individuals simultaneously occupy the roles of both parent and child. For the sake of simplicity, let us consider direct linkages within a hypothetical lineage. The oldest living generation in a lineage, G_1, is the only one that occupies the role of parent only. This individual occupies the *omega position*. At the other end of the generational spectrum, G_n, which may be anywhere from one to six links removed, is the lineage member who occupies only the role of child. This individual is in the *alpha position*.

From a structural, synchronic perspective, we can see each circle as representing one *generational station,* and we can consider the number of stations which exist in a lineage at a given time. From a diachronic perspective, we can trace the careers of individuals or parent-child pairs as they move across stations. Howev-

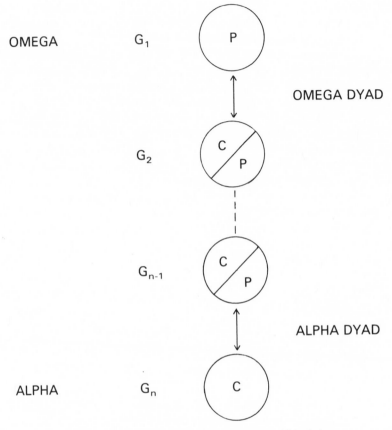

FIG. 5.1   A multigenerational model of parent-child relations

er, the number of stations change over time. When G_1 dies, the lineage loses one link; when a new generation is born, a link is added. We therefore also need to consider *generational turnover,* which can occur in the alpha position, the omega position, or both.

PARENT-CHILD RELATIONSHIPS FROM A MULTIGENERATIONAL PERSPECTIVE: SOME RESEARCH ILLUSTRATIONS

The framework sketched above has emerged over several years of work on a fairly massive data set from a study of three-generational families. The more I pondered those data, the more convinced I became that adults who are both parents and children deserve a good deal of scholarly attention. Not only can they help us fill the data gap left by the alpha and omega traditions, they are also essential to building understanding of parent-child relations across dimensions of time. Three aspects of parent-child dynamics have been of particular interest to me: socialization and influence, patterns of support, and what I have come to call "developmental reciprocities." For all of them, I have explored differences between men and women. Most of my work has pursued these issues in three-generation families and much of my attention has focused on middle-aged individuals who relate "up" as children of aging parents and "down" as parents of children who are in the early phases of adulthood. My thinking has been shaped by three research endeavors: a study of influence patterns in three generations of Chicago area families, an exploratory study of divorce among middle-aged couples, and a pilot study of middle-aged women who discussed feelings about two sets of relationships: that of daughter to an aging parent and that of mother to a young-adult child. Before I discuss themes which have emerged from these three data sets, let me briefly outline the studies.

Three Data Sets

The Chicago study: Patterns of Influence in Three Generations.   With funding from the National Institute on Aging, a University of Chicago team headed by Cohler, Hagestad, and Neugarten studied members of three-generation families in the Chicago area.

A requirement for participation in the study was that at least one member from each of the three adult generations live in the Chicago metropolitan area. The township of Evanston was used as a geographical point of entry. Most of the families were initially located through a door-to-door survey. The families, all Caucasian, were interviewed between July and November, 1977. From each family, we conducted separate interviews with one young adult grandchild, both the middle-aged mother and father, and one aged grandparent. There were 148 families, 592 respondents. In all the families, the middle-aged parents had an intact marriage and both parents were the grandchild's natural parents.

Approximately equal numbers of grandsons and granddaughters were interviewed. Slightly more than one-fourth of the third generation were married, and about 80% of those married had children. Thus, in at least one-fifth of the sample, there were actually four generations in the family. Median age for grandsons was 21; for grandgranddaughters it was 22.

As would be expected, the sample had many more grandmothers than grandfathers. Forty grandfathers were interviewed, 108 grandmothers. The sample was rather evenly divided between maternal (parents of the mother) and paternal (parents of the father) grandparents: 83 maternal and 65 paternal. The median age of grandfathers was 80; for grandmothers it was 76. The middle generation parents had a median age of about 50. However, the two older generations had a wide spread on age/cohort and there was considerable overlap in ages between the "parent" and "grandparent" groups. This pattern has also occurred in other three-generations research to date (e.g., Bengtson, 1975; Hill, Foote, Aldous, Carlson, & MacDonald, 1970).

The basic research design was a dyadic one. Across intergenerational pairs, we asked both members to discuss each other and their relationship. We therefore had reciprocal data, reflecting the two individuals' views of their relationship. The only exception was that the grandparents were not asked to discuss their child-in-law. This decision was made because of fatigue problems among the older respondents. The interview was open-ended with the exception of three attitude checklists and a personality Q-sort measure. Interviews ranged from 1 to 5 hours, with an average length of 2½ hours. Fig 5.2 represents the data from a family in which a paternal grandmother and a grandson were interviewed.

The central focus of the study was intergenerational influence. In pilot studies, we found the word influence to be a red flag, particularly among grandparents. Many of them would make emphatic statements about *never* wanting to interfere—to meddle—in the lives of children and grandchildren. Nevertheless, they would, in the course of the interview, relate numerous attempts to set the younger generations straight. Based on pilot interviews with a wide range of families and age groups, we developed a list of 11 topic areas with numerous

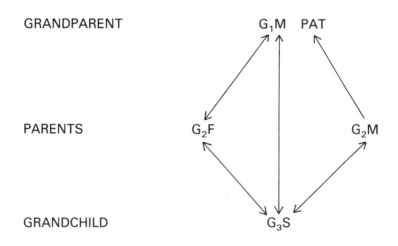

GRANDPARENT G_1M PAT

PARENTS G_2F G_2M

GRANDCHILD G_3S

M = Mother

F = Father

S = Son

FIG. 5.2.   Data from paternal lineage

subtopics. Each area was printed on a card and these cards were presented to the respondent during the interview. The interviewer then said, ''Take a look at this list. . . . Have you and _____ talked about any of these?'' If the answer was yes, the interviewer followed up by asking, ''Can you remember the last time it came up between you? What happened?'' Interviewers were trained to code the responses into ''shared information,'' ''R sent influence,'' ''R received influence,'' or ''R both sent and received influence.'' If the respondent related attempts to influence, a follow-up question was asked about whether any change resulted as a consequence of the attempt. Summary scores were developed for each dyadic discussion, counting reports of sending and receiving across the 11 areas. Each respondent was also given a total score for sending and receiving across all dyadic discussions. Across each pair, comparisons were made between the two partners' reports and an intradyadic congruence measure was computed.

The Study of Divorce in Middle Age.   During the academic year 1979–1980, M. Smyer and I (Hagestad, Smyer, & Stierman, 1983) conducted a study on middle age divorce in an Eastern metropolitan area. Working from court records, we contacted and interviewed 93 men and women who had been divorced for about 1 year. The respondents ranged in age from 41 to 61, with a mean of 50 for men and 49 for women. Prior to the divorce, they had been married from 16 to 37 years, with an average marriage duration of 25 years. All of them had children, the majority of them grown. Only one-fourth of the sample had children under the age of 16. Sixty percent of the respondents also had at least one living parent, ranging in age from the early sixties to the upper eighties. The in-depth interviews concentrated on the divorce process, but considerable information was obtained about relationships with two other generations: maturing children and aging parents.

Being in the Middle: Exploring Women's Views of Parents and Children. During 1981–1982, I collected a set of preliminary interviews with 79 middle-aged women who had at least one parent living and whose oldest child was over the age of 19. The interviews, which were semi-structured, asked the women to discuss their relationships with the parent and with their oldest child. Some questions asked for comparisons of the two relationships.

The three studies which I have briefly outlined focused on different sets of key issues. The Chicago research had as its main goal to map patterns of socialization and influence across three generations. However, it also had data on patterns of support. A deepened interest in support patterns led to the study of middle age divorce. This research, in turn, made my view of interdependence among lives in the family more complex. The recent interviews with middle-aged women have explored perceptions of such interdependencies.

My discussion in the next three sections focuses on the middle-generation's relationship with parents and children in patterns of socialization and influence, support, and interdependence. In each section, I attempt to relate conceptual issues in the study of parent-child relations to findings from my own work.

Socialization and Influence

The Chicago study of three-generation families was inspired by the late 1960s reconceptualizations of socialization as a process between parents and children. As two key papers by Bell (1968) and Rheingold (1969) indicated in their titles, we increasingly came to stress influence from child to parent, not only from parent to child.

It has often puzzled me that the emphasis on reciprocal influence between parent and child emerged within the alpha tradition of research. A reconceptualization of socialization came as a result of new views of "the chronological child," most importantly discarding what Hartup (1978) called "the social mold view" of the first decade of life. However, I believe that a view of socialization as reciprocal also says something about parents, recognizing that adults are changeable and change too. For some reason, the growing emphasis on individual development as a lifelong process, which characterized the field of psychology in the last decade, did not lead to a major push for research on how adults and their parents mutually shape each other's life patterns and behaviors. However, a number of authors have provided *discussions* of how patterns of socialization may change as parents and offspring mature and age (e.g., Bengtson & Black, 1973: Brim, 1968; Mortimer & Simmons, 1978; Riley, Johnson, & Foner, 1972). Brim (1968) argued that, as parents age and become more dependent, we see "reversed socialization" where the children call the shots. Thus, he sees changing patterns of influence between parents and offspring as a result of individual maturation and aging. Other writers see the shift as necessitated by historical change. The best-known exponent of this latter view is Mead's *Culture and Commitment* (1970), with its discussion of the older generations as "immigrants in time" who must rely on the young for needed knowledge and skills.

For either view of socialization from young to old, there is a great scarcity of data, as recent reviews demonstrate (Lerner & Spanier, 1978; Mortimer & Simmons, 1978). It would seem quite safe to conclude that at the present time, we know considerably more about patterns of mutual influence between infants and their mothers (e.g., Lewis & Rosenblum, 1974) than we know about how parents and offspring influence one another throughout adulthood.

As a matter of fact, the only major body of empirical work on influence between parents and children beyond the early phases of their relationship has tended to take a *unidirectional* view of such influence. The events of the 1960s gave rise to considerable concern about societal cohesion, stability, and continuity because of apparent conflict between young and old. Fears that the young were taking dramatically different paths and possibly threatening social order focused a good deal of attention on "generation gaps." Often, empirical investigations of such possible gaps included comparisons of youth and their parents' political orientations and views on ethical and social issues. Frequently used concepts in this work were continuity, similarity, and transmission. A typical piece of research gave attitude measures to college students and their parents. Data analysis explored similarities between these two generational groups. Often, statistical agreement was translated into "consensus" or "intergenerational continuity," which in turn were interpreted as results of successful *parental transmission* of values or attitudes. In a fair amount of work, party affiliation or voting behavior was explored in a similar mode. Recent work of this type has often been done under the rubric of "political socialization." (For an overview of this research and some of its problems, see Bengtson & Troll, 1978.)

Work on "transmission" from parent to child has primarily concerned itself with *outcomes,* or products of influence. Research on mutual socialization between parent and child has emphasized *process.* I believe the Chicago three-generation study is fairly unique in exploring how parents and adult children perceive processes of influence in their relationship. As I have worked on the data from our interviews with these families, I have been struck with the importance of considering outcomes of transmission from old to young, as well as processes of mutual influence, up and down generational lines. We need to consider both the issue of intergenerational continuity and the fact that relationships across family generations bring together individuals from different cohorts and different stages of individual development. An ongoing process of negotiation seeks to develop and maintain a common base for relating, in spite of contrasting historical anchorings and individual developmental tasks. I believe that in order to understand these two kinds of phenomena, the creation of family continuity across generations, and the "bending and stretching" necessary to accommodate individual and societal change, we should focus a great deal of attention on individuals who are both parents and children. Such individuals are critical *generational bridges* (Hill et al., 1970) who serve as "brokers" of stability and change across generational lines.

My discussion of findings from the Chicago study concentrates on the middle-generation's position in patterns of family influence. I touch on the following questions: How do middle-aged men and women see their position in the flow of influence between generations? Do they report about equal numbers of influence efforts "up" to aging parents and "down" to young adult children, or do they concentrate more on their children? How do they talk about themselves as the "targets" of influence from the two other generations? Does more come from "above"—their parents—or from "below,"—their children? What *types* of influence efforts are directed "down" and "up?" To what extent are they perceived as successful?

I concentrate on direct ascendant/descendant connections, and do not discuss relations between the middle-aged and their parents-in-law. Thus, in the families in which a maternal grandparent was interviewed, the focus is on the middle-generation mother. If we interviewed a paternal grandparent, I discuss the father. As mentioned earlier, we had 65 paternal and 83 maternal lineages.

Both among men and women, the majority appeared to concentrate more influence efforts on their child than on their parent, although about one-third reported equal numbers of attempts to influence each of the two other generations. About 10% spoke of more efforts to influence the parent than the child. While men concentrated more on the younger generation, women tended to balance influence up and down the generational ladder. Cases in which more influence was aimed at the aging parent than the young adult child most commonly occurred in families where a maternal grandmother was interviewed. When we examined how the middle-aged respondents discussed attempts on behalf of others to influence *them*. nearly one-half reported equal numbers of such attempts from the child and the parent. Only about 15% said the child made more efforts to influence them than did the parent. Thus, a simple conclusion seems to be that parents never give up trying!

Some interesting patterns emerged when we examined how the respondents perceived the success of their own, the parent's and the child's efforts. Both men and women thought their attempts to change the other person's behaviors or outlooks had about a 50% "success rate." This was the case for influence to parent as well as child. However, when they discussed how the two others had tried to change *them,* there were clear contrasts between parent and child in perceived success. Parents were seen as having been successful in their influence attempts about one-third of the time, while children were perceived to have considerably better luck. Their reported success rate was about three out of four. Among men who discussed a daughter's attempts at influencing them, the child was reported to be successful nearly all the time. A similar pattern emerged when we looked at how the grandparent generation spoke of their middle-aged children's efforts to influence *them.* Aged parents reported about a two out of three success rate when their children had tried to influence them. Again, fathers saw offspring, especially daughters, as highly successful in their attempts to influence them, considerably more so than the children (the middle generation) thought they were. Another aspect of this study was that children, both young adults and middle-aged, typically reported "sending" more influence than was even registered by the parent. Thus, a number of influence messages did not seem to reach the target, but those that *did* appeared to penetrate. This may be in part because there were some kinds of influence messages parents were ready to hear from offspring and some that fell on deaf ears.

The one area of influence that cut across all the relationships we examined in the study was *health*. Family members in all three generations struggled to keep the others healthy by trying to get them to watch their diets, stop smoking, see the doctor, and take their medicines. In the 16 dyadic reports we are comparing here (sending and receiving influence as reported by men and women in four types of parent-child pairs, depending on gender of parent and child), *13* had health among the top two "high traffic areas." Beyond that, we see considerable variation by generation and gender.

"Up" to their parents, middle-aged respondents concentrated on *practical advice* on where to live, household management, dress and grooming, money, and the uses of time. It was clear that a number of them served as consultants on money management for widowed mothers and mothers-in-law. The aged parents were less likely to recall instances when the middle-aged child tried to influence them, but when they did, their reports were fairly similar to those from the child. However, there were some important exceptions. Messages regarding *internal family dynamics,* such as parent-child relations or the relative importance of family and friends, often appeared to fall on deaf ears among the parents. The same thing happened with regard to views on *current social issues.* The former sorts of messages were often geared to aging mothers; the latter to fathers. In both cases, the recipient tended not to "hear," or at least recall them. Further light was shed on these discrepancies when we asked our respondents if there were topics which "made things difficult" between them and the other family members they were discussing. In discussions of grandmothers and mothers, the clear trouble spots were topics dealing with interpersonal issues, particularly in the family realm. The most frequent mention of such touchy subjects was found among mothers discussing grandmothers, but they were also commonly identified in middle-generation fathers' discussions of grandmothers, and by both sets of partners in mother-grandchild pairs. Grandmothers were more likely than grandfathers to identify difficult topics, and their reports, like those of other family members, most frequently mentioned interpersonal family issues as creating difficulties between them and younger generations. When grandfathers were discussed, views on social issues were by far the most commonly mentioned. Among the 40 families where a grandfather was interviewed, nearly all of them had at least one family member who said that such questions created difficulties with grandpa. Race relations, social policy, and sex roles were social issues which frequently came up. Reports of such "sticky subjects" came from the two younger generations, while grandfathers typically insisted that everything was fine and dandy.

Discrepancies between the views of the middle and the older generation also appeared when we asked about influence "down," to the middle-aged child. Parents emphasized health, work, and finances as areas where they had sought influence and had reasonable success. However, they underestimated their influence in the areas of parent-child relations and questions of how to manage other interpersonal relations. Both middle-aged men and women saw issues related to childrearing as an area where the parent had shaped their behaviors and outlooks, considerably more than the parent seemed to recognize or be ready to report.

The middle-aged respondents were considerably more ready to listen to advice on how to parent from their parent than from their child. Women, more than men, recalled such efforts from offspring, but seldom reported that the efforts led them to change their behaviors as mothers. Aside from health, the areas in which men and women were most likely to recognize influence attempts from off-spring—and take them to heart—were views on current social issues and the uses of free time. Many of them stated that the child helped them "keep up with the times." I refer to this as "cohort-bridging" processes within the family.

Where did parents concentrate most of their efforts to influence their grown children? Most commonly, they reported that they had attempted to shape behaviors and outlooks related to the child's transition into adulthood: education, work, money, and personal life-style, such as dress and grooming. This was the case for both men and women, and applied to both sons and daughters. Practically all young adults could recall at least one incident when their mother and father had tried to influence them. The majority (about 80%) recalled four or more such incidents for each of the parents.

When I pondered *interviews* rather than computer print-outs, I was struck by how the same issues came up over and over again as I read the four sets of interviews from a given family. Furthermore, I was impressed by the variability of such issues, across families. That is what led me to qualitative readings of entire family sets. So far, we have read 34 families (Hagestad & Kranichfeld, 1982).

We identified the families which had all male or all female lineage connections in the members we interviewed. In the all-male lineage subgroup, a paternal grandfather, a father, and a grandson were interviewed. There were 10 such families. In the all-female lineage subgroup, we talked to a maternal grandmother, a mother, and a granddaughter. Twenty-four families fell in this pattern. In these 34 families, we again focused on "the straight line" and did not read the middle-generation parents who did not have their own parents interviewed. In the reading, we concentrated on identifying *family themes* (Bengtson & Troll, 1978). In order to be counted as a theme, the same issue had to be brought up by at least two of the three people and indirectly involve all three family members. For example, if a granddaughter reported that she and her mother discussed health problems and her mother reported that she and the grandmother discussed such problems, this would constitute a family theme. Approximately half of all the identified themes were mentioned by all three generations. In the all-female units we found an average of three themes, for the all-male slightly over two. Most of these themes came up several times in the interviews. Indeed, about one-fifth of the themes were mentioned seven or more times across the three interviews.

We grouped the themes into five main categories: (1) views on social issues; (2) work, education, and money; (3) health and personal appearance; (4) daily living at home (e.g., household maintenance); and (5) interpersonal relations. Table 5.1 shows the percentage distribution of the recorded themes by these five areas in all-male and all-female lineage units. As is quite clear from the table, there were some striking differences in what men and women paid attention to

TABLE 5.1
Percentage Distribution of Family
Themes in All-Male and All-Female
Three-Generation Lineage Units*

	All Male Units	All Female Units
Views on social issues	32%	9%
Work, education, money	59%	9%
Health and appearance	9%	15%
Daily living	—	14%
Interpersonal relations	—	53%
	100%	100%

*Percentage distribution of *themes*, not families. Most families had more than one theme.

and talked about in their relationships across generations. For men, themes fell into domains of instrumental concerns and social issues in society at large. For women, they were typically focused on interpersonal relations, mostly within the family.

Let me give some examples. In one of the all-male units, the grandfather and the father had worked together in the labor movement for 15 years. The grandfather retired and the father was asked to resign. His decision to comply caused much family upheaval, because the life of the entire family had been heavily focused on union activities. After losing this focus, they were struggling to find a new common ground. The father said about the grandfather: "Ours was a work relationship. After we left the union, he has been looking for ways to keep him and me tied together." He went on to tell of how the grandfather, his father, had asked for a sizable loan, even though he did not need the money. The father's interpretation was that this was the grandfather's way of trying to get them "into business together again."

In one of the all-female units, themes revolved around how to relate. All three women discussed how the mother tended to criticize the granddaughter, who was very sensitive to the criticism. This issue came up *twelve times* in the interviews. The grandmother and the granddaughter both discussed an occasion when the grandmother told the young woman that she needed to become less emotionally dependent on her parents, and then the criticism would not hit as hard and interaction would be smoother. The mother spoke of similar issues and stated that since the granddaughter, her daughter, was becoming more independent, she was better able to verbalize her feelings when criticism hurt. The mother said that as a result of these changes, she had come to treat the daughter with more respect, more as an adult equal.

During the qualitative analyses of the data, I have become increasingly impressed by the great variability in what issues engage attention, time, and energy in families. I have come to think that in seeking a common ground for relating across generations, the critical question may not be *how* to think about certain issues, but *what to think about* at all. Families vary a great deal in what they consider worthy of attention; what they think should be taken seriously. For example, many of the families in our study emphasized money and the management of finances. However, the issue was not necessarily that there was *one* "family way" of dealing with money. Rather, the critical assumption seemed to be that money merits time, attention, and conversation. Family members work at finding a set of concerns which engage all of them, but which are not likely to bring out differences great enough to be disruptive. It is my impression that some issues considered important by members of *one* generation sometimes do not come into play in interactions with other family members because the potential for conflict and open discontinuity is too great. This is what I have come to call "family demilitarized zones": unspoken agreements on what *not* to speak about.

The Chicago data also point to differences between men and women in what they emphasize in their search for "common ground" across generations. Contrasts between the sexes fell along the lines of Parsons and Bales' (1955) distinction between "instrumental" and "emotional-expressive" leadership. Grandfathers and fathers chose as their focus of attention relationships with the wider society through work, education, and finances. Particularly for grandfathers in the study (most of them born around the turn of the century), cohort changes in the rest of society appeared to present potential threats to a common family base. Women, on the other hand, concentrated attention on relationships *within* the family. The mothers in the study appeared to think of themselves as "ministers of the interior," specialists on internal family dynamics.

As mentioned earlier, the two older generations of Chicago women did not appear too open to advice from younger members on how to handle family affairs. Between middle-generation women and their mothers or mothers-in-law, there appeared to be some tension between two "specialists," two "kin-keepers." However, as I also mentioned, middle-generation mothers were more ready to acknowledge, and take to heart, influence regarding parent-child relationships from their mothers, the grandparent generation, than from their children in the third generation. In the recent pilot interviews with middle-aged women, we found that a number of them expressed the view that "you don't understand what it means to be a parent until you've been there." Many of them added the expectation that their children, particularly their daughters, would develop new sensitivity to them after experiencing the transition to parenthood. Work on these interviews and the study of divorce in middle age have again pointed to the greater internal family focus of women. One area in which earlier research has found consistent sex differences is in patterns of intergenerational support.

Patterns of Support

Much of my curiosity about parents and children has focused on how they constitute interpersonal resources for one another throughout adulthood. Above, I touched on how children may serve as "cohort bridges" for their parents, softening the impact of social change in the wider society. Now, let me comment on emotional support. A sizable research literature within the omega view of parent-child relations has explored patterns of exchange across the generations. Repeatedly, it has been shown that even though this society does not have an extended family structure, there is an impressive exchange of gifts and services between older people and their children. Hill, (Hill et al., 1970) Shanas (Shanas, Townsend, Wedderburn, Fries, Milhoj, & Stehouwer, 1968). Streib (1972), and Sussman (1976) are some of the key researchers in this tradition. However, there has been little work in which the flow of support and concern "up" and "down" generational lines has been explored on an intra-family, rather than on an aggregate, group level. Again, members of a middle generation are an interesting research target.

Little work has explored the relative importance of children and parents as sources of support for middle-aged men and women. In my dissertation research at the University of Minnesota (Hagestad, 1975) I was struck by questionnaire responses from nearly 800 undergraduate students who were asked about their relationships with their parents. The majority of both male and female students said their mother was more likely than their father to discuss personal problems and worries with them. Recent work on primary relationships in later adulthood has found that women, significantly more than men, use children as confidants. Our study of divorce in middle age (Hagestad et al., 1983) found a similar trend. Two findings stood out. First, during the divorce process, women utilized their "vertical connections" to parents and children more than men did. Women more frequently turned to the two other generations to discuss marital problems and to seek emotional and material support. Second, when family supports were relied on during the divorce process, children were both turned to more and seen as more helpful than parents, especially by women. Two-thirds of the women, compared to one-fourth of the men, said they had discussed their marital problems with their children. When the respondents were asked to identify the person who was the most helpful during the worst part of the divorce process, nearly one-fourth of the women named a child. Only 5% of the men did so. Our data suggest that women. more than men, approached children as adult equals, to whom they could turn for advice and support. One man said, "I underestimated the children. . . . I just figured they were kids, even the older ones. They're young men, but I thought. 'what the hell do they know . . . they're kids.' " A number of our respondents also turned to their parents. Three-fourths of the women and half of the men who had surviving parents said they had discussed marital problems with them. However, only *one* respondent in the sample mentioned a parent as most helpful during the crisis of marital breakup. The tendency for these middle-aged individuals, particularly women, to rely more on help from grown children than from aging parents made me curious as to whether this in part reflected negative attitudes toward divorce on behalf of the parent. In the interviews with middle-aged women we asked them: "If you had a personal problem or worry, would you discuss it with your parent or your (oldest) child, do you think?" More than half of them (54%) said the child, less than one-fourth (21%) said the parent. The remainder said "both," "neither," or "it depends." When we followed up by asking why they would rather turn to the child, two responses were most common: "My child is involved in today's world and more likely to understand," and "I would not want to burden my parent." For those who said they would talk to the parent, the parent's wisdom and maturity was a commonly mentioned reason.

One finding from the divorce study has given me considerable food for thought. Since about 40% of the sample were in the omega position (i.e., they had no living parents), we examined patterns of help seeking during the divorce crisis by generational location of the respondents. Our data suggested that having parents still living appeared to make the middle-aged individuals, particularly men, more ready to turn to other family members, such as children and siblings. For those with no parents, there was less overall use of family supports. Among men who had at least one parent living, 60% talked to children during the most difficult part of the divorce process. Among those with no parent living, 24% did so. The corresponding figures for women were 54% and 47%. The same contrast was found with regard to seeking support from siblings. Among men *with* parents living, 20% turned to neither a child nor a sibling. For men *without* parents, the corresponding figure was 53%. Clearly, these findings are from a small sample and have to be interpreted with caution. However, I think they illustrate the importance of seeing a given parent-child relationship in a wider generational context and considering generational succession (Marshall & Rosenthal, 1982).

So far, I have concentrated on members of the middle generation as *recipients* of support from parents and children. However, the middle-aged are also *providers* of support and concern. I believe this is an area where it is again important to look "up" as well as "down" generational lines. As we saw from the Chicago study, middle-aged women and men tended to concentrate more influence efforts on children than on parents. In the recent interviews with women, we asked, "Do you worry more about your parent or your child, would you say?" Two-thirds of them said they worried more about their child; only one out of six said their parent. Typical comments were: "My mother has lived her life; my daughter has hers ahead of her. So many things can go wrong . . . there is lots to worry about." When we asked them who worried more, the parent about them or they about the parent, responses were about equally divided between those who said "*I* do" and those who thought the parent worried more. When the same question was posed about the relationship to the young adult child, most of the women said without hesitation: "There is no comparison—*I* worry much more!" A few of them added: "I wish she *would* worry a little about me." Others said: "I wish it would change, with me worrying less and him worrying more!"

Recently, a number of authors in the omega tradition of research have discussed the growing pressures on the middle-aged who are faced with aging parents in need of help and support. A student whose thesis I helped supervise (Smith, 1983) found that when middle-aged women experienced a sense of overload in caring for aged parents, they tended to have young adult children who were "off track" in their life course development. For example, one woman had a son in his late twenties, still without a job; another had a daughter whose marriage had failed and who had moved back into her old room. This study points to the importance of considering support patterns, as well as expectations, across more than one parent-child link. This brings me to my last issue: the complex interdependence of lives across generations.

Developmental Reciprocities

Many of the respondents in the midlife divorce study were attempting to verbalize a sense of being "off track," things not working out right. Not only did they express a sense that their own life course progress had been interrupted; they were also aware that their transition created ripple effects for other family members, such as children and parents. A number of the women who were receiving considerable financial and emotional support from adult offspring expressed a dilemma of interdependence. On the one hand, they felt that the support they were receiving had been earned through years of caregiving, chauffeuring, and girl scouts. On the other hand, they knew that by providing the help, their children might have their own adult life career disrupted, which again threatened the women's sense of accomplishment as mothers. Some of the youth whose parents divorce in middle age not only may lose stability and parental support which they had counted on, but also may be asked for accelerated, off-time maturity, confronting parental needs for which they would be more prepared 20 to 30 years later.

Pondering these interviews made me increasingly aware of how the lives of parents and children are interdependent throughout their relationship. They are what Plath (1980) calls *consociates*, fellow life-travellers, whose lives are closely interwoven. Such life interdependencies, or developmental reciprocities (Klein, Jorgensen, & Miller, 1978), have been the topic of countless literary works, but have generally been neglected by social scientists. Let me point to two topics which I think deserve considerable attention by scholars interested in parents and children: contingent life course expectations and countertransitions.

Anthropological work and historical records provide many examples of how societal age norms made life careers of parents and children contingent on one another. For example, under a system of primogeniture, the oldest son could not marry and start his own family until his father died or relinquished the farm (Arensberg & Kimball, 1968). I cannot think of institutionalized norms stating such career contingencies in our society. Nevertheless, *informal* expectations recognize that "your own life course progress hinges on the uncertain progress of others in their life-stage tasks" (Plath, 1980, p. 23). Children count on a period of strength—almost invulnerability—in their parents, up to old age. Illness and deaths which upset such expectations represent more severe crises than when they come as expected, on time. Recently, a colleague whose parents both died before he was 40 exclaimed: "I'm orphaned!" A listener responded that he was *too old* to be an orphan. The answer came quickly: "But I'm also too young to be next in line!"

His statement reflects expectations about timing of parental death, based on demographic changes which were discussed in the first part of this chapter (see also Treas & Bengtson, 1982). In addition, it shows that we anticipate rhythms of generational turnover. We count on spending some time in a middle generation, between two other adult generations. We are not ready to be "the last one in line" when we are 40. We do not expect to have only one generation *below* us when we are 60. In the recent interviews with middle-aged women, we explored their perceptions of what being in the middle generation meant to them. When asked what her mother currently gives to her, one woman said: "I think it's the security of knowing that I still have one parent. I think that once both of them are gone, there will be a feeling that part of your life is gone."

Parents also build strong developmental expectations regarding children. Couples plan on "slowing down" when the children have finished school and found work. Often, their personal sense of accomplishment and security is built on the knowledge that the children have mastered *their* life tasks successfully. Erikson's concept of generativity in late adulthood is linked to the "reflected glory" obtained from the younger generation's successful mastery of the tasks of early adulthood (Plath, 1980).

Many of the middle-generation women expressed how they counted on new relationships with maturing children in the near future. One said of giving and receiving in the relationship with her daughter: "I give much more, but I anticipate that she'll give to me as I get older and she becomes more mature. Like how it was for me and my mother."

Recent work on the "empty nest" shows that when children *do not* leave on time and do not "turn out right," parents are left with a sense of strain and personal failure (Harkins, 1978; Nydegger & Mitteness, 1979; Wilen, 1979). A father in the Chicago three-generational study expressed his anger and bewilderment with his son:

> Last night we had a confrontation. . . . A disgust on my part for a 20-year-old not in school, not working, not putting anything into the house . . . it's all tak-

ing . . . food, car, clothing. . . . He said "I'll get out, leave now!" I said, "No, stay, but *do* something, get a job!" (Wilen, 1979).

In our interviews with middle-aged women, we asked if the relationship with the child had changed over the last few years. One woman exclaimed: "*No!* And that's the problem!" When we asked if she thought it *would* change in the near future, she said:

> I certainly hope so! She still lives at home. . . . I hope she becomes financially secure enough to move away. I hope she gets a job and that she can live somewhere else. If these things happen, I won't worry so much. . . . She *is* 25 years old!

I believe the frustration expressed by some of these parents stems from a sense that *their* ability to move on with their lives, *their* life tasks, hinges on the children's progress. Only when their children have been successfully launched into adulthood do many parents have the freedom to attend to some of their own developmental concerns, such as signs of aging and old parents' increasing dependency. Nearly two decades ago, Blenkner (1965) discussed her concept of *filial maturity*—the readiness to accept a new dependence from aging parents. It is seldom recognized that such maturity builds on a transformation of the relationship with a third generation—young adult children.

The divorce study reminded us of how life decisions and transitions by one family member may create involuntary and unplanned changes for others. Because the lives of family members are intimately interconnected, person A's experience of a transition may create a different transition for person B. Building on an idea discussed by Riley and Waring (1976), I have come to speak of these phenomena as *countertransitions*. Marriage by one member creates in-lawhood for others. Parenthood creates grandparenthood and great-grandparenthood. Recent work has presented a strong argument for the need to study life events in a total life context (Danish, Smyer, & Nowak, 1980). We now need to take the logical next step and recognize that people's coping abilities and available supports are influenced not only by a constellation of personal events but also by family constellations of events, affecting individuals and their significant others. Parent-child relations are a good place to start.

Future Work

The three previous sections have discussed how the parent-child relationship is a continuous presence in the lives of adults—a steady source of influence through mutual socialization, intergenerational support, and interdependent lives. I have suggested that an interest in parent-child relations among adults inevitably leads the researcher to the study of intergenerational relations, because most adults spend a number of years when they simultaneously occupy the roles of parent and child. I have also argued that if we take a dynamic, diachronic perspective on parent-child systems, we need to consider several dimensions of time. Recently, historical changes in mortality and fertility patterns have drastically altered the pulse of family time. Parents and children may now anticipate sharing nearly half a century of life. For about half that time, the child is also a parent and forms a link in a multitiered set of vertical ties that connect family generations. The fact that we can now observe two or more tiers of parents and children in a given family presents researchers with some exciting new opportunities and challenges. Let me briefly mention a few which I feel we need to address in future work.

If we seek to bridge the current gap between the alpha and omega traditions of research, many of our theoretical concerns will center on issues of continuity and change. Such questions can be posed on three levels of analysis: individual, dyad, or family lineage.

In some of my own recent work, I have pondered questions about *styles* on all three levels. How much stability do we expect to find in parenting behaviors across the parent's adult years? Do individuals exhibit "parenting styles" which remain characteristic of them through the ages of 25, 45, 65, and 85? Do parent-child pairs display consistency in interactional patterns across the different phases of their relationship? Are there normal, predictable changes in parent-child relations across the spans of their individual lives and the career of their relationship? What triggers such changes? On what dimensions would it make sense to start looking for continuity and change? Do parenting styles and interaction patterns "run in families?" The answers to all these questions, I believe, is that we do not know. However, I am confident that if we begin to pose them, we will have to confront basic assumptions, often implicitly held, about the nature of individual development and family dynamics over time. Furthermore, the pursuit of such questions would push us to reexamine core theoretical constructs, to rethink issues of measurement and research design, and to explore new avenues in data analysis.

Let me give a few examples with regard to parenting style. Nearly all the research in this area has been done on parents and young children. There is little or no work on parenting or patterns of parent-child interaction beyond the alpha phase. Indeed, there is a general lack of attention to parents as a continuous presence in the lives of adults. I believe such trends in past work reflect assumptions about individual development. It is still commonly assumed that most, if not all, molding of behavior and outlooks occurs in the first decade of life. Consequently, parental behavior is seen as reflecting early life experience and is expected to remain fairly stable throughout the adult years. Work on dysfunctional family patterns often reflects such assumptions. For example, discussions of abusive parents typically attempt to trace such parental behaviors to experiences in the individual's family of orientation. Often, it is assumed that abusive parents were abused children. Indeed, it is commonly argued that there is intergenerational transmission of family violence—that it "runs in families." Data to back up such claims are skimpy at best (for excellent recent discussion, see Kadushin & Martin, 1981). Most commonly, abusive parents are asked to provide retrospective accounts of their own childhood experiences. To my knowledge, no systematic work has examined these parents' *present* relationship with their own parents.

A number of research questions which would help us understand troubled families would also contribute to our general knowledge of developing individuals in developing family systems. How much consistency do we find in parenting behaviors and patterns of interaction over time? To what extent does a young parent's behavior reflect current relationships with his or her parents, and to what extent does it reflect their earlier relationship history? On what dimensions should explorations of continuity and change in their relationship be concentrated? Is there more intergenerational transmission of dysfunctional patterns than of positive ones?

If we assume plasticity and change throughout life, would we not expect changes in parenting behaviors as the parent moves through adulthood, beyond changes which reflect responses to developing children? Do we nevertheless see a consistency in basic style, on some key dimensions? Would we expect to find greater similarity on an intra-individual level, across time, than inter-individually, across parents in a similar phase of parenting? If we take a life-span view of development, do we not take a skeptical stance to retrospective accounts of parent-child relations, because we recognize that such reports reflect the past through the lens of a given present? Explorations of changes in parent-child relations across phases of the relationship career do not have to rely solely on retrospection regarding earlier phases. We now have possibilities to study both observable changes over time and individuals' perceptions of such changes. Present knowledge does not allow us to hypothesize about the extent to which the two kinds of data would show parallels.

Past work on continuity and change in parent-child relations over time has not used available research strategies to their full potential. Within a cross-sectional approach, it is possible to examine patterns of parental behavior and dyadic interaction across generations within families, exploring similarities and differences in two or more sets of parents and children. A search for similarities and contrasts in behaviors or relationship styles leads researchers to some fundamental issues in conceptualization and measurement. Can constructs be developed which allow for the description and comparison of such patterns, across different ages, stages, generational locations, and historical experiences? Work on parenting style has put a great deal of emphasis on disciplining. Clearly, constructs will need to be on a higher level of generality in order to be applicable to parents and children from alpha to omega. For example, disciplining may be seen as a subdimension of a broader construct of control. One could argue that the basic dimensions of control and support, identified in early work on parenting (Sears,

Maccoby, & Levin, 1957), could be used to characterize parent-child interaction at any stage. Interviews from the Chicago families provided vivid pictures of how the issue of parental control is still alive between 80-year-olds and their offspring. The family members' verbal reports also provided glimpses of how parent-child dyads differed on such dimensions as degree of mutuality or the ratio of positive, supportive interactions and controlling, negative interactions. Such constructs have been used in observational research on troubled families (e.g., Burgess, 1979; Patterson & Reid, 1970), but to my knowledge, no work on parent-child relations in later life has sought to measure them. It would seem quite feasible to use the same sorts of constructs to describe patterns of interaction in *family lineage units,* representing several generations. In attempts to operationalize these constructs it is time to explore new research strategies. As a survey researcher, I find myself increasingly impatient with the limitations of verbal reports and have started to explore possible ways to observe intergenerational interaction directly, preferably in a naturalistic setting. It is rather amazing that research on adults and their parents has seldom or never used direct observation of the type which is so common in work on young children and their parents. Particularly in the exploration of family styles, such an approach would hold a great deal of promise. One could for example observe members of three generations and first watch $G1$ interacting with $G2$; $G2$ with $G3$, and then compare each of these dyads with the third generation present and absent.

Observational techniques would also lessen some problems related to units of analysis. In a multigenerational view of parents and children, we inevitably move beyond the dyad and face the problem of finding ways to describe families as units, including the statistical headaches it presents (Hagestad & Dixon, 1980). For those of us whose main research tool is the social survey, there are complex issues of dependence of measures, since a major way in which we can create variables to characterize dyads and larger units is to combine individual verbal reports into secondary, derived variables. Observational techniques offer the possibility of describing family units more directly, for instance in frequencies or ratios between certain types of interactions.

Finally, I think researchers in the 1980s can move beyond the limitations of cross-sectional comparisons and address dimensions of family time through longitudinal research. For example, it should be possible to construct longitudinal data sets by building on earlier research. Some of the work done on parenting in the 1950s and 60s, focusing on young adults and their children, should allow for possibilities to restudy the same individuals as middle-aged parents and young adult offspring, themselves parents. There are also some valuable longitudinal data sets which are currently being "mined." For instance, the Berkeley studies now have data on parent-child relations over half a century. For part of that time, there is information on three generations from the same family (see Eichorn, Clausen, Haan, Honzik, & Mussen, 1981).

Longitudinal research will allow us to address a much-neglected aspect of family time, namely generational turnover. We have extremely limited understanding of what happens to individuals and relationships when families add a new generation or lose the last member of the omega generation. For example, the few researchers who have studied changes in parent-child relationships as a result of the child becoming a parent (e.g., Fischer, 1981) have not, to my knowledge, controlled for whether the birth represented the parents' first grandchild or not. Theoretically, this would seem to be an important issue, since it has a bearing on whether observed changes in the relationship, such as greater sense of closeness, stem from new orientations in the child (in which case grandparental status of the parent would not be an important factor) or in changed roles for the parents (in which case presence or absence of other grandchildren would be important). Similarly, recent work on the life course has pointed to death of parents as an important life transition (e.g., Marshall & Rosenthal, 1982; Winsborough, 1980). As far as I know, no work has explored how the personal impact of parental death is different when it entails a change in generational structure and ends the role of child for the surviving adult.

CONCLUSIONS

Given recent demographic change, one could argue that parent-child relations represent a more compelling force in shaping the human experience from birth to death now than in any previous historical period. Such an argument rests on two demographic facts. First, because mortality patterns have stabilized and become more predictable, parents and children can now count on multiple decades of shared lives. Second, altered fertility patterns and increased life expectancy make it normal for adults to participate in two sets of parent-child relations—one with their parents and one with their children. Being a parent and being a child are both at the core of the modern adult experience. Consequently, the study of parent-child relations over time brings the researcher into the field of intergenerational relations.

Parents and children form evolving, vertical linkages that make families continuous social systems. In this continuous chain of interlocked lives, identities begin to be shaped before children are born and continue to be shaped beyond the span of individuals' lives.

We have long recognized that the study of parent-child relationships is critical to understanding *child development*. With an increasing awareness that development and change are lifelong processes, we need to expand our research focus to examine the impact of parent-child ties on *human development*. In seeking such wider understanding, developmental psychologists and family sociologists would have much to gain by crossing disciplinary boundaries and integrating their research efforts.

ACKNOWLEDGMENTS

In addition to the volume editor, the following colleagues provided valuable comments on earlier drafts of this paper: Vern Bengtson, Robert Burgess, Glen Elder, Reuben Hill, Mary Jo Ward, and Jack Wohlwill.

REFERENCES

Aldous, J. *Family careers: Developmental change in families.* New York: Wiley, 1978.

Arensberg, C. M., & Kimball, S. T. *Family and community in Ireland* (2nd. ed.). Cambridge, Mass: Harvard University Press, 1968.

Baumrind, D. Current patterns of prenatal authority. *Developmental Psychology Monographs,* 1971, *4*(1), 1–102.

Bell, R. Z. A reinterpretation of the direction of effects in studies of socialization. *Psychological Review,* 1968, *75,* 81–95.

Bengtson, V. L. Generation and family effects in value socialization. *American Sociological Review,* 1975, *40.* 358–371.

Bengtson, V. L., & Black, D. Intergenerational relations: Continuities in socialization. In P. Baltes & K. W. Schaie (Eds.), *Life span developmental psychology.* New York: Academic Press, 1973.

Bengtson, V. L., & Troll, L. E. Youth and their parents: Feedback and intergenerational influence in socialization. In R. Lerner & G. Spanier (Eds.), *Child influences on marital and family interaction.* New York: Academic Press, 1978.

Blenkner, M. Social work and family relationships in later life with some thoughts on filial maturity. In E. Shanas & G. F. Streib (Eds.), *Social structure and the family.* Englewood Cliffs, N.J.: Prentice-Hall, 1965.

Block, J., von der Lippe, A., & Block, J. H. Sex-role and socialization patterns: Some personality concomitants and environmental antecedents. *Journal of Consulting and Clinical Psychology,* 1973, *41,* 321–341.

Brim, O. G. Adult socialization. In J. A. Clausen (Ed.), *Socialization and society.* Boston: Little Brown, 1968.

Bronson, W. C. Adult derivatives of emotional expressiveness and reactivity-control: Developmental continuities from childhood to adulthood. *Child Development,* 1967, *38,* 801–817.

Burgess, R. L. Child abuse: A social interactional analysis. *Advances in Clinical and Child Psychology* 1979, *2,* 171–172.

Danish, S. J., Smyer, M. A., & Nowak, C. A. Developmental intervention: Enhancing life-event processes. In P. B. Baltes & O. G. Brim, Jr. (Eds.), *Life-span development and behavior* (Vol. 3). New York: Academic Press, 1980.

Eichorn, D. H., Clausen, J. A., Haan, N., Honzik, M. P. & Mussen, P. H. *Present and Past in Middle Life.* New York: Academic Press, 1981.

Elder, G. H., Jr. *Children of the Great Depression.* Chicago: University of Chicago Press, 1974.

Elder, G. H., Jr. Family and kinship in sociological perspective. In R. Parke (Ed.), *Review of child development research (Vol. 7): The family.* Chicago: University of Chicago Press, in press.

Fischer, L. R. Transitions in the mother-daughter relationship. *Journal of Marriage and the Family,* 1981, *43,* 613–622.

Hagestad, G. O. *Middle-aged women and their children: Exploring changes in a role relationship.* Ph.D. Dissertation, University of Minnesota, 1975.

Hagestad, G. O. Problems and promises in the social psychology of intergenerational relations. In R. W. Fogel, E. Hatfield, S. B. Kiesler, & E. Shanas (Eds.), *Aging: Stability and change in the family.* New York: Academic Press, 1981.

Hagestad, G. O. Parent and child: Generations in the family. In T. M. Field, A. Huston, H. C. Quay, L. Troll, & G. E. Finley (Eds.), *Review of human development.* New York: Wiley, 1982.

Hagestad, G. O., Croft, C., & Waitsman, S. *Family reality and family texts: A content analysis.* In final preparation.

Hagestad, G., & Dixon, R. *Lineages as units of analysis: New avenues for the study of individual and family careers.* Paper presented at the NCFR Theory Construction and Research Methodology Workshop, Portland, Oregon, 1980.

Hagestad, G. O., & Kranichfeld, M. *Issues in the study of intergenerational continuity.* Paper presented at the NCFR Theory and Methods Workshop, Washington, D.C., October, 1982.

Hagestad, G. O., Smyer, M. A., & Stierman, K. L. Parent-child relations in adulthood: The impact of divorce in middle age. In R. Cohen, S. Weissman, & B. Cohler (Eds.), *Parenthood: Psychodynamic perspectives.* New York: Guilford Press, 1983.

Hareven, T. K. Family time and historical time. *Daedalus, 1977, 106,* 57–70.

Harkins, E. B. Effects of empty nest transition on self-report of psychological and physical well-being. *Journal of Marriage and the Family,* 1978, August, 549–556.

Hartup, W. W. Perspectives on child and family interaction: Past, present, and future. In R. M. Lerner & G. B. Spanier (Eds.), *Child influences on marital and family interactions: A life-span perspective.* New York: Academic Press, 1978.

Hartup, W. W., & Lempers, J. A problem in life-span development: The interactional analysis of family attachments. In P. B. Baltes & K. W. Schaie (Eds.), *Life-span developmental psychology: Personality and socialization.* New York: Academic Press, 1973.

Hill, R., Foote, N., Aldous, J., Carlson, R., & MacDonald, R. *Family development in three generations.* Cambridge, Mass.: Schenkman, 1970.

Hill, R., & Rodgers, R. H. The developmental approach. In H. T. Christensen (Ed.), *Handbook of marriage and the family.* Chicago: Rand McNally, 1964.

Kadushin, A., & Martin, J. A. *Child abuse: An interactional event.* New York: Columbia University Press, 1981.

Klein, D. M., Jorgensen, S. R., & Miller, B. Research methods and developmental reciprocity in families. In R. M. Lerner & G. B. Spanier (Eds.), *Child influences on marital and family interaction: A life-span perspective.* New York: Academic Press, 1978.

Lerner, R. M., & Spanier, G. B. (Eds.). *Child influences on marital and family interaction: A life-span perspective.* New York: Academic Press, 1978.

Lewis, M., & Rosenblum, L. A. *The effect of the infant on its caregiver.* New York: Wiley, 1974.

Marshall, V. W., & Rosenthal, C. J. Parental death: A life course marker. *Generations,* 1982, Winter, 30–31.

Mead, M. *Culture and commitment: A study of the generation gap.* New York: Langman, 1970.

Mortimer, J., & Simmons, R. Adult socialization. *Annual Review of Sociology,* 1978, *4,* 421–454.

Nydegger, C. N., & Mitteness, L. *Role development: The case of fatherhood.* Paper presented at the annual meeting of the Gerontological Society, Washington, D.C., 1979.

Oppenheimer, V. K. The changing nature of life-cycle squeezes: Implications for the socioeconomic position of the elderly. In R. W. Fogel, E. Hatfield, S. B. Kiesler, & E. Shanas (Eds.), *Aging: Stability and change in the family.* New York: Academic Press, 1981.

Parsons, T., & Bales, R. F. *Family: Socialization and interaction process.* New York: Free Press, 1955.

Patterson, G. R., & Reid, J. B. Reciprocity and coercion: Two facets of social systems. In C. Neuringer & J. D. Michael (Eds.), *Behavior modification in clinical psychology.* New York: Appleton-Century-Crofts, 1970.

Plath, D. W. Contours of consociation: Lessons from a Japanese narrative. In P. Baltes & O. Brim, Jr. (Eds.), *Life-span development and behavior* (Vol. 3). New York: Academic Press, 1980.

Rheingold, H. L. The social and socializing infant. In D. A. Goslin (Ed.), *Handbook of socialization theory and research.* Chicago: Rand McNally, 1969.

Riley, M. W., Johnson, M. E., & Foner, A. (Eds.). *Aging and society: A sociology of age stratification* (Vol. 3). New York: Russell Sage Foundation, 1972.

Riley, M. W., & Waring, J. Age and aging. In R. K. Merton & R. Nisbet (Eds.), *Contemporary social problems* (4th ed). New York: Harcourt Brase Jovanovich, 1976.

Rodgers, R. H. *Family interaction and transaction: The developmental approach.* Englewood Cliffs, N.J.: Prentice-Hall, 1973.

Ryder, N. The cohort as a concept in the study of social change. *American Sociological Review,* 1965, *30,* 843–861.

Sears, R. R., Maccoby, E. E., & Levin, H. *Patterns of child rearing.* Evanston, Ill.: Row, Peterson, 1957.

Shanas, E. Social myth as hypothesis: The case of the family relations of old people. *Gerontologist,* 1979, *19,* 3–9.

Shanas, E., Townsend, P., Wedderburn, D., Fries, H., Milhoj, P., & Stehouwer, J. *Old people in three industrial societies.* New York and London: Atherton & Routledge Kegan Paul, 1968.

Smith, L. *Meeting filial responsibility demands in middle age.* Unpublished M. A. Thesis, The Pennsylvania State University, 1983.

Streib, G. F. Older families and their troubles: Familial and social responses. *Family Coordinator,* 1972, *21,* 5–19.

Streib, G. F., & Beck, R. W. Older families: A decade review. *Journal of Marriage and the Family,* 1980, *42,* 937–956.

Sussman, M. B. The family life of old people. In R. H. Binstock & E. Shanas (Eds.), *Handbook of aging and the social sciences.* New York: Van Nostrand Reinhold, 1976.

Treas, J., & Bengtson, V. L. The demography of mid- and late-life transitions. *The Annals,* 1982. *464,* 11–21.

Troll, L. E. The family of later life: A decade review. *Journal of Marriage and the Family,* 1971, *33,* 263–290.

Troll, L. E., & Bengtson, V. L. Generations in the family. In W. R. Burr, R. Hill, F. I. Nye, & I. L. Reiss (Eds.), *Contemporary theories about the family* (Vol. 1). New York: Free Press, 1979.

Troll, L. E., & Smith, J. Attachment through the life-span: Some questions about dyadic bonds among adults. *Human Development,* 1976, *19,* 156–170.

Uhlenberg, P. Death and the family. *Journal of Family History,* 1980, *5,* 313–320.

Walters, J., & Walters, L. H. Parent-child relationships: A review, 1970–1979. *Journal of Marriage and the Family,* 1980, *42,* 807–822.

Wilen, J. B. *Changing relationships among grandparents, parents, and their young children.* Paper presented at the annual meeting of the Gerontological Society, Washington, D.C., 1979.

Winsborough, H. H. A demographic approach to the life cycle. In K. W. Back (Ed.), *Life course: Integrative theories and exemplary populations.* Boulder, Col.: Westview Press, 1980.

6 Commentary: Psychological and Sociological Perspectives on Parent-Child Relations

Jeylan T. Mortimer
University of Minnesota

My comments highlight sociologists' and psychologists' distinctive perspectives on the study of parent-child relations.[1] There are certainly numerous differences in the approaches of the two disciplines to this important topic. Most obviously, psychologists concentrate on the early years, with major emphasis on the parent-child dyad; sociologists usually focus on subsequent periods of the child's life—parent-child relationships in adolescence, youth, young adulthood, and even later—within the context of the family as a unit of social organization.

The papers presented in this symposium, however, highlight two other important points of divergence. First, sociological and psychological perspectives tend to emphasize different determinants of variation in parent-child relations. To the psychologist, differences are largely a function of the child's age, developmental status, and ongoing parent and child behaviors. For example, Uzgiris places major emphasis on age as a determinant of the child's imitation of the mother's acts; Shatz points to age differences in infants' attentiveness and other responses to maternal gestures. The psychologist focuses on the immediate actions and reactions of parent and child as determining the dynamic pattern of parent-child relations—as in Uzgiris's examination of imitative behavior and Shatz's concern with infant selectivity to maternal communicative acts.

For the sociologist, in contrast, parent-child relationships are seen as grounded, preeminently, in the social context in which they occur. For students of "social structure and personality" (House, 1981) position in the broad structural frame-

---

[1]I am using these field designations rather loosely, recognizing the great diversity within each of these disciplines. For example, within sociology, structural functionalists, symbolic interactionists, and exchange theorists would have quite distinctive approaches to parent-child relationships.

work of society will have major implications for parent-child relationships, which, in turn, lead to differences in children's development and attainment.

As an illustration of the manner in which the structural context can affect parent-child relations, let us briefly attend to the influence of social class (Gecas, 1979). Whereas the psychologist, as in some of the research presented here, may select a sample from a rather restricted socioeconomic range, the sociologist more typically designs research in such a way that parent-child relations at different socioeconomic levels can be compared. As class position increases, parents have been found to be more supportive, empathic, and equalitarian in relations with their children. In discipline, there is greater use of reasoning as opposed to physical punishment. Kohn (1977) hypothesizes that class differences in socialization stem from distinct occupational conditions. Middle-class occupations place a premium on independent thought and responsibility, whereas in working-class occupations traits like punctuality and the following of rules assume greater importance. According to Kohn, parents value in their children those traits that are useful to them in their work. For example, middle-class fathers emphasize self-direction and working-class fathers, obedience. One might expect that if middle-class parents are concerned with development of the child's capacities to be independent and self-directed, this would encourage greater use of reasoning, more equalitarian family relations, and more supportive parent-child behaviors.

A second major difference in sociological and psychological approaches lies in the outcomes of parent-child relations that are given greatest attention. For the psychologist, parent-child relations seem to be of interest with respect to relatively immediate outcomes, that is, the development of rudimentary communicative understandings between child and mother (Uzgiris), the development of language as assisted or deterred by maternal gesturing (Shatz), or the implications of maternal employment in the preschool years for children's cognitive development (Clarke-Stewart, Hoffman). Underlying this concentration on short-term outcomes may be an assumption that features of cognitive and personality development in the early years are likely to have lifelong consequences.

Sociologists tend to be interested in the more long-range effects, particularly pertaining to the child's placement, as an adult, in the social structure. That is, to what extent do differences in parent-child relations lead to differences in children's achievement, socioeconomic attainment, and the acquisition of adult social roles? The many studies of status attainment in sociology focus on parental social-class position as limiting the life chances of children (see, e.g., Sewell & Hauser, 1975). Much attention has been given to the manner in which advantages and disadvantages, associated with social-class origin, are mediated by the character of parent-child relationships, for example, through the level of parental encouragement to attend college or to have high occupational aspirations (Sewell & Hauser, 1976) or parental structuring of the child's environment so as to stimulate cognitive growth (Williams, 1976).

Some of my own research reflects this interest in the consequences of parent-child relations for adult attainment and role acquisition. For the past several years I have been studying a panel of male college graduates who participated in the 1962–1967 Michigan Student Study, initiated by Theodore Newcomb and Gerald Gurin. While still in college, the panel members were given a battery of psychological tests and were also queried about their relations with their parents. In 1976, about 10 years after their graduation from college, these men were surveyed by mail. The survey included several of the original instruments, as well as questions regarding their adult lives.

What is most pertinent about this study for the perspective of this volume is the far-reaching consequences of the character of the earlier (in late adolescence) parent-child bond. Those college students who reported a greater degree of closeness with their parents had a stronger sense of individual competence, more strongly crystallized occupational value orientations, and they attached greater importance to work as a central life sphere. These psychological attributes proved to be highly stable over time. Moreover, the findings show quite conclusively that the attitudes and values, fostered by close and empathic parent-child bonds, influenced the adult life course, promoting educational achievement and the attainment of diverse occupational rewards, including income and work autonomy (Mortimer, Lorence & Kumka, 1983). Moreover, the father-son relationship was found to be important in the process of intergenerational occupational transmission, particularly along professional and business lines (Mortimer & Kumka, 1982).

I have included this brief discussion of some sociological work on the subject of parent-child relations to highlight the features of this perspective. The examples I have given show how structural contexts (e.g., social class) lead to differences in parent-child relationships (e.g., on the dimension of supportiveness), which, in turn, are expected to foster differences in child outcomes (e.g., in occupational values and attainments). Surely, psychological and sociological studies complement and extend one another. Whereas the psychologist focuses on the more immediate determinants, the sociologist seeks sources of variation in the wider social structure. While the psychologist concentrates on parent-child relationships in the early years, and attends to concurrent developmental outcomes, the sociologist is more interested in subsequent relations and their implications for adult role acquisition and attainment. Let us now turn to the chapters of this symposium.

Hagestad's chapter, "The Continuous Bond: A Dynamic, Multigenerational Perspective on Parent-Child Relations between Adults," is exemplary of sociologists' concern with the structural context in which parent-child relationships are embedded. She focused on how the changing structure of the family influences the character and outcomes of parent-child bonds, particularly in the middle and later phases of life. In recognition that parent-child relations do not occur in a structural vacuum, but in a multigenerational family context, Hagestad considered the length of the family line, the number of living generations (does the closeness between parent and child increase when there are no competing relationships "up"?), the implications of position as "alpha" or "omega," and the presence of continuities and discontinuities in parent-child relationships across generations. Further expressing her concern with the structural embedment of relations, she examined the effects of one intergenerational bond on others (e.g., how overload due to care for an aging parent may affect the middle-aged parent's relations with children.) Moreover, she recognized the dynamism and reciprocity in relationships when parent and child are older. Not only does the parent influence the child, but intergenerational similarities in attitudes may reflect influence "up" generational lines as well.

Hoffman's presentation, "Maternal Employment and the Young Child," reflects elements of both sociological and psychological perspectives. Her approach is sociological in its concern with maternal employment, an important social role in the wider society, as a source of variation in parent-child relations and child outcomes. Hoffman is highly sensitive to change in the implications of maternal employment dependent on the social milieu in which it occurs. The differences that she observes in the effects of maternal employment indicate the complexity of the causal relations involved. Maternal employment appears to have no uniform effect on parent-child relationships or child outcomes, but its effects depend on its broader life context, particularly as defined by social class and the sex of the child. Her approach is psychological, at least in this paper, in its concern with rather immediate individual outcomes (e.g., infants' and children's psychological status, the child's attachment to the parent, and related variables.)

It is evident that research on the subject of maternal employment has made major advances, moving from rather simplistic studies and conclusions to more complex multivariate assessments, incorporating more sophisticated study designs including important control variables. It may be important, in future work, to further attend to the possible reciprocities of causation with respect to the mother's employment decision making and the child's developmental outcomes. In spite of greater continuity of employment among women in their childbearing and childrearing years, family responsibilities still promote intermittent and part-time employment (Moen, forthcoming). If women can choose whether to work (of course, not all can), maternal employment may be more probable and continuous if the child is perceived to be faring well. Though generally we only attend to the effects of maternal employment on children, if maternal employment, even to a small extent, "selects" the better adapted children and families, child outcomes may "cause" maternal employment as well. Longitudinal studies focusing specifically on parental decision-making processes may be useful in identifying (or ruling out) such reciprocal processes (Heyns, 1982).

Clarke-Stewart's contribution, "Day Care: A New Context for Research and Development," is psychological in its focus on relatively immediate outcome variables: the child's cognitive development, the relationship with the mother, reactions to unfamiliar adults and to peers, and so forth. But this chapter has elements of a sociological approach as well in its concern with maternal employment and the manner in which external social structures—in this case, day-care homes and centers—impinge on the family and the developing child. Her research findings will be most reassuring to highly educated parents worried about the possible negative impacts that dual labor force participation may have on their children's development. They also indicate important criteria for choosing a center or day-care home.

My main reservation to this study is that the composition of the sample appears to maximize the likelihood that child care, outside the home, will have optimal consequences: It overrepresents highly educated, professional-managerial parents, whose resources (money, information) would be especially great; many of the parents had expressed interest in an early reading program, indicating their concern with the child's intellectual achievement; they were willing to volunteer for this study, which could also be indicative of special attentiveness to child development and the absence of major family or child problems. Finally, these parents, because of their generally high socioeconomic status, are optimally situated regarding choice of parental work pattern—these mothers may be particularly likely to adjust their labor force involvement to the developmental status of their child. Though the findings are of interest with respect to this type of population, the reader should be careful not to generalize Clarke-Stewart's findings to other socioeconomic groups, nor to children who are younger than two.

The chapter by Uzgiris, "Imitation in Infancy: Its Interpersonal Aspects," will be of interest to both sociologists and psychologists. Many psychologists will focus on its implications for the early developmental progress of infants—social, cognitive, and communicative. As maternal imitation of the child is found to stimulate reciprocal responses on the part of the infant, it could foster quite positive outcomes. And if such maternal behavior is indeed beneficial, might it be enhanced by early training? If so, such training could be an effective point of very early childhood intervention.

But instead of focusing on infant imitative behavior as mainly an indication of the child's developmental status, Uzgiris views this behavior as embedded in a social context—representing a rudimentary, preverbal form of communication between mother and child. Sociologists in the tradition of Cooley (1902) and Mead (1934) might consider early parental imitative behavior and child "matchings" as an initial form of what Mead called "taking the role of the other." Mead considered this a necessary precondition for the ability to participate in social life. Such imitative behaviors may also be implicated in the development of the self-concept, the differentiation of the self from others, and the attribution of qualities to the self—as in Cooley's "looking glass self." Sociologists would also be interested in the implications of the family's social structural position for these interactive behaviors. Does the frequency of maternal imitation of the child differ by education, occupational status, race, or ethnicity?

In her chapter, "Contributions of Mother and Mind to the Development of Communicative Competence: A Status Report," Shatz also focuses on the immediate mother-child dyad—the mother's communicative behaviors and the child's responses to them. She highlights the developmental status of the child as a determinant of language acquisition. Thus, while the younger participants in her study often failed to understand the connections between gesture and language, older children were able to integrate these communicative behaviors. Shatz's work emphasizes the constraints to communicative development arising from the child's own developmental status. The child actively organizes and selects those aspects of communication that are meaningful at a given stage of development. At the same time, Shatz points out that the communicative attempts of the child, even if highly rudimentary and nonverbal, may function to stimulate adult interest and further communicative attempts. Thus, the child is far from a passive recipient of parental influences; it instead selects from, and even molds, the environmental context. This emphasis on the active character of the "socializee" has become increasingly prominent in the study of development—within and across life stages—by both sociologists and psychologists (see, e.g., Gecas, 1981; Lerner & Busch-Rossnagel, 1981; Mortimer, Finch & Kumka, 1982).

I found Shatz's distinction between parents as "speakers" and parents as "teachers" of language particularly interesting. Parents, acting as teachers of language, may use gestures to attract their children's attention and to help them understand the meaning of vocabulary and grammatical forms. It is ironic, however, that gestures, perhaps intended to assist in the child's language acquisition, may make learning more difficult if they limit exposure to language and serve as substitutes for more explicit verbal referents. The fact that children were found to give more verbal responses in the ungestured experimental conditions indicates that they may obtain more practice in language use, a factor that is probably very important for linguistic development, when gestures are not used.

From a more sociological perspective one might ask, how does location in the social structure, or the social features of the family, affect parents' behaviors as speakers of language, and their impact on children's communicative development? Are there differences, for example, in the amount of language to which the child is exposed depending on the parent's education, socioeconomic position, the number of siblings, and so on? Might the child less frequently hear the spoken language in a single-parent household, with no other adults present? It may be that the sheer amount of language heard has consequences for learning, even when the child is not being spoken to directly. Thus, the sociologist would urge an extension of the study of enviromental influences on communicative development beyond the immediate mother-child dyad.

In conclusion, this excellent set of chapters demonstrates the rich diversity of approaches to the study of parent-child relations and their outcomes in the social and behavioral sciences. They suggest the fruitfulness of sociologists and psychologists coming together and sharing their conceptualizations, findings, and conclusions. Such juxtaposition suggests new questions to be asked, and useful modes of extending and enriching one another's work. Applying both sociological and psychological perspectives to this subject matter certainly broadens our understanding beyond what would be obtained from consideration of either one alone. Clearly, the confluence of psychological and sociological approaches is necessary for a full understanding of the determinants and consequences of parent-child relationships.

REFERENCES

Cooley, C. H. *Human nature and the social order.* New York: Scribner's, 1964. (Originally published 1902.)

Gecas, V. The influence of social class on socialization. In W. R. Burr, R. Hill, F. I. Nye, & I. L. Reiss (Eds.), *Contemporary theories about the family* (Vol. 1). *Research based theories.* New York: Free Press, 1979.

Gecas, V. Contexts of socialization. In M. Rosenberg & R. H. Turner (Eds.), *Social psychology: Sociological perspectives.* New York: Basic Books, 1981.

Heyns, B. The influence of parents' work on children's school achievement. In S. B. Kamerman & C. D. Hayes (Eds.), *Families that work: Children in a changing world.* Washington, D.C.: National Academy Press, 1982.

House, J. S. Social Structure and Personality. In M. Rosenberg & R. H. Turner (Eds.), *Social psychology: Sociological perspectives.* New York: Basic Books, 1981.

Kohn, M. L. *Class and conformity: A study in values* (2nd ed.). Chicago: University of Chicago Press, 1977.

Lerner, R. M., and Busch-Rossnagel, N.A. *Individuals as producers of their development: A life-span perspective.* New York: Academic Press, 1981.

Mead, G. H. *Mind, self and society.* Chicago: University of Chicago Press, 1934.

Moen, P. Continuities and discontinuities in women's labor force participation. In G. H. Elder, Jr. (Ed.),*Life course dynamics: 1960's to 1980's.*New York: Social Science Research Council (forthcoming).

Mortimer, J. T., Finch, M. D. & Kumka, D. Persistence and change in development: The multidimensional self-concept. In P. B. Baltes & O. G. Brim, Jr. (Eds.), *Life-span development and behavior* (Vol. 4) New York: Academic Press, 1982.

Mortimer, J. T., & Kumka, D. A further examination of the "occupational linkage hypothesis". *Sociological Quarterly 1982, 23*(Winter): 3–16.

Mortimer, J. T., Lorence, J., & Kumka, D., *Work, family, and personality: The early life course.* Unpublished Manuscript, 1983.

Sewell, W. H., & Hauser, R. M. *Education, occupation and earnings: Achievement in the early career.* New York: Academic Press, 1975.

Sewell, W. H., & Hauser, R. M. Causes and consequences of higher education: Models of the status attainment process. In W. H. Sewell, R. M. Hauser, & D. L. Featherman (Eds.), *Schooling and achievement in American society.* New York: Academic Press, 1976.

Williams, T. Abilities and enviroments. In W. H. Sewell, R. M. Hauser, & D. L. Featherman (Eds.), *Schooling and achievement in American society.* New York: Academic Press, 1976.

7

Commentary: Family Interaction and Child Development

W. Andrew Collins
Institute of Child Development
University of Minnesota

Resonances of two traditions in the study of parent-child relations have been heard at this symposium: a concern with *outcomes* of parental behavior toward children; and an interest in *processes* of interaction between parents and children. The outcome tradition has been predominant, and its yield in socialization research has been rich. I need only mention the empirical studies of Baldwin; Sears, Maccoby, and Levin; and more recently Hoffman, Baumrind, and the Blocks to conjure up the impact of this work. In this volume, chapters by Clarke-Stewart and Hoffman continue this tradition.

Work on processes has only recently become prominent. Its focus on parent-child interaction complements research on outcomes by encouraging theory and research on relatively molecular issues of the sources, nature, and direction of influences. Uzgiris's contributions to this 17th Minnesota Symposium extend this interactional research tradition. They illustrate some of the important issues highlighted by a focus on the process of interaction, and they demonstrate several significant lines of thought that are currently becoming more influential in the study of the family and parent-child relations. My comments are addressed to these trends and some distinctions that emerge from them. I should hasten to say that I believe the trends have their backgrounds in the field of developmental study as a whole, not just the study of family relationships.

PARENT-CHILD RELATIONS AS A CONTEXT OF DEVELOPMENT

The dominant trend is a tendency towards examining parent-child interactions as a context for development. This is not entirely a new emphasis, of course. The long-time dominance of a unidirectional model of socialization certainly cast

167

parents as major environmental factors in development. But little attention has been given to the functioning of parent-child dyads and related systems that would explain the course of the child's development.

In the chapters of this symposium, the nature of interaction is accorded a much more central role in understanding behavioral development in several domains. Shatz has given us a sense of the ways in which parent-child verbal interaction might support or fail to support the acquisition of a fully functional corpus of language and has thus illumininated important issues in early language development. Uzgiris has suggested that conceiving of imitation as something that goes on between parent and child, rather than as isolated instances of child behavior, may give us insights into functions of imitation in development that have not yet been extensively considered. Hagestad has outlined some apparently powerful generational and social-structural factors that constrain parent-child interactions, with attendant implications for socialization functions of family ties. These more process-oriented analyses of the characteristic interaction of individuals in families represent a significant elaboration of the questions commonly addressed in studies of parents as aspects of children's environments.

I hasten to note that focus on factors in skills and performance is becoming increasingly influential in the study of development generally and indeed in many areas of the psychological study of behavior. The impetus is an interest in a particular type of question, on the order of "What features of the natural environment of the child enable functioning at developmentally appropriate levels?" Related concerns recently have been raised in such diverse formulations as Gibson's ecological theory of perception and in the perspectives advanced by ethological researchers. Among other things, the analysis of parent-child interaction makes possible a functional analysis of significant aspects of interpersonal experience for behavior change across time.

This functional approach entails a number of methodological difficulties, some of which have been addressed in a number of recent volumes (e.g., Cairns, 1979; Lamb, Suomi, & Stephenson, 1979). A superordinate issue deserves mention here, namely, the need for researchers to diversify methodologically. A focus on naturalistic interactions exerts considerable pressure for researchers to work both in the field and in the laboratory. An ideal protocol would go something like this: We would make astute and careful observations of focal interactions between parents and children under naturalistic conditions. We would then use information derived therefrom to construct laboratory analogues to examine the operation of the apparent elements of those interactions and, if appropriate, their causal status with regard to the phenomena of interest. The common pattern, however, is for researchers to work in one setting or the other, leaving the related tasks to (unspecified) others. If a functional analysis is to be accomplished, we need more work in which multiple approaches to the same phenomena are undertaken within the same programs of research, to maximize interrelationships between more and less molar levels of analysis and also to specify the nature of relationships among theoretically and empirically associated variables.

Shatz's chapter gives a pertinent example. Her naturalistic studies of gesturing were supplemented by laboratory procedures with the result that she now proposes a more restricted view of the role of gestures in the influences of maternal speech than had previously been assumed. Uzgiris's finding on mother's matching of child behaviors and its functional relationship to further matching by the child is an opportunity for micro-studies to similarly supplement the leads from in-context analyses.

The notion of family contexts for development is complicated in a significant way by the view represented in this volume by Hagestad's work. That family interactions are embedded in a series of larger contexts, such as extended family, community, society, and culture, is widely recognized by developmentalists. These contexts constrain and inform the nature and effects of parent-child relations, but the difficulty is incorporating these concerns into empirical approaches. The most widely recognized implication of this point is the cohort or historical-milieu effect. As Hoffman and Clarke-Stewart have reminded us, social change has an impact upon the questions researchers ask and the results they get in studies of parent-child relations. There is a certain sense in which some of the questions we ask about outcomes trap us in a scientific time warp in which research questions must be repeatedly re-addressed to keep up with the changing milieu.

A somewhat different implication of this ecological view, moreover, is that studies of parent-child interaction must take account of the contexts that constrain the behavior of both parent and child. We do not yet have formulations for examining the role of extra-family factors in intra-family behavior. Hagestad's work on intergenerational perceptions is promising in this regard. The remaining challenge is to find ways of linking perceptions to the behavioral exchanges that seem to characterize particular parent-child relationships.

RELEVANT CHARACTERISTICS OF FAMILY ENVIRONMENTS

The question of developmental processes in the family context brings us to the interesting problem of how we might think about the qualities of family environments that are optimal for interaction and for the development of the child. Through the years the most frequently offered generalization is that parental responsiveness is the essential quality of "good" family environments. Two related characteristics have been widely suggested—and they have been echoed in various forms by the papers at this meeting. The first characteristic is *contingency,* which includes the clarity of the links between child's action and parent's reaction. I think of contingency as an essential ingredient in the widely invoked notion of *reciprocity* in relationships. Certainly the notion of contingency is critical to the formulation presented by Uzgiris. The idea of the mother reacting to the infant imitatively and vice versa is implied to be important, at least largely if not entirely, because of the contingency between the two actions. The second commonly identified characteristic of parental responsiveness is *demandingness*. By demandingness is usually meant the explicitness of behavioral requirements laid out by parents, their expectations for the child's actions, and so forth.

There are several reasons why these two characteristics of parental behavior have repeatedly been found to be influential ones (cf. Maccoby & Martin, in press). Certainly one of the reasons is that both contingency and demandingness are associated with setting standards and monitoring children's behavior, both of which have repeatedly emerged in studies of socialization as especially significant dimensions of differences among families. Examples are the work of Baumrind, with her distinctions between authoritarian and authoritative families, and the work of Hoffman on the distinctions between physical and psychological discipline. Studies of variables like mother's teaching style and other social-class and educational correlates of parents' influences on cognitive development address related issues, again at a very global level of analysis. In addition to standard setting and monitoring, a dimension of affect appears to be correlated with contingency and demandingness; affective factors have been addressed in studies in which families are characterized as either warm and accepting or cold and rejecting.

Other characteristics may also eventually emerge as important dimensions of parental environments, in addition to these standard ones. To discover them, however, we will need to break out of the observational frames that have come to us from the assumptions that have guided the classic studies of childrearing. For example, Fischer (Fischer & Bullock, in press) has recently noted two aspects of parental behavior that appear relevant to cognitive development. These distinctions may serve as one example of useful categories as we begin to try to describe what happens between parents and children in the course of normal interactions.

First, Fischer has borrowed from Vygotsky the notion of ``scaffolding.'' What Fischer intends to capture by this metaphorical term is parents' behavior that helps children to participate in activities long before the children are capable of sustaining those activities by themselves. The idea is that the early scaffolding of action by an interactive partner leads to internalization of the structure of the activity. One frequently suggested example of scaffolding is the early turn-taking routines between mother and infant, which are almost certainly due entirely to the mother's imposition of conversational patterns around the infant's verbal and motor action. Although at the time they probably do not indicate an initiatory capacity of the infant, such scaffolding by the mother may nevertheless later contribute to social turn taking in conversation, play, and other situations in which the child is a full initiator and participant. Uzgiris's instances of interpersonal imitation probably often fall into the same category. Indeed, she suggests that such instances may be one way of providing scaffolding for symbolic functions as well as conversational routines. We lack evidence for the *necessary* role of these proposed precursors of more complex performance and skills; a number of experiences undoubtedly contribute to both conversational and symbolic competence. We may be able to broaden our knowledge of developmental processes, however, by looking for ways in which parents typically seem to try to enhance their children's competent functioning before the children show evidence of being able to perform adequately alone.

Fischer's second category of parent action, *support,* occurs in instances in which a child has the capacity to perform at a given level of complexity or sophistication. In these circumstances, parents may merely provide the environmental supports necessary for performance at the highest level of which children are capable. We have seen instances in the chapters delivered here of parental behaviors that might well function as scaffolding and as support at different points. I understood both Uzgiris and Shatz to argue, for example, that parental actions that signal or maintain engagement or get and hold the child's attention for interaction and task accomplishment may serve scaffolding and support functions. Neither gesture, in Shatz's case, nor imitation, in Uzgiris's, is apparently thought to provide a full account of language acquisition or symbolic competence, but both may help advance the child's manifestations of competence in a wide range of situations.

Our efforts to analyze parent-child relations as contexts for development should include attention to instances of categories like scaffolding and support activities. Besides serving to specity further what aspects of parent-child relations are functional aspects of the child's everyday environment, this approach may also be one avenue to understanding parent-child environmental factors that do not lead to optimal outcomes. For example, one particularly intriguing finding cited by Hoffman is that sons of working mothers achieve less well in school than sons of nonworking mothers. An analysis of the parent-child environment, including both the extent and kind of scaffolding and support activities that parents typically provide for children in families with different work statuses, might elucidate this finding.

DEVELOPMENTAL CHANGE IN PARENT-CHILD INTERACTION

A third major theme in the study of parent-child interactions is more apparent from its omission from these symposium chapters than from its salience. The theme concerns understanding the nature and impact of parent-child relations as children grow older. The chapters in this volume, with the exception of Hoffman's, have dealt essentially with the early and late periods of development.

Indeed, in the entire body of psychological literature on parent-child relations, the years of middle childhood and adolescence are neglected.

When these periods are addressed, the most common focus is the greater difficulty of parent-child relations, relative to other periods of life, and the phenomena of increasing independence from parents and greater orientation to peers. One increasingly compelling suggestion, however, is that the change in parent-child relationships with age is not a shift away from parent influences, but is more nearly a transformation in the direction of co-regulation. In his book *The Urban Villagers,* Gans (1962) described the nature of the implicit rule system that governs the interactions between parents and their adult children. For example, there are certain occasions on which they are expected to be together, and there are certain life events in which members of extended families are regularly called upon. A picture emerges of children growing toward continuing relationships with parents that are different from the relationships of childhood, but still systematic and governed by rules widely understood in the subculture. Shifts in middle childhood and even in adolescence are partial transformations in the gradual movement toward co-regulation in parent-child relations. The available data by and large indicate that although the transformation may not always be smooth, transformation probably is a better metaphor than disjunction or disruption in the patterns that exist prior to puberty.

In this and in other aspects of parent-child relations, the question of real moment is not whether there are difficulties and conflicts at major developmental transition points, but the nature of the difficulties and how they are typically responded to within the family across time. Maccoby and Martin (in press) argue that the problem to be attacked in understanding parent-child relationships is two fold: We must understand their patterning through time, and, simultaneously, the quality and nature of moment-to-moment action and reaction from which adequate descriptions of relationships can be derived.

Maccoby (forthcoming) has recently suggested several considerations that are relevant to the shifts in parent-child relations over time. These considerations encompass relatively global surface variables such as the amount of conflict and difficulty at a given period and also illuminate moment-to-moment interactions that require more fine-grained analyses. One factor is the increasing capacity of children for selectivity in their experiences. Although there is ordinarily little choice in the family about who is available for interaction, as children grow older they are often able to determine to a greater extent than earlier how extensively they are in contact with different family members. To be sure, this is constrained by physical space features, such as whether the child has a private room to retreat to; it is also constrained by ecological niche factors, such as whether there is a ready momentary alternative to being at home and how early in children's lives such alternatives are accessible to them. We know little at this point about how selectivity works in determining the social environment of children, nor do we know very much about its impact upon the general effect of the environment upon them. Nevertheless, we should view the increasing selectivity of the child as a factor in changes with age in the nature of parent-child relations.

Even more important are the patterns of expectations of both parents and children that are the natural but subtle products of relationships that continue over long periods. Maccoby makes the point that parents form impressions of their children's behavior that govern behavior toward them. For example, parents of hyperactive children behave toward their children more in terms of the children's typical level of activity than in terms of their behavior in a particular situation in which they are being observed. The same parents, however, respond to an unfamiliar child in terms of more proximal cues, even though the unfamiliar child generally had been independently rated as having the same level of activity overall as the parents' own child (Halverson & Waldrop, 1970).

Some of the expectations formed of children's behavior have to do with patterns that are related to age period, such as cognitive skills, nature and range of extra-family social experiences. Within an age period, parents and children may often prematurely "stabilize" reactions to each other. Transition points in development, such as the shift into school and the changes that accompany puberty, are especially ripe for violations of expectations that have been prematurely stabilized. As developmental change takes place, the child may begin to react differently to parents' attempts to produce compliance, for example. Parents in turn may then make initial attributions about the child's behavior that are extreme and may react strongly on the basis of them. Thus, the lag between parental expectations and children's behavior can increase tension, so that family interactions become notably conflictful for a time.

Several examples may illuminate this point. In late middle childhood, children's raising questions about, or asking for rationales for, parental demands may be interpreted as insolent or uncontrolled behavior, and parents may respond to such behavior with extra firmness. The child may interpret this response as rigidity, and conflict ensues. Successive instances feed these interpretations on both sides. In this account, conflict results at least in part from changed behavior patterns of the child that reflect changing cognitive skills and new patterns of intra- and extra-family social involvements and, on the parents' side, the violation of parental expectations based on typical behavior in the preceding age period. Hagestad's finding that parents believe their children's attempts to influence them are generally successful, whereas children believe they send more messages than are received may reflect a similar process.

A number of questions can be raised about the nature of these changes around different transitions. For example, what are the norms of age changes in family relations? At this point we have no data available on the typical patterning of interactions across time. Thus, we actually know little about how cataclysmic age changes in parent-child relations are, in spite of theorizing in which they are presumed to be extensive and dramatic. We may ask whether age-related changes typically occur as bursts of conflicts or whether they tend to be more gradual. Parents and children may settle into stable interaction patterns over a period of time, which then break up when the stress from the child's growth becomes too great. Information about the usual ways in which these things occur is badly needed.

Second, we know very little about the role of various family members in helping to negotiate such changes. Most information that is available at this point focuses on mother and child; information is lacking on fathers, siblings, grandparents. Nor do we know very much about emerging family patterns in our society today and how interactional characteristics may vary across time. While we have some information on effects of divorce on children at different ages, this literature focuses mostly on outcomes for parents and children, not on the process of negotiating the readjustments that are neccessary when divorce takes place. Hoffman reminded us that in the area of dual-employment families, there is little focus on the nature of interaction and how such factors may be manifested when children are at different ages.

Finally, although hypotheses have been suggested about the nature of factors in changing interaction from one age period to another, we have virtually no information concerning the perceptions of parents and children about various aspects of their lives together. Goodnow (1982) has been engaged in some work of this sort in Australia with parents of young children. She found pronounced differences across subcultural groups in expectations of children's development at different ages and expectations of the kinds of childrearing procedures, if any, that are likely to be effective in modifying the course of development. Uzgiris's procedure for interviewing mothers while watching videotapes of their interactions with their infants is an especially useful technique for examining expectations pertinent to moment-to-moment interactions. Such information is needed for parents of children in other age periods. It also needs to be amplified by information about the typical attributions for various patterns of child behavior at different ages as a function of behavioral expectations in arenas that are especially central to smooth functioning of family relationships.

CONCLUDING COMMENTS

Points such as these are in the future for the study of parent-child relations if we pursue the general tack taken by several contributors to this symposium. They are somewhat more complex points than previous approaches to parent-child relations have obliged us to think about. They require new formulations about parent-child relations that go beyond the fountainhead theories of development, or at least oblige us to think more deeply about them than we often do. They also require imaginative use of different research strategies within the same programs of research to enable us to converge upon the complex patterns of processes that we undoubtedly will need to understand if we are to chart the role of parent-child relations in development. We are at a pioneering stage, in spite of a long history of research on parent-child relations. I have appreciated the opportunity to think about the topography of the frontier, and I am grateful to these symposium participants for the opportunity they have given all of us to look ahead to the future of work in this important area.

REFERENCES

Cairns, R. (Ed.). *The analysis of social interactions*. Hillsdale, N.J.: Lawrence Erlbaum Associates, 1979.

Fischer, K., & Bullock, D. Cognitive growth in middle childhood. In W. A. Collins & K. Heller (Eds.), *Middle childhood: Status of the research*. Washington, D.C.: National Academy Press, in press.

Gans, H. *The urban villagers*. New York: The Free Press of Glencoe, 1962.

Goodnow, J. *Unpublished manuscript*, 1982.

Halverson, C., & Waldrop, M. Maternal behavior toward own and other preschool children: The problem of "ownness." *Child Development*, 1970, *41*, 839–845.

Lamb, M. E., Suomi, S., & Stephenson, G. *Social interaction analysis*. Madison: University of Wisconsin Press, 1979.

Maccoby, E. E. Socialization in the context of the family in middle childhood. In W. A. Collins & K. Heller (Eds.), *Middle childhood: Status of the research*. Washington, D.C.: National Academy Press, in press.

Maccoby, E. E., & Martin, J. A. Socialization in the context of the family: Parent-child interaction. In E.M. Hetherington (Ed.), *Handbook of child psychology*, (Vol. 4) Social development. New York: Wiley, in press.

8 Commentary: Relationships and Child Development

Willard W. Hartup
Institute of Child Development
University of Minnesota

The dialectical issues threaded through this volume are among the most exacting challenges in child development research. We no longer conceive of socialization as the processes through which parents "mold" the social repertoires of their children; nor do we seek merely to identify sequences through which the child, *in vacuo*, constructs its vision of reality. The contemporary view of child development is a constructivist view: a view of the child that emphasizes the transactions occurring between a changing individual and a changing social environment.

Cognitive functions, language, and affect regulation arise primarily in social contexts: Many of us now argue that their determinants cannot be understood in the absence of a detailed analysis of the structure and functions of social relations. These considerations are as basic to understanding the determinants of adult development and aging as to understanding the development of the child. To grasp the significance of social relations for the individual, the entire life history, including the changes in transactions that coincide with major developmental transitions, must be charted. Since many transactions occurring within the family and in other social contexts are constrained by societal change, the study of behavioral development is extraordinarily complex.

THE IMPORTANCE OF RELATIONSHIPS

Not stated in the essays comprising this volume is the observation that childhood socialization occurs mainly within relationships, that is, within focused, enduring, affect-laden ties existing between the child and other individuals. None of the contributors would argue with the contention that the construction of relationships is a major developmental challenge for the child, its caretakers, and its companions. Missing, however, is a statement that relationships constitute the principal nexus within which the child adapts to the world, and that ontogeny cannot be conceived except in terms of the dyadic processes that are involved in those close and enduring encounters we call "relationships." Strong versions of this agrument implicate relationships in the development of basic cognitive and communicative functions as well as in the adaptation of children to changes in the social environment.

Numerous writers (see Hinde, 1979) argue that we do not yet know the best ways to describe relationships, let alone understand their functions or dynamics; prediction and outcome remain shrouded in the developmental mists; causation and consequence are difficult to delineate. Moreover, there are optimists and pessimists among us as to whether we will ever be able to do so. Nevertheless, new studies are converging in broad outline to confirm the thesis that the dialectics between the developing child and the development of relationships may be the most critical issue in our science.

THE NATURE OF PARENT-CHILD RELATIONSHIPS

Parent-child relationships can be described in various ways. Relationships between children and their caregivers are unique in terms of their *content* (what the actors do, including what they talk about), their *diversity* (the range of activities encompassed), *patterning* (their structural ebb and flow), and their *developmental course*. To me, one of the most interesting properties of adult-child relations is their basic asymmetry; these interactions involve individuals who are psychologically and socially dissimilar. Parents and children are individuals of dissimilar competencies and statuses, and their interaction is basically complementary rather than equilitarian.

These complementarities may take the form of structural regularities (e.g., one individual "gives," the other "takes"). But complementarities are also evident in the initiation and termination of social interaction (e.g., one "drives the interaction," the other is "driven") and in the determination of content. Thus, caretaking and teaching are interactional contents that are mainly complementary in nature; and these are hallmarks of the parent-child relationship—especially in the early years of the child's life and in the final years of the parent's. Note that these complementarities do not involve "activity" by one individual (e.g., the parent) and "passivity" by the other (e.g., the child). To the contrary, submission by the young child is as active a process as dominance by the parent, in the same way that learning is a process that is as active as teaching. Similarly, the acceptance of care is a process that is as active as caregiving.

The young infant is well adapted to asymmetries in social interaction: orientation and attentional biases in both infant and mother work as a complement; infant reflexive actions and maternal caregiving behaviors work similarly. Even the contingencies in maternal behavior toward the child and the infant's bias for detecting these contingencies (Watson & Ramey, 1972) work to establish a socialization complementarity in the early weeks and months of life.

Socialization refines these complementarities but does not remove them. With the emergence of a focused attachment between the child and the mother, the relationship continues to constitute a complement. A "goal-corrected partnership" may be an appropriate metaphor to describe the mother-child relationship at the end of the first year (Bowlby, 1969) but, even though certain equivalencies come to be manifest in their interaction, this partnership is not typified by equal-to-equal interaction. Rather, the mother gives protection; the child receives it. The mother gives care; the child accepts it. And, even if we remark proximity as a "set goal" of attachment in both the mother and the child, the child's overt actions dovetail with the mother's in a manner that complements rather than duplicates them.

Over time, the mother and child gradually interact with one another on more equal terms, for example, in initiating or "driving" the interaction. As the child grows older, the child's responsibilities for determining the content of the interaction increases. Nevertheless, the caregiver-child relationship remains mainly complementary throughout the first two decades, and there is some indication that this complementarity is never entirely relinquished. ("Your children are always your children.")

In childhood, the asymmetrical relationship between parents and their children is expressed largely by the complementarity of instruction. Even though mothers may be speakers first and teachers second (Shatz, this volume), the adult is wise in the ways of the world and effective in transactions with it; the child, on the other hand, is largely ignorant. Whatever children seek to teach adults and that adults may learn from them, children rarely attempt deliberately to alter what adults know or how they think. Thus, a complementarity of instruction, in which parents demand compliance and children give it, is the main basis of the parent-child relationship. Even in middle age, most individuals believe they learn more from their aging parents than from their nearly mature children (Hagestad, this volume).

The asymmetries contained in parent-child interaction are actually mixed with symmetries—incidents in which parent and child engage in equal-to-equal interaction. For example, mothers accomodate to the cognitive status of their babies and engage them in imitation (Uzgiris, this volume). Initially, the mother imitates the baby or "prompts" the infant's imitations by matching its vocalizations or moving its hands through trajectories that match her own. These incidents constitute a "mix" of asymmetrical and symmetrical elements. The mother initiates the imitation; her actions, not the child's, bring it about. But the exchange itself is symmetrical; the actors engage in the same movements. With time, these exchanges become more completely symmetrical: the child initiates and terminates many imitations as well as the mother; the mother's prompting declines. By the middle of the second year, the child imitates complex as well as simple acts, multi-unit chains as well as single units, and "inappropriate" actions as well as "appropriate" ones (see Uzgiris). Imitative symmetries thus become embedded within the basic asymmetries that mark the relationship between mother and child. More than likely, this new "mix" of symmetries and asymmetries in mother-child relations constitutes a better basis for socialization in childhood and adolescence than would be the case with asymmetries alone.

Peer relations, in contrast to adult-child relations, are basically symmetrical; these relationships involve individuals who are psychologically and socially similar and whose interactions are mainly equalitarian. In peer interaction, beginning in the earliest years, dominance is met with resistance; chase is met with chase; give-and-take is followed by take-and-give; sociable behavior is matched with sociable behavior. Within these situations, one individual does not invariably teach and one invariably learn. Rather, teacher and learner roles are passed back and forth. Capacities for engaging in equalitarian relationships emerge only slowly during the first several years of life, seeming to require some sense of self, capacities for "driving" social interaction as well as being "driven," and the ability to integrate and coordinate action schemes so that interaction with immature companions can be sustained over time. Imitation, which initially emerges in the mother-child interaction, is well suited to the coordinations required in peer interaction. Thus, the symmetries mixed into the asymmetries of mother-child interaction may serve as a bridge into child-child interaction.

Mothers may not invite their infants into imitative interaction in a conscious effort to prepare them for child-child socialization. Nevertheless, it is known that mothers whose relationships with their young children are "secure" arrange more frequent contacts between their children and other children than do mothers whose relationships with their children are "insecure" (Lieberman, 1977). One can suppose, then, that mothers support the introduction of symmetries into their own interactions with their children partly to facilitate the child's exploration of the wider social world. To support this supposition, however, we need better information than is currently available about maternal "theories of child development."

MOLAR VERSUS MOLECULAR ANALYSIS

Currently, we have a better grasp on the content and structuring of adult-child complementarities using molar levels of analysis than using molecular ones. For example, both cross-cultural and indigenous studies indicate that children's actions toward adults consist mainly of appeals for information and things that are important to the child; in contrast, adult actions toward children consist of information giving, nurturance, and dominance (Barker & Wright, 1955; Whiting & Whiting, 1975). Interview studies confirm that this state of affairs is well understood by both parents and children, and that power distinctions are clearly recognized as a hallmark of adult-child relations. These complementarities are seen as "natural" and "right." Using interviews, for example, Youniss (1980) established that "kindnesses" are understood by children to be actions confirming this complementarity (by both children and adults) whereas "unkindnesses" are understood to be actions disconfirming it. And, even in the middle age, there is a greater willingness to "listen to" one's parents than to one's children, confirming the persistence of this complementarity through the life span.

More molecular analyses of these complementarities have been slow to mature. Clearly, it is difficult to obtain a data base from naturalistic observation that is sufficient to examine the complementarities involved in assertiveness training, verbal exchanges, imitation, and other theoretically relevant behavior classes. Progress is being made, however, in various laboratories. Patterson (1982), for example, has examined coercive processes in family interaction, showing how parents and children are connected in cycles of coercion that are associated with changes over time in aggression among family members. In these studies, the notion that contingencies of positive reinforcement must underlie aggression training in parent-child interaction has been disconfirmed; rather, it seems to be negative reinforcement that supports the familial socialization of aggression (Patterson, 1979). In addition, there is a complex interplay among parents, siblings, and the child that occurs in those conditions most conducive to coercive exchanges in the family (Patterson, 1982). Finally, in recent work, these micro-processes seem to bear a consistent relation to macro-processes (e.g., the family consequences of stress and social change).

Current evidence suggests that cognitive and communicative competencies in the child may be more buffered within the social context and less sensitive to the nuances of social relationships than personality development. In this volume, the essay by Shatz indicates that neither developmental changes nor individual differences in early communication development depend extensively on modeling, shaping, or similar processes. But we must be cautious in deciding what the evidence tells us, and what it does not. First, social interaction may be a necessary but insufficient basis to account for individual differences in cognitive abilities. Second, and more likely, we may not have examined the molecular dimensions of mother-child interaction that generate these differences. For example, mothers may "manage" or manipulate the conditions for communication in order to "open the gates," "set demands," or "set the direction" for more mature functioning on the part of the child rather than provide an exemplar for it. But we know little about this.

Even in social development, the contribution of mother-child interaction to the emergence of social skills may not be through direct reinforcement but through more subtle machinations. First, the security she provides the child for exploration of the environment (a well-established function) "sets the stage" for contact with objects other than herself (e.g., other children). Second, mothers arrange the child's schedule so that these objects are available to be explored. Monkey mothers position themselves so that agemates are nearby and available for contact (Hinde, 1974). Human mothers do the same thing. These arrangements increase slowly during the first 2 years of the child's life and mothers accelerate their occurrence subsequently. We do not know, however, whether individual differences in these maternal managements are antecedents of individual differences among their children.

Other studies (see Matas, Ahrend, & Sroufe, 1978) suggest that, from the relationship with the caregiver, the child carries forward self-confidence, persistence, and modes of utilizing resources (including social resources) rather than specific cognitive skills or IQ points. Two-year olds who were securely attached to their mothers in the first year, for example, do not solve difficult problems in the presence of their mothers more quickly and completely than less-securely attached children. Rather, they work more persistently and creatively at the task, make more appropriate requests for help, and *their mothers give it.* Conventional studies of cognitive socialization, which do not focus on the child's utilization of cognitive skills in context, may thus miss the mark. It may be that "indirect" intrusions into cognitive socialization, communication training, and affect regulation are the primary contributions of the mother-child relationship to cognitive development, and that conventional pedagogics (e.g., modeling and reinforcement) are secondary.

These same considerations may be necessary in understanding the caretaker's role in individuation, self-awareness, and the emergence of mastery motivation. There was a time when early independence training was thought to be the primary antecedent of individual differences in achievement motivation (Crandall, 1963). Contemporary studies, however, have yielded a welter of weak and inconsistent results relevant to this hypothesis. Newer studies suggest that a more extensive "ecology of achievement motivation" may account for individual differences in this area (Trudewind, 1982). Independence training may be one element in this ecology, but more important elements seem to consist of "setting up the child" for mastery or "arranging appropriate challenges" rather than the direct shaping of achievement behavior. More and more, then, the complementarity of instruction that distinguishes parent-child relations from other close relationships must be examined with reference to the parent's functions as "manager," "scaffold," (both cognitive and affective), and "resource," and less and less as "teacher" or "pedagogue." Years ago, Anna Freud remarked to an audience of education students that "parents are not teachers." I am only now beginning to understand what she meant.

Childhood socialization is "full of attributions" (Radke-Yarrow, Zahn-Waxler, & Chapman, 1983). The child's earliest experiences with social attributions are not well documented, especially as these occur within close relationships.

Experimental studies with school-aged children suggest that, when adults overtly attribute motives or abilities to the child, social interaction changes accordingly. For example, Jensen and Moore (1977) provided boys with either cooperative attributions ("you work well with others") or competitive ones ("you're a real winner"), observing corresponding differences in cooperation and competition in their subsequent interactions with other children. Similarly, Miller, Brickman, and Bolen (1975) reduced littering among fifth-graders by telling them each day that they were tidy. Other studies (see Grusec & Rendler, 1980) demonstrate that self- and other-attributions affect children's altruism. Nevertheless, the manner in which these attributions are woven into parent-child relations is unstudied. We know nothing about social attributions in this context during early childhood— the emergence of attributions in parent-child interaction, the circumstances under which they occur, and changes in them over time. Again, the main issue may not be the occurrence or nonoccurrence of relevant attributions or their frequencies of occurrence. For example, the consequences of specific attributions may depend on their credibility to the child in the context in which they occur. The mother's sensitivity in deploying certain attributions may thus be more important developmentally than how often she uses them (Radke-Yarrow et al., 1983). To verify this notion, however, requires fine-grained examination of parent-child interaction beginning in the earliest years.

CONCLUSION

Individuation begins within parent-child relationships, social contexts that are mainly asymmetrical. Symmetries (i.e., equal-to-equal social interactions) appear within these relationships. These symmetries diversify adult-child relations and probably enhance their functioning. These symmetries, for example, may provide the child with a basis for entering into child-child relationships.

Close relationships need to be better understood, especially in relation to the manner in which these ties may enhance or interfere with cognitive and affective socialization. We need serious investigation into the connections between micro- and macro-processes in parent-child interaction. The effects of day care or maternal employment on child development, for example, may be constrained by the relationships existing between these individuals. Understanding the connections between these elements is the unique subject matter of child psychology and a major need in extending our knowledge base from "what happens" over the life course to "how it happens."

REFERENCES

Barker, R. G., & Wright, H. F. *Midwest and its children.* New York: Harper & Row, 1955.
Bowlby, J. *Attachment.* New York: Basic Books, 1969.

Crandall, V. J. Achievement. In H. W. Stevenson (Ed.), *Child psychology: The sixty-second yearbook of the National Society for the Study of Education.* Chicago: University of Chicago Press, 1963.

Grusec, J. E., & Rendler, E. Attribution, reinforcement, and altruism: A developmental analysis. *Developmental Psychology,* 1980, *16,* 525–534.

Hinde, R. A. *Biological bases of human social behavior.* New York: McGraw-Hill, 1974.

Hinde, R. A. *Towards understanding relationships.* New York: Academic Press, 1979.

Jensen, R.. & Moore, S. G. The effect of attribute statements on cooperativeness and competitiveness in school age boys. *Child Development,* 1977, *48,* 305–307.

Lieberman, A. F. Preschoolers' competence with a peer: Relations with attachment and peer experience. *Child Development,* 1977, *48,* 1277–1287.

Matas, L., Arend, R. A., & Sroufe, L. A. Continuity of adaptation in the second year: The relationship between quality of attachment and later competence. *Child Development,* 1978, *49,* 547–556.

Miller, R. L., Brickman, P., & Bolen, D. Attribution versus persuasion as a means of modifying behavior. *Journal of Personality and Social Psychology,* 1975, *31,* 430–441.

Patterson, G. R. A performance theory for coercive family interaction. In R. Cairns (Ed.), *The analysis of social interaction.* Hillsdale, N.J.: Lawrence Erlbaum Associates, 1979.

Patterson, G. R. *Coercive family process.* Eugene, Ore: Castalia, 1982.

Radke-Yarrow, M., Zahn-Waxler, C., & Chapman, M. Children's prosocial dispositions and behavior. In E. M. Hetherington (Ed.), *Handbook of child psychology: Socialization, personality, and social development* (Vol. 4). New York: Wiley, 1983.

Trudewind, C. The development of achievement motivation and individual differences: Ecological determinants. In W. W. Hartup (Ed.), *Review of child development research* (Vol.6). Chicago: University of Chicago Press, 1982.

Watson, J. S., & Ramey, C. T. Reactions to responsive contingent stimulation in early infancy. *Merrill-Palmer Quarterly,* 1972, *18,* 219–227.

Whiting, B. B., & Whiting, J. W. M. *Children of six cultures.* Cambridge, Mass: Harvard University Press, 1975.

Youniss, J. *Parents and peers in social development: A Sullivan–Piaget perspective.* Chicago: University of Chicago Press, 1980.

Author Index

Subject Index